DURA-EUROPOS

Archaeological Histories

Series editor: Thomas Harrison

An important series charting the history of sites, buildings and towns from their construction to the present day. Each title examines not only the physical history and uses of the site but also its broader context: its role in political history, in the history of scholarship, and in the popular imagination.

Avebury, Joshua Pollard and Mark Gillings
Pompeii, Alison E. Cooley
Tarquinia, Robert Leighton
Troy: Myth, City, Icon, Naoíse Mac Sweeney
Ur, Harriet Crawford

DURA-EUROPOS

J. A. Baird

BLOOMSBURY ACADEMIC
LONDON • NEW YORK • OXFORD • NEW DELHI • SYDNEY

BLOOMSBURY ACADEMIC
Bloomsbury Publishing Plc
50 Bedford Square, London, WC1B 3DP, UK

BLOOMSBURY, BLOOMSBURY ACADEMIC and the Diana logo are trademarks of
Bloomsbury Publishing Plc

First published in Great Britain 2018

Cover design: Terry Woodley
Cover image © Yale University Art Gallery

A catalogue record for this book is available from the British Library.

A catalog record for this book is available from the Library of Congress

ISBN: HB: 978-1-4725-2211-5
         PB: 978-1-4725-3087-5
         ePDF: 978-1-4725-2365-5
         eBook: 978-1-4725-2673-1

Typeset by Integra Software Services Pvt. Ltd.

To find out more about our authors and books visit www.bloomsbury.com
and sign up for our newsletters.

For Dan

CONTENTS

LIST OF FIGURES

ACKNOWLEDGEMENTS

The idea to write this book for Bloomsbury's *Archaeological Histories* series was that of Tom Harrison, to whom I am very grateful, both for having the idea and bringing it to me. I hadn't planned such a project, but at the time he approached me in 2011, the war had begun in Syria and Dura-Europos had become inaccessible. I hoped then, and continue to hope now, that this small contribution of a general book on the site might help stop us from forgetting this incredible polyglot, multicultural place on the Syrian Euphrates.

I have many debts of gratitude. Above all, Susan Matheson and Simon James have been, from my perspective, the two Gaddé of Dura. Susan Matheson, the Molly and Walter Bareiss Curator of Ancient Art, welcomed me to the Yale University Art Gallery, first in 2004. Together with Lisa Brody, who has since joined the gallery as associate curator of Ancient Art, and Megan Doyon, senior museum assistant, Susan ensured the Dura-Europos archive is a welcoming, open, productive, and inspiring place to work. On that first trip, I had hoped to find enough material in the archive to include something from it in my PhD on Roman-era housing in Syria. More than a decade later and with their help and collaboration, I'm still finding new treasures. It was Simon James, now Professor of Archaeology at the University of Leicester, who first encouraged me to go both to the Yale archive and to the site itself. In his unfailing encouragement and support, he has been a model doctoral supervisor and then colleague. I've also been fortunate to have worked at Dura with the *Mission Franco-Syrienne d'Europos-Doura* and have learned much especially from Pierre Leriche, but also Ségolène de Pontbriand, Shaker Al Shbib, Gaëlle Coqueugniot, Ben Gourley, and many others on site.

In addition to the Yale Dura archive, I've been lucky to have had assistance from a range of others during the writing of this book. Tom Rosenbaum, an archivist at the Rockefeller Archive Centre at Sleepy Hollow, kindly helped me to access the files there relating to Dura and its funding. David Langbart, of the textual records division at the National Archives in the United States, helped me locate the surviving records relating to the work of archaeologists in the Office of War Information, including Margaret Crosby. Fredrika Louise Loew, in the Division of Rare and Manuscript Collections at Cornell University Library, helped me access A. H. Detweiler's writings on his archaeological experiences. I am grateful to them all for their time and expertise.

I've also learned much from conversations with other scholars of Dura, including Susan Downey, Stephen Dyson, Maura Heyn, Lucinda Dirven, and Sanne Klaver, and the boundlessly enthusiastic Ted Kaizer. I'm grateful to all of them. At Birkbeck, the School for Social Sciences, History and Philosophy provided funding for a trip to Yale in 2015, which allowed me to gather the material I needed for the third chapter of this book. My colleague Rebecca Darley kindly advised me on the coin hoards, and I've had the encouragement of a vibrant Department of History, Classics and Archaeology throughout the writing of this book. A few close Birkbeck colleagues and friends in particular have helped me through the process: Jessica Reinisch, Lesley McFadyen, and Serafina Cuomo never failed to have good advice, smart ideas, and, most importantly, lunch.

There will never be a last word on Dura. Not only do we await Pierre Leriche's assessment of the site in light of the twenty-five years of fieldwork he directed there, no single book could do justice to the site: the material is too rich and plentiful, and too much work remains to be done on the excavated material. Nonetheless, I hope this book will allow those new to the site to be able to envisage it. I've tried to make clear not just what we know but how we know it, and to provide the references so that anyone might be able to consult the original evidence themselves. The sage edits of Tom Harrison, Simon James, and Daniel Stewart have been invaluable to the present text, but I alone am to blame for the failings that remain.

Finally, this book is dedicated to my husband, Daniel Stewart, in thanks for being the best partner over two continents, two kids, and almost two decades, and for never once telling me to stop talking about Dura.

ABBREVIATIONS

Dura F. R. 3.1.1   Downey, S. B. 1969. *The Excavations at Dura-Europos Conducted by Yale University and the French Academy of Arts and Letters. Final Report 3, Part 1, Fascicle 1. The Heracles Sculpture.* Ed. C. B. Welles. New Haven: Dura-Europos Publications.

Dura F. R. 3.1.2   Downey, S. B. 1977. *Excavations at Dura-Europos, Final Report Volume 3, Part 1, Fascicle 2. The Stone and Plaster Sculpture.* Los Angeles: Institute of Archaeology, University of California.

Dura F. R. 4.1.1   Toll, N. 1943. *The Excavations at Dura-Europos Conducted by Yale University and the French Academy of Inscriptions and Letters. Final Report 4, Part 1, Fascicle 1. The Green Glazed Pottery.* Ed. M. I. Rostovtzeff, A. R. Bellinger, F. E. Brown, and C. B. Welles. New Haven: Yale University Press.

Dura F. R. 4.1.2   Cox, D. H. 1949. *The Excavations at Dura-Europos Conducted by Yale University and the French Academy of Inscriptions and Letters. Final Report 4, Part 1, Fascicle 2. The Greek and Roman Pottery.* Ed. M. I. Rostovtzeff, A. R. Bellinger, F. E. Brown, and C. B. Welles. New Haven: Yale University Press.

Dura F. R. 4.1.3   Dyson, S. L. 1968. *The Excavations at Dura-Europos Conducted by Yale University and the French Academy of Inscriptions and Letters. Final Report 4, Part 1, Fascicle 3. The Commonware Pottery, The Brittle Ware.* Ed. C. B. Welles. New Haven: Yale University Press.

Dura F. R. 4.2   Pfister, R., and L. Bellinger. 1945. *The Excavations at Dura-Europos. Conducted by Yale University and the French Academy of Inscriptions and Letters. Final Report 4, Part 2. The Textiles.* Ed. M. I. Rostovtzeff, A. R. Bellinger, F. E. Brown, Nicholas Toll, and C. B. Welles. New Haven: Yale University Press.

Dura F. R. 4.3   Baur, P. V. C. 1947. *The Excavations at Dura-Europos Conducted by Yale University and the French Academy of Inscriptions and Letters. Final Report 4, Part 3. The Lamps.* Ed. M. I. Rostovtzeff, A. R. Bellinger, F. E. Brown, Nicholas Toll, and C. B. Welles. New Haven: Yale University Press.

Dura F. R. 4.4.1   Frisch, T., and N. Toll. 1949. *The Excavations at Dura-Europos. Final Report Volume 4, Part 4, The Bronze Objects. Fascicle 1: Pierced Bronzes, Enameled Bronzes, and Fibulae.* New Haven: Yale University Press.

Dura F. R. 4.5   Clairmont, C. W. 1963. *The Excavations at Dura-Europos Conducted by Yale University and the French Academy of Inscriptions and Letters. Final Report 4, Part 5. The Glass Vessels.* Ed. Ann Perkins. New Haven: Dura-Europos Publications.

Dura F. R. 5.1	Welles, C. B., R. O. Fink, and J. F. Gilliam. 1959. *The Excavations at Dura-Europos Conducted by Yale University and the French Academy of Inscriptions and Letters, Final Report V, Part I, The Parchments and Papyri*. Ed. Ann Perkins. New Haven: Yale University Press.
Dura F. R. 6	Bellinger, A. R. 1949. *The Excavations at Dura-Europos. Final Report 6. The Coins*. New Haven: Yale University Press.
Dura F. R. 7	James, S. 2004. *The Excavations at Dura-Europos Final Report 7. Arms and Armour and Other Military Equipment*. London: British Museum.
Dura F. R. 8.1	Kraeling, C. H. 1956. *The Excavations at Dura Europos Conducted by Yale University and the French Academy of Inscriptions and Letters, Final Report 8, Part 1. The Synagogue*. Ed. A. R. Bellinger, F. E. Brown, Ann Perkins, and C. B. Welles. New Haven: Yale University Press.
Dura F. R. 8.2	Kraeling, C. H. 1967. *The Excavations at Dura-Europos Conducted by Yale University and the French Academy of Inscriptions and Letters, Final Report 8, Part 2. The Christian Building*. Ed. C. Bradford Welles. New Haven: Yale University Press.
P. Dura	Papyri or Parchment from Dura, following numbering in: Welles, C. B., R. O. Fink, and J. F. Gilliam, eds. 1959. *The Excavations at Dura-Europos Conducted by Yale University and the French Academy of Inscriptions and Letters, Final Report V, Part I, The Parchments and Papyri*. New Haven: Yale University Press.
Dura P. R. 1	Baur, P. V. C., and M. I. Rostovtzeff, eds. 1929. *The Excavations at Dura-Europos Conducted by Yale University and the French Academy of Inscriptions and Letters. Preliminary Report of First Season of Work, Spring 1928*. New Haven: Yale University Press.
Dura P. R. 2	Baur, P. V. C., and M. I. Rostovtzeff, eds. 1931. *The Excavations at Dura-Europos Conducted by Yale University and the French Academy of Inscriptions and Letters. Preliminary Report of Second Season on Work, October 1928-April 1929*. New Haven: Yale University Press.
Dura P. R. 3	Baur, P. V. C., M. I. Rostovtzeff, and A. R. Bellinger, eds. 1932. *The Excavations at Dura-Europos Conducted by Yale University and the French Academy of Inscriptions and Letters. Preliminary Report of Third Season of Work, November 1929-March 1930*. New Haven: Yale University Press.
Dura P. R. 4	Baur, P. V. C., M. I. Rostovtzeff, and A. R. Bellinger, eds. 1933. *The Excavations at Dura-Europos Conducted by Yale University and the French Academy of Inscriptions and Letters. Preliminary Report of Fourth Season of Work October 1930-March 1931*. New Haven: Yale University Press.
Dura P. R. 5	Rostovtzeff, M. I., ed. 1934. *The Excavations at Dura-Europos Conducted by Yale University and the French Academy of Inscriptions and Letters. Preliminary Report of Fifth Season of Work, October 1931-March 1932*. New Haven: Yale University Press.
Dura P. R. 6	Rostovtzeff, M. I., A. R. Bellinger, C. Hopkins and C. B. Welles, eds. 1936. *The Excavations at Dura-Europos Conducted by Yale University and the French Academy of Inscriptions and Letters. Preliminary*

                        Report on the Sixth Season of Work, 1932–1933. New Haven: Yale
                        University Press.

Dura P. R. 7/8   Rostovtzeff, M. I., F. E. Brown, and C. B. Welles, eds. 1936. *The
                        Excavations at Dura-Europos Conducted by Yale University and the
                        French Academy of Inscriptions and Letters. Preliminary Report of the
                        Seventh and Eighth Seasons of Work, 1933–1934 and 1934–1935.* New
                        Haven: Yale University Press.

Dura P. R. 9.1   Rostovtzeff, M. I., A. R. Bellinger, F. E. Brown, and C. B. Welles, eds.
                        1944. *The Excavations at Dura-Europos Conducted by Yale University
                        and the French Academy of Inscriptions and Letters. Preliminary
                        Report on the Ninth Season of Work, 1935–1936. Part 1, The Agora and
                        Bazaar.* New Haven: Yale University Press.

Dura P. R. 9.2   Toll, N. P. 1946. *The Excavations at Dura-Europos Conducted by
                        Yale University and the French Academy of Inscriptions and Letters.
                        Preliminary Report on the Ninth Season of Work, 1935–1936. Part 2,
                        The Necropolis.* Ed. M. I. Rostovtzeff, A. R. Bellinger, F. E. Brown, and
                        C. B. Welles. New Haven: Yale University Press.

Dura P. R. 9.3   Rostovtzeff, M. I., A. R. Bellinger, F. E. Brown, and C. B. Welles, eds.
                        1952. *The Excavations at Dura-Europos Conducted by Yale University
                        and the French Academy of Inscriptions and Letters, Preliminary
                        Report of the Ninth Season of Work 1935–1936. Part 3: The Palace
                        of the Dux Ripae and the Dolicheneum.* New Haven: Yale University
                        Press.

YUAG   Yale University Art Gallery.

Plan of Dura-Europos

Figure 1 Plan of Dura-Europos by A. H. Detweiler, annotated with names of structures and block names. YUAG.

Chapter 1

THE EXCAVATION OF DURA-EUROPOS

The ancient site now known as Dura-Europos was founded in the aftermath of Alexander the Great's conquests, under the Seleucid dynasty, which held sway in much of what is now the Middle East and Central Asia. The city which developed would eventually be controlled by a range of powers including the Arsacids, another dynasty which the Romans called the Parthians, and eventually by the Romans themselves. Archaeological expeditions in the first half of the twentieth century revealed this site to be one of incredible linguistic and religious diversity, as testified by many religious buildings, paintings, sculptures, objects, inscriptions, parchments, and papyri. Such was the wealth of archaeological material recovered that almost a century later work continues on the many findings from the place known simply as Dura by those who study it. Dura is a place now being destroyed anew, as the site is pillaged for antiquities and Syria's past is ravaged, a victim of the power struggles between more recent empires and dynasties.

Dura-Europos was never truly lost (Figure 1.1). While the name of the site was buried in its inscriptions and papyri beneath the earth, and within a few scant mentions in ancient literary sources, its city walls, citadel, and palace never fully disappeared. The ancient city, overlooking the fertile plain of Mesopotamia and the Euphrates river in the valley to its east and the Syrian steppe and the route to Palmyra to its west, was never substantially reoccupied after its capture by Sasanians in the mid-third century CE, but its walls continued to provide shelter to occasional travellers, and roads wound their way through the site.[1]

With Western travellers' and archaeologists' early forays into the Middle East in the nineteenth century, the site was noted and photographed if not recognized for what it would eventually be known as: one of the richest archaeological sites of the Greco-Roman Near East, site of some of the earliest examples of Jewish and Christian religious buildings anywhere, source of hundreds of ancient parchments and papyri, a polyglot city of dozens of cults and languages, and eventually a Roman military garrison. In what may be the earliest photograph of the site, taken in 1885 by John Henry Haynes, an early archaeological photographer and later the first American Consul to Baghdad, the main gate of the city, called the Palmyrene gate by its later excavators (or the Arabic *Bab al-Hawa*, the gate of the winds, by local people), is visible, still standing several metres above ground level, and towering above Haynes' horses, held steady as scales for his camera (Figure 1.2).[2]

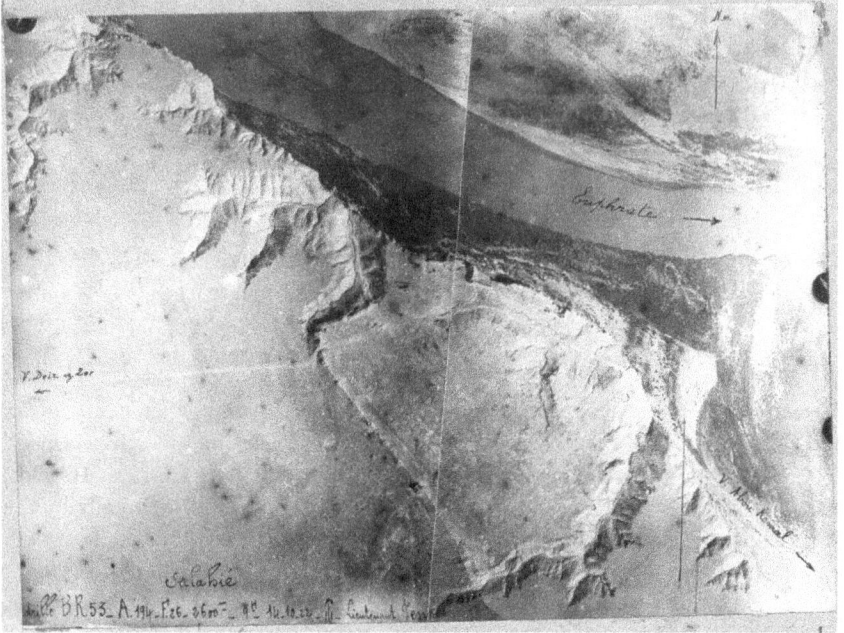

Figure 1.1 Aerial photograph of Dura-Europos, taken by the French military in October 1922. The city walls around the site are clearly visible, as is the road through the site, towards the cities of Deir ez-Zor to the north and Abu Kemal to the south. YUAG.

Figure 1.2 The 'Palmyrene Gate' of Dura-Europos, taken by John Henry Haynes, 1885. Courtesy of Special Collections, Fine Arts Library, Harvard University, HayAr.259.

The mining of ancient sources to locate 'lost' Classical sites meant that other explorers were on the lookout for the site which Roman historian Ammianus Marcellinus described as abandoned in the fourth century, and which Isidore of Charax had described centuries earlier in his itinerary of overland routes as 'Dura, the city of Nicanor, a Macedonian foundation, which the Greeks call Europos'.[3] The substantial ruins were noted by a number of travellers and archaeologists, including John Punnet Peters, on the first campaign of the University of Pennsylvania to Nippur in 1888.[4] Gertrude Bell was among those who noticed the site, and her diary entry on 8 March 1909 mentions the ruins of Salihiyeh, the name of the town which remains just south of the archaeological site, below the plateau, although it was the following day, and closer to Abu Kemal, when the impressive tower tombs made her wonder if she was seeing the ancient city of Dura.[5]

It would be more than a decade, after the First World War, before the ancient names of the site were restored to it. Like so much of the site's later investigation, this discovery was entangled in larger networks – of foreign scholars and universities working in the Middle East, of Western military operations, and international jostling for power in the region as it was carved into Mandated territories (Figure 1.3). So it was that on 31 March 1920 that Captain M. C. Murphy of the British Royal Veterinary Corps reported that the previous day he had discovered 'some ancient wall paintings in a wonderful state of preservation', sepoys having accidentally uncovered them while making a rifle pit.[6] Murphy's dispatch found its way along with photographs of the paintings into the hands of Gertrude Bell, by then writing a review of the civil administration of Mesopotamia, and subsequently via the civil commissioner, Colonel A. T. Wilson, the British governor general of Mesopotamia, to James Henry Breasted, of the Oriental Institute of the University of Chicago.[7]

Figure 1.3 Map of Dura-Europos in its regional context made by H. Gute, of the Yale expedition, in 1933, showing Dura with other major sites (ancient and modern) and contemporary borders.

The British military and civil authorities provided transportation in the form of seven Model 'T' Fords for Breasted, in late April the same year, when he set out on the 300-mile journey from Baghdad up the Euphrates to Salihiyeh, which he reached on the fourth of May, a journey he likened, for its dangers, to 'putting our heads in the lion's mouth'.[8] He studied the paintings, which were excavated further by several squads of East Indian troops, took photographs, made drawings and notes, and by the very next morning was headed for Aleppo, having swapped his convoy of automobiles for Turkish horse-drawn *arabanahs* (Figure 1.4). He reached Aleppo safely despite worries of being trapped on 'fighting ground' by Arab and British forces or set upon by brigands.[9] The boundaries of what would become modern Syria and Iraq were coalescing at the very same time, and territory shifted from British to Arab hands as Breasted moved across the landscape, the British withdrawing from the region around Salihiyeh the day after Breasted had recorded the paintings. Breasted's journey would continue, via Cairo and then London, where he stayed in the Savoy hotel at the expense of His Majesty's Government and delivered political and military intelligence on the Middle East directly to the British foreign minister, Lord Curzon, before arriving home in America in July 1920.[10] Dura had been but a brief chapter on his expedition of 1919–1920, which had been the first expedition of the Oriental Institute (and indeed the expedition was a fundamental part of the Institute's foundation), financed with money from John D. Rockefeller Jr, of one of the wealthiest families in America, whom Breasted knew personally.[11] The impact of the discoveries at Dura would be far out of proportion with the duration of time Breasted spent there. Near the time Breasted got back to America, hopes for Syrian independence had been crushed by the French.

Figure 1.4 Photograph from Breasted's expedition with British Officers posing in front of the interior of the Palmyrene Gate, with British East Indian troops stationed at the top. Courtesy of the Oriental Institute of the University of Chicago. Negative 3293, Photograph 6853.

Breasted's work at Dura made its way into the popular press, including the *New York Times*, which reported on 10 June 1922 that 'This ruined Roman fortress at Salihyah has thus furnished a new and unparalleled example of the transition from decadent Orientalized Hellenistic art to the Byzantine art from which reviving Europe inherited so much', the Associated Press having interviewed Breasted on the eve of his presentation of his work in the 'remote and inhospitable region' to the French Academy. His presentation was made at the insistence of Franz Cumont, an eminent Belgian scholar who was lecturing in America and had seen Breasted's photographs of the paintings and realized their importance.[12] In the newspaper article, Breasted described the paintings and the temple in which they had been found as 'of Roman legionaries but likewise of some Oriental cult'.

Breasted's single day of work would become, four years after his visit to the site, the book *The Oriental Forerunners of Byzantine Painting: First-Century Wall Paintings from the Fortress of Dura on the Middle Euphrates*. The name of the site – Dura – was now known from the painted inscription of the Fortune of the site, the Tyche of Dura, on one of the paintings.[13] His recording and judgements about the nature of the site would set the tone for much of what was to follow. Breasted had been among the first American archaeologists working in the Middle East, collecting antiquities and laying the groundwork for the study of the Orient by Americans, preparing the possibility of excavations across the region. Having founded the Oriental Institute and having been the first American to get a PhD in Egyptology, Breasted was a formidable figure.[14] His work was widely read and his reputation well established by the time he visited Dura, which was but a small blip on his expedition of, as he put it, 'grubbing in the dirt'.[15]

Breasted's description and judgements on the paintings he had recorded at Dura set the scholarly tenor. Breasted had coined the term 'Fertile Crescent' and was interested in the pre-Classical and Eastern past. His grand narrative of the ancient world, in his earlier book *Ancient Times*, was that civilization was something which 'arose in the Orient' and then was 'obtained' by Europe.[16] In broad terms, his characterization of the ancient world and the triumph of an Indo-European race, the movement of power and civilization Westward from the Persians via the Greeks and Romans to Europe was a re-imagining of his own times, with the Fertile Crescent being much of the same territory of the Ottoman Empire carved up by the Sykes-Picot agreement between Britain and France.[17] Dura itself would not have been discovered by Captain Murphy and his men had the British not been in command on the upper Euphrates. *Oriental Forerunners* introduced Dura to the modern world, and it was grounded in Orientalism and an archaeological adventure story, devoting much of the text to the expedition itself, that is, to the exertions of travel, and many of the images used to illustrate the book were not of archaeology but of the convoy, and the roads and rivers they travelled on and across, the procession equipped with the starry American flag.[18] The characterization of the paintings themselves as 'Oriental' framed a paradigm of East versus West (and in the paintings, naturalism versus abstraction), which continues to dominate descriptions of the site.[19] The idea of Forerunners was also typical of Breasted's world view: civilization had begun in this region, but its true realization, and inheritors, were in the West.

Breasted was, then, the first of Dura's excavators to have a troubled and troubling relationship with the workers at the site and local people, writing openly of his physical abuse of his driver, complaining of 'oriental palaver' on his travels (while simultaneously praising the hospitality of local people), even altering photographs to exclude them: the turbaned head of one of the troops helping to excavate was painted out, leaving only Breasted himself in the frame as the discoverer of Durene treasures.[20]

Those first treasures, the main impetus for the later work at Dura, were two painted scenes from a temple in the northwest corner of the site which would come to be known as the temple of Bel or the temple of the Palmyrene Gods, although it was likely not known by either of these names in antiquity.[21] Both paintings were scenes of sacrifice annotated with short texts: one sacrifice was being performed by a family of Dura's elite, that of a man named Conon, and the other, later, painting depicted a sacrifice by Roman soldiers led by the tribune Julius Terentius.[22] The latter included the labelled figure of the Tyche, or Fortune, of Dura, which had confirmed the name of the site. Like other of Dura's riches, the paintings were to be distributed to museums, in this case the former painting moving to what would become the National Museum in Damascus, and the latter to Yale University Art Gallery in New Haven, Connecticut.

By the time Breasted's *Oriental Forerunners* appeared, French rule under a United Nations mandate of Syria and Lebanon had begun. Salihiyeh now being under the control of France, the *Académie des inscriptions et belles-lettres* began work, sent by the High Commission of the French Republic, and led by the Belgian Franz Cumont.[23] Cumont was himself a formidable figure in early-twentieth-century archaeology and ancient history, and was at the time already particularly well known for his work on Mithraism and Eastern religions. Cumont began at Dura in 1922, and wrote the introduction to *Oriental Forerunners*; Breasted's work had been, in turn, dedicated to him. In 1922 and 1923, officers and soldiers of the *Armée du Levant* were the workers for Cumont's excavation; in 1924 Syrian legionaries conducted further work in his absence.[24] These excavations revealed more of Breasted's temple and another, the temple of Artemis, as well as more of the city's fortifications, a single house near the centre of town, a palace he called the *Redoute*, and associated inscriptions, parchments, and objects (Figure 1.5). Cumont's work was published in 1926, as *Fouilles de Doura-Europos*, and many of the objects found their way to the Louvre.[25]

In Cumont's work, the chronology of the site began to come into focus, and he recognized Seleucid, Parthian, and Roman phases at Dura from the documents and inscriptions. These periods would come to be problematic, as the material evidence could not be as easily phased. Indeed, nearly a century later, the periodization of the site has not been completely resolved. Despite this, Dura has later become a type site for both the Roman Near East and for Parthian art. In his first season of work Cumont's team excavated a papyrus which gave the name of the city as Europos, which, together with the Tyche of Dura named on the paintings, allowed the site to be definitively identified with that mentioned by the ancient geographer Isidore, a site known in antiquity both as Dura and Europos. Cumont also recovered an inscription which confirmed that the town had eventually been granted *colonia* status by Rome.[26] Later scholars would owe much to Cumont's characterization of the site, in particular his view of the nature of the Hellenistic settlement. Precisely why the site had two names, Dura and Europos, remains a matter of debate, which will be returned to in a later chapter. The amalgam Dura-Europos is modern.

The figurehead who presided over most of the excavations at Dura – and indeed over the field of ancient history in the first half of the twentieth century – was Mikhail Rostovtzeff. By 1925, before the final publication of his excavations had been made, Cumont had received a letter from Rostovtzeff expressing interest in Cumont's work at Dura.[27] Rostovtzeff was already world renowned for his work. He had left Russia after the Bolshevik Revolution in 1918, and he would become one of the most important ancient historians of the twentieth century.[28] In particular at this early date, he was interested in one of the documents excavated by Cumont at

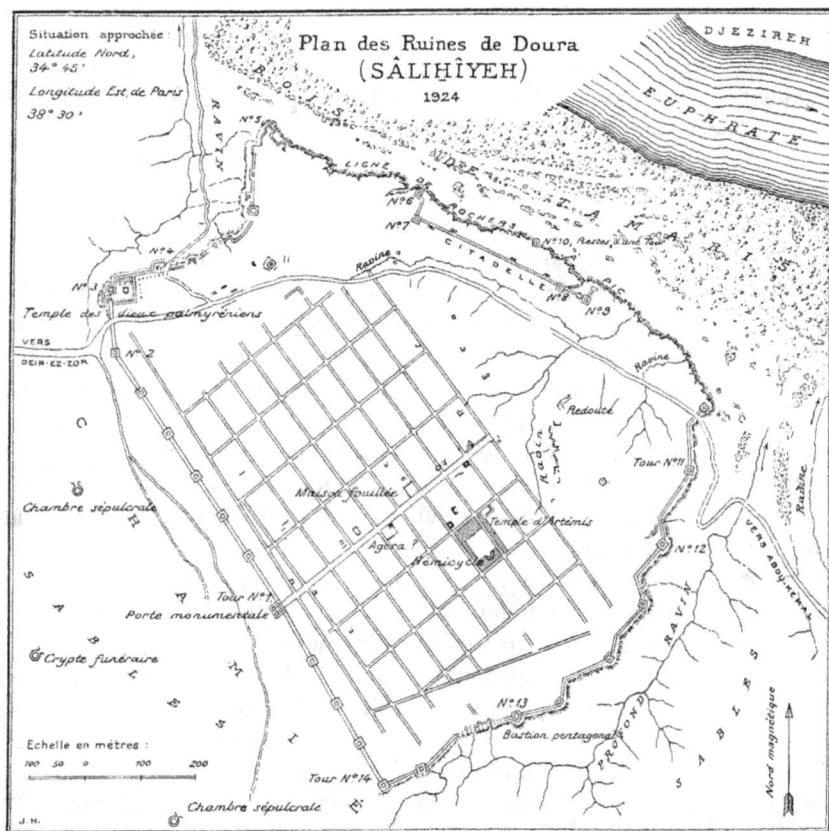

Figure 1.5 Cumont's plan of Dura. Cumont 1926, plate 2. The Palmyrene gate is 'Tour No. 1', then labelled only as the monumental gate.

Dura, specifically as it related to his interest in the Hellenistic Orient: the Middle East in the wake of the death of Alexander the Great.[29] Dura's ability to provide such documents would remain a key facet of Rostovtzeff's interest in the site. Rostovtzeff joined Yale in 1925 as Sterling professor of ancient history and archaeology, and it was from Yale the excavations would be run and to which the archive and objects would largely go. The next year, in 1926, he published his landmark *Social and Economic History of the Roman Empire*, further cementing his reputation.[30]

Cumont published his magisterial *Fouilles de Doura*-Europos in 1926, only two years after his excavations completed. Rostovtzeff published a breathless review which appeared the following year, admiring not only the results of the work but also the rapidity and volume of the publication, writing 'Glory and honor to him! He has set an example which ought to be followed by all excavators!'[31] In the same review, Rostovtzeff likened Dura to a Syrian Pompeii, not only because of its preservation but because it showed the 'gradual absorption' to Hellenistic civilization of the local Syrians (just as, in this reading, Italians had been absorbed at Pompeii).[32] This model of culture change would remain important in Dura's scholarship, and Rostovtzeff would repeat the comparison to Pompeii many times. Because of what Rostovtzeff recognized as the enormous historical importance of the site, he asked in the review that given the French and Syrian governments could not continue work, 'Is there no institution or private person in the United States to understand all the importance of the enterprise and to help with money those who are ready to devote their time and their energy to this task?'[33]

The review was, of course, a contrivance to be able to make such assertions and demands publicly, and the correspondence between Cumont and Rostovtzeff reveals this directly.[34] Rostovtzeff would answer his own call. Dura may have been rediscovered by chance, but its excavation under his scientific direction (as his title appeared in the publications) was a deliberate choice. Dura fitted with Rostovtzeff's interests in Hellenism in the East, and in Dura he saw the potential for understanding a Roman frontier town.[35] Yale University, in addition to wanting to assist their illustrious new professor, stood to gain papyri for its burgeoning collection, as well as paintings. Perhaps more importantly, Yale wanted the status of conducting work at a major site in the Middle East, particularly as the University of Chicago and other institutions were establishing excavations, and other countries had already begun work.[36]

The president of Yale at the time was James Rowland Angell, and he would become deeply involved with running the excavations for the duration of his tenure. While he left intellectual direction to Rostovtzeff, it was Angell who had ultimate authority over the budget, the appointment of staff including the field director, and was responsible for agreements with Syria. Each field director of the excavation reported to Rostovtzeff but also to Angell, and major finds always merited a cable to him. Angell also oversaw the launch of the project, which was approved by the Yale Committee for excavations, and agreed by the Syrian government in 1927, and he secured the funding for the excavations to proceed.

The *Accord* regarding the excavations at Salihyeh-Doura sur l'Euphrate was technically between the president of Yale and the French High Commission.[37]

The first of these, made in July 1927 for six years, made a number of specifications, including the appointment of Maurice Pillet as technical (field) director, and the movement of objects to Damascus at the end of each campaign. There, it specified 'unique' objects would remain in the collections of the Syrian state, and that other objects would be divided with Yale such that Syria had a representative example of each; objects requiring special study including parchments were to be sent to Paris and returned to Syria after their publication, although this seems not to have happened in practice, and most were retained by foreign institutions.[38] Yale was responsible for publication of the work and, together with the French Academy, had exclusive rights to publish. The budget was $22,000 a year for the first three years. The funding for the expedition would come, just as Breasted's had, from Rockefeller, albeit now indirectly via his General Education Board.[39] The General Education Board's methods were to quietly engineer: it did not seek nor want mentions in publication, and asked Yale not to make a public announcement of its contributions.[40] The French Academy was also considered a collaborator with Yale, although they contributed no funds. Cumont was, however, a joint scientific director with Rostovtzeff, and while Cumont was not involved in the detailed running of the expedition, he was consulted on major matters, copies of reports were sent to him, and he continued his correspondence, not limited to Dura, on matters both practical and intellectual with Rostovtzeff.[41] After preliminary investigations in June 1927, *The Times* in London would report from New York in January 1928 that 'Yale University, acting through the French Academy, has obtained permission from the Syrian government for an expedition, headed by one of its archaeologists, Professor Michael I. Rostovtzeff, to excavate the buried city of Dura on the Euphrates. The expedition will start work in the spring with the support of the General Education Board'.[42]

Work began in earnest in April 1928.[43] The initial seasons focused on the fortifications, including the Palmyrene gate and citadel, and other monumental structures, such as the Redoubt, a large palatial structure whose massive wall had remained exposed. This was from the outset a heavily militarized operation, as Cumont's had been. For instance, in the spring 1929 season, forty men of the Syrian legion were on the site under French command, and the commander supervised excavation work on the Palmyrene gate; 'order in the camp' and policing was undertaken by ten *gardes mobiles*, and Pillet's assistant Duchange had also been a sergeant in the French army.[44] Local workers were recruited with the help of the regional Intelligence Department.[45] A detachment of Syrian soldiers continued to guard the expedition when it was present at Dura throughout the later seasons as well.[46]

Maurice Pillet would prove to be a contentious choice for field director. The period 1928–1929 was the second season, but the first major one running from October to April. In addition to Pillet, Yale's staff included Clark Hopkins, who had a post at Yale, and Jotham Johnson, a graduate student, as 'scientific assistants'. Pillet's reports after each campaign were addressed to Angell: these were detailed, including descriptions of the voyage to the site, the organization of the workers, detailed tables concerning the weather, and the excavations themselves.[47] Much other correspondence, though, between Rostovtzeff and Angell, and the reports from field staff including Clark Hopkins, is dedicated to the 'problem' of Pillet himself.[48] While much of this involved a clash of personalities, Pillet's methods, including paying workers for artefacts, were often problematic in terms of archaeological methodology: from the time of Pillet's directorship, there are virtually no records of the objects excavated which note their find-spot.

Under Pillet much more of the city was revealed, and the expedition moved from tents huddled inside the citadel to a purpose-built excavation house.[49] In addition to the Palmyrene gate, the fortifications, and citadel, he continued work on the Redoubt, on the temple of Bel, bath buildings, two blocks of houses, the arch of Trajan outside the city walls, the temple of Atargatis, and the temples in the southwest corner of the site. The focus on fortifications was not only due to an interest in monumental architecture but because the deep ramparts and depth of earth in the towers and along the city walls allowed the preservation of fragile documents which were otherwise seldom preserved. The state of affairs was summed up well by Henry Rowell, a recent Yale graduate who had been appointed as Hopkins' successor as Yale assistant on site in a letter written at Dura to Alfred Bellinger (a member of the Classics department who had earlier been on site, as a Yale representative, and would later edit the publication series and study Dura's coins):

> I feel sure that if Cumont had not found his documents here, Rostovtzeff would have thought twice about engaging us in this expensive venture. On the other hand we are conducting a useful investigation of a frontier town which has been a sort of melting pot of three or four civilisations and which has already permitted us to rewrite or write for the first time several chapters on Rome in the East. All well and good.[50]

The preliminary reports chronicling the excavations of Pillet and his frontier town including his yearly expedition reports and chapters by a number of scholars appeared rapidly between 1931 and 1933.[51]

The lack of concern for archaeological context (as it would now be called) continued until the end of the fourth season, in spring 1931, which was Pillet's last, after which Angell wrote to him formally notifying him that his services were no longer required.[52] There had been other major problems under Pillet, including most notably in December 1930, when excavation work on the fortifications of the city led to a collapse of part of a wall, resulting in the deaths of three workmen and the injuries of others.[53] Rostovtzeff went to the site and decided that the accident had been Pillet's fault, caused by digging unsafe trenches to save time and money.[54] Even before Angell received the letter notifying him of that incident, however, he had written to Pillet signalling that the excavations might not continue. In the event, they would continue, but without Pillet.[55]

The fifth season began in 1931 with Clark Hopkins as director (Figure 1.6). There is undoubtedly a marked change in the quality of the records from this time onwards.[56] Hopkins kept a field diary, and Susan Hopkins, his wife, kept a detailed finds register when she was present on site. Photographs and photographic records were also kept in a systematic fashion. Architects joined the expedition and produced plans of the site, and from 1931 onwards the archaeological archive is much more detailed and more systematic in its records. This is in part due to the growing and skilled team. In particular, architect Henry Pearson, who first travelled to Dura in 1931 with his mother, made detailed plans on many of the buildings that were (and had been) excavated. Back at Yale, further faculty joined the team working on Dura material, including Alfred Bellinger, on the coins.

On site, the number of workers rose steadily, from what had been about 100 in the first season to an average of 300 by the fourth and later, employing both men and young boys (the latter being paid much less).[57] In the fifth season, a number of important finds were made, including more temples (those of Aphlad and Azzanathkona), buildings in what would be identified as the agora, Roman military structures, and most sensationally, the Christian building with its paintings.[58] Hopkins' tenure as director also changed the tone of the correspondence from the tight formality with and worry over Pillet; Angell was happy with the progress, and in one of the few mentions of the prevailing economic climate in America at the time, he wrote to Hopkins of the work that 'It is most gratifying to hear,

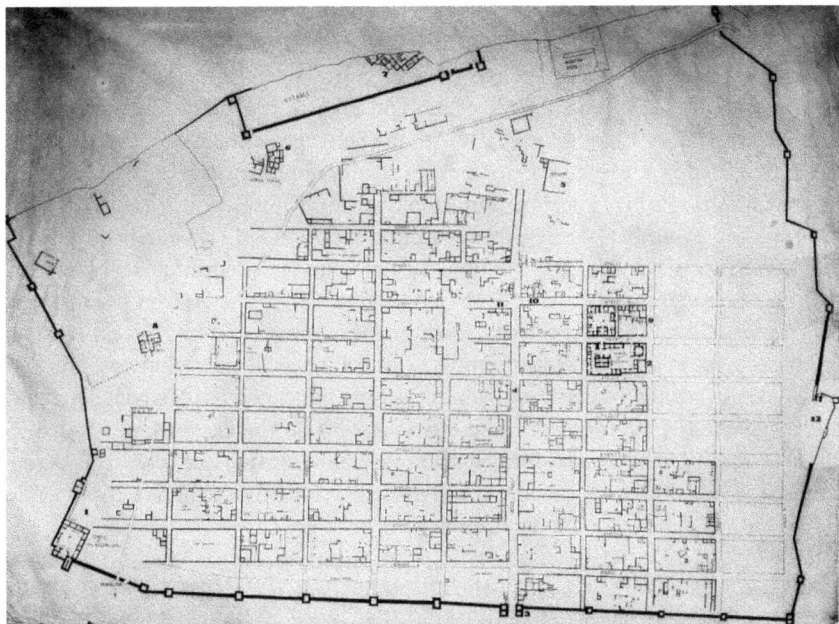

Figure 1.6 Hopkins' plan of the site. By the end of Pillett's tenure, a revised city plan had been published, drawn by Hopkins, but not all the walls indicated had actually been excavated; rather, it was based in part on Hopkins' survey of the site and sketches of standing remains. Site north is on the left of the plan; the 'modern house' at the top of the plan is the expedition house. YUAG.

in these days of general depression, so encouraging and optimistic an account of any undertaking'.[59] While the team was thrilled by the excavation of the Christian paintings, they were not received with much fanfare by scholars, much to Hopkins' disappointment.[60] The lack of engagement with the discovery seems to have been because they were not within the Holy Land proper in Palestine. As a result they did not fit easily into the archaeological narratives of religious legitimacy tied to specific places in the landscape of the contemporary Middle East.[61]

The Rockefeller Foundation meanwhile continued its funding of the project. In 1931, the internal foundation rationale considered a number of factors pertinent, including the importance of the site, the completion of work which had been started, the prestige of Rostovtzeff personally, and the 'extraordinary record' of Yale in supplementing Rockefeller funds with money from other sources.[62] Rostovtzeff was interviewed by the foundation in 1932, and the report on this interview emphasized the importance of exploiting the opportunity of the French occupation of Syria, and the notion that the excavations would help bring the US leadership in archaeological work in the future: both in the use of Dura as a place of training for American archaeologists and in the collection of antiquities for Yale.[63]

In the sixth season, 1932–1933, Le Comte Robert du Mesnil du Buisson joined the expedition, representing the French Academy; he had excavated elsewhere in Syria and had been a captain in the French army.[64] Du Mesnil had worked as an antiquities inspector under the French High Commission, and he always wore his military uniform on site. From Yale, Frank Brown, still a PhD student, joined as an assistant.[65] Hundreds of Syrian men and boys continued to be employed on the site, with more than 360 in 1932, when the wages were lowered so that the workforce could be expanded, apparently so that employment could be offered to the famine-stricken area.[66] Susan Hopkins, the wife of Clark, travelled with him and had a number of roles, from running the kitchen to cleaning coins, from identifying papyri to making the object catalogue, all in addition to caring for their infant daughter, Mary Sue Hopkins (Figure 1.7).[67] This season would see a wide range of discoveries at the site, including the Roman amphitheatre, the block of houses next to the citadel, the temple of Adonis, but all else was overshadowed by the discovery for which Dura would become best known: the synagogue and its paintings. In 1933 there was also a new *Accord* on the excavations, signed in October that year by Angell on behalf of Yale for a further six years.[68] The new agreement was similar to the first, specifying the *partage* of the finds between Yale and Syria was to be agreed to by the antiquities service.

In Hopkins' description of the synagogue discovery, which was found after a search along the embankment of the city walls looking for painted plaster, it is interesting that it is not biblical revelations that spring to his mind but differently Oriental ones: it was, to him, like 'a page from the Arabian Nights. Aladdin's lamp had been rubbed, and suddenly from the dry, brown, bare desert, had appeared paintings.'[69] The synagogue was initially agreed to go to Yale in the *partage* but the decision was reversed, and Hopkins' attempts to secure even some of the scenes were unsuccessful.[70] The synagogue paintings remained together and were placed

Figure 1.7 Clark Hopkins in front of Palmyrene gate with his daughter, Mary Sue, in her pushchair, and one of the workmen with his back to the camera. 1932–1933 season, from Hopkins' personal photograph album. YUAG.

in their own specially built structure in the new National Museum in Damascus, expertly installed by Henry Pearson, who had himself carefully removed them from the mudbrick walls on the site. The discoveries of the Christian building and the Jewish synagogue were among the primary justifications for the continuation of work at the site, which had been planned to be wound down.[71] While the full publication of the Dura synagogue would have to wait until the 1950s, the paintings were immediately recognized for their importance and have been the continued topic of scholarly debate since.[72] Key to their importance was the fact that they were not meant to have existed at all, as such graven images were prohibited by the second commandment. In addition to their value for understanding Dura's community and ancient Judaism more broadly, the discovery of Dura's synagogue paintings would instigate art historians to study Jewish art as a field.[73] Like so much other material at Dura, the synagogue paintings had a mixed reception in part because they could not be easily categorized.[74] The paintings were also destabilizing to contemporary understandings of ancient Judaism and to the primacy of the textual canon, and they were consequently treated in some cases as anomalous or otherwise artistically subordinate.[75] The discovery of the synagogue just before the Nazis came to power in Germany was also significant in many ways. For instance, Kurt Weitzmann (then in Germany but later at Princeton), having attended a seminar in Germany during 1933–1934 on the topic of Dura led by Hans Lietzmann, studied the synagogue as a means of quietly resisting the Third Reich.[76]

After the synagogue discovery, more impressive finds came thick and fast, including the Mithraeum, the temples of Zeus Kyrios, Zeus Theos, and the Gaddé.[77] The discovery of the Mithraeum at Dura in 1934 was a significant milestone in the excavations, in part because of Cumont's existing scholarship on the topic of Mithraism. Cumont had told Rostovtzeff that he would return to the site should one be discovered there, and indeed it came to pass. Rostovtzeff, too, travelled to Dura, and together they posed for a photograph, each with a hand placed on the altar of the third-century Mithraeum.[78] By 1935 at least some of the scholarly community was finally impressed with Dura, including William Albright, director of the American Schools of Oriental Research, who wrote that it was 'where extraordinarily important discoveries continue to be made with such regularity that the observer is left breathless'.[79] The eighth season, in 1934–1935, saw the expedition shortened, in part due to the depreciation of the dollar.[80] Hopkins completed his directorship at the end of the 1934–1935 season, when he resigned from Yale to take up a post at Michigan and excavate on their behalf at Seleucia on the Tigris in Iraq.[81] By this time, it was becoming more problematic to secure funding and to travel to the site. In 1935 the Rockefeller Foundation agreed to provide $30,000 for Dura, but this was given on the condition it would be the last funding they would deliver.[82]

Frank Brown succeeded Hopkins as field director for the final two seasons of work, from 1935 to 1937. By this time, Rostovtzeff knew the expedition would be winding down, and the expedition concentrated on completing work which had already begun, including in the agora in the centre of the city, and more work on the Roman military structures, including the Palace of the Dux, the Dolicheneum, and the temple of the Gaddé. During this time, other buildings fully excavated included the temple of Zeus Megistos and the adjacent House of Lysias, and the temple in block X9, but all of these would remain unpublished for decades. So too would blocks of housing which were converted for Roman military use in the third century, including block E8.[83] One of the major accomplishments of the later seasons, however, was the plan that was made by A. Henry Detweiler, which remains the most useful published plan of the site (Figure 1). It was included as a large folded map inserted in the first fascicle of the ninth preliminary report and was based on a site survey which recorded each block in preparatory drawings: some of these records are the only plans of blocks which were otherwise undocumented.[84]

Yale's Secretary's Office was responsible for the press releases concerning Dura, and in these 'Yale University News Statement' documents written for release to the newspapers, it is possible to get a sense of the official narratives of the site, as they were packaged for popular consumption. The titles frequently included the epithet 'Pompeii of the Euphrates' and publicized the antiquities collected and displayed by Yale.[85] The scholarly status of Rostovtzeff and other team members is emphasized, as is their position as 'scientists' in the field. Photographs were also used for popular news coverage, and Dura was the repeated topic of reporting in the *Illustrated London News*, with articles written by Hopkins in 1932–1935. These public reports were very consciously about the recovery of 'treasure' and emphasize not only the unique character of the finds but the status of the Christian and Jewish paintings as the earliest known examples, and their relationship to the origins of Christian art, in the terms framed by Breasted (or, in the case of the synagogue, 'Jewish prototypes of early Christian art'). The discovery narrative is also foregrounded, with headlines including 'A Flood of New Light on Mithraism', in an article describing the Mithraeum excavation. In his 1934 article 'The Tragedy of a Buried City Told by Its Ruins', Hopkins writes of the dramatic destruction of the site at Persian hands, and he concluded that 'No one ever uncovered the paintings so carefully concealed, or dug up the hoards of coins so hastily laid aside, until in our own day the spade of the excavator began the exploration of that mysterious buried city'.[86] His description not only emphasizes Dura's status as an eastern Pompeii (in being untouched since antiquity) but also uses a number of contemporary tropes regarding archaeology, including its mysterious or uncanny nature. It also neglects the labour of the workers doing the actual excavation: the spade of the excavator is a dramatic device, but Hopkins and the other directors of the site rarely touched such tools themselves.

Archaeology was useful not only to Yale's standing but also to American interests in the Middle East more broadly. The US Department of State in Washington was regularly in contact with Angell about the excavations at Dura, and this relationship worked both ways. For instance, Angell asked for assistance when, in 1936, he thought there were going to be changes to the system of *partage* which secured so many finds for Yale and he appealed to the Department of State for information and assurances that they would be able to continue to export antiquities.[87] There is a very conscious understanding, both by Yale's leadership and by the State Department, that culture *was* politics, and that American involvement in archaeology served national interests.[88] Archaeology was a means by which nations, and institutions, competed with each other. And indeed, Frank Brown would work for the United States in the Office of War Information, which generated wartime propaganda, in Syria and Lebanon during the Second World War.[89] Later, he would be seconded from Yale by the Department of State to be director of Antiquities for Syria.[90]

After Angell's retirement, the new president of Yale Charles Seymour wrote to Henri Seyrig, director of the Antiquities Service for Lebanon and Syria, in 1938 asking to renew the concession at Dura for a further six years after the second *Accord* expired in October 1939.[91] This was granted, with six years from October 1939 agreed retrospectively in 1940, but it was never taken up.[92] The excavation house at Dura had been closed up, and equipment sold and otherwise dispensed with, in 1937.[93] The expedition has been halted, amongst other reasons, primarily by lack of financing. The Rockefeller Foundation, in 1938, accounted that it had spent a total of $254,000 on Dura, between its direct allocations and the money apportioned to Dura from Yale's Rockefeller Fluid Research grant. They did not, however, want to continue funding, instead pointing to the future of American work in the Near East being assured by the American Schools of Oriental Research in Jerusalem.[94]

As will be seen in the chapters that follow, the end of the expedition's excavations in Syria was not the end of the project, and the objects and records at Yale would continue to be studied for decades to come. No further sanctioned archaeological excavation would occur at the site, however, until the 1980s. At this time, a joint Franco-Syrian expedition was founded by Pierre Leriche and Assad Al Mahmoud, the *Mission Franco-Syrienne de Doura-Europos*, created by the French Ministry of Foreign Affairs and the Syrian Directorate of Antiquities and Museums. The expedition began in 1986, with aims of re-examining the previously excavated areas, preserving them, and conducting new excavations. This included work on previously unexcavated houses and religious buildings, as well as new trenches in streets and fortifications to clarify dating with stratigraphy.[95] Leriche also re-christened the site Europos-Doura, reordering the modern name for the site to give precedence to its Hellenic foundation.[96] Work on the site ceased with the outbreak of the Syrian conflict, with the final field season in 2011.[97]

From the excavation by British and then French troops to the funding provided by the oil wealth of the Rockefeller Foundation, from Breasted's intelligence reports to Lord Curzon in London to the links between the Yale expedition and the American State Department, Dura's excavation is a good example of how archaeology was never an independent science despite the way it characterizes itself. Archaeology was militarized, politicized, captured, exported, and displayed. Archaeological knowledge was borne out of these contexts, and archaeological interpretations were deeply if not consciously imbued with contemporary politics. The archaeology of the ancient Middle East that would emerge from Dura-Europos was deeply entangled with the modern one. Archaeology at Dura-Europos was born out of militarized Western intervention in the Middle East, was funded by oil money, and was an instrument of 'soft' cultural power, and this has an important legacy both for the interpretation of archaeology's historiography and for future archaeological engagements in the region. As will be seen, the place of archaeology and of Dura itself in broader conflicts continues to the present day. Despite these contexts, entanglements and complications, what was uncovered at Dura was no less than one of the most well-preserved and well-documented urban environments to survive from Greco-Roman antiquity.

Chapter 2

THE SITE OF DURA-EUROPOS

The importance of Dura-Europos is unusual in the history of significant Classical sites. It was not an important city in antiquity, if we can judge from the few references in preserved historical sources of the period. While it was the site of massive battles, these were unremarked by extant Roman historians. Rather, Dura's importance has, since its discovery, been as an archaeological site, and from the time of the Yale-French Academy expedition, its value was in the sheer volume of material produced as they excavated almost a third of the ground within the city walls. That archaeological material was evidence of a Seleucid colony, taken by the Arsacid (Parthian) empire, then by the Romans, although that chronology, as we will see, is not without its major complications.

Due to the lack of mention elsewhere in ancient documentary sources, Dura's history and chronology had to emerge almost entirely from the site itself, from its material culture and its written records.[1] The unique place of Dura, with its many languages and religions, and geographically and politically at the edges of empires (be they Seleucid, Arsacid, Roman, or Sasanian), was both its greatest asset and its greatest difficulty. Asset because of the sheer wealth and variety of material, and difficulty because there was no easy means of comparison for the material culture or texts, and no other sites with a similar profile. When it came to periodizing the site, that is, splitting it into different phases, arguments have often hinged on single, sometimes problematic, pieces of evidence coupled with simplistic historical assumptions. Any date which hinges on a single coin can be overturned with the find of a single new one, and the priorities of the excavators and the methodologies they used shaped what we know. This chapter gives an overview of Dura's historical development, of how we know it, and why this has been significantly rewritten over the past three decades as scholars have revisited the evidence of the original excavations and conducted new work on the site.

Dura lies at the edges: between the steppe and the Euphrates valley, between the Arsacid capitals of Mesopotamia and the cities of Roman Syria (Figure 2.1). The Euphrates river, which runs alongside the eastern side of the site at the base of the plateau on which the site sits, flows south, feeding a fertile floodplain now much diminished by modern dams upstream, between the Shamiyeh plateau to the west and

Figure 2.1 Aerial photograph of Dura-Europos, taken from north of the site while excavations were ongoing (the northeast corner of the site is still unexcavated here). The Euphrates river is visible to the left of the site, overlooked by Dura's citadel. Outside the city walls to the right and bottom of the photograph, large spoil heaps are visible where the expedition dumped its backdirt over the city walls. YUAG z1.

to the east the Jezireh. The climate in the Roman era was probably relatively similar to the modern one, with hot dry summers, cold winters, and relatively meagre rainfall.[2]

The foundation of the site which we now call Dura-Europos happened in late fourth or early third century BCE, with a colony called Europos. However, given its situation on the fertile valley and on a promontory strategically overlooking the river, it is not surprising that there is evidence for much earlier inhabitation in its immediate vicinity. The earliest textual record that has been recovered from Dura is not in Greek script, but cuneiform, and the earliest pottery not Hellenistic, but Assyrian.[3] These are very ephemeral traces of the site's earlier histories, and in the Old Babylonian cuneiform tablet discovered, re-used in a mudbrick used to construct the temple of Atargatis, a place called *Da-wa-ra* is named, which was probably a much older form of the toponym 'Dura' itself, meaning 'fortress'.[4] This fortress may refer to the naturally protected topography of the citadel, at a high point and surrounded by natural wadis on three sides, and river cliff on the other. This place name seems to have remained attached to the site, alluding to some continuity, if not at the site then in the local landscape, from much earlier times into the Arsacid and Roman periods at the site.

The Hellenistic Period

The Hellenistic period of Dura had been one of Rostovtzeff's chief interests when he set up the excavation, but by the time the excavations ended, he wrote that 'Little has been found in the city dating from the Hellenistic period', and generally (and relatively) speaking, this remains the case.[5] As we have already seen in the first chapter, in one of the few ancient mentions of Dura, Isidore described Dura as 'the city (*polis*) of Nicanor, a Macedonian foundation, which the Greeks call Europos'.[6] The identity of this Nicanor is problematic, as there are several historically known possibilities bearing this common name. It is also possible that Isidore's preserved text is incorrect and should be read Nicator, that is, Seleucos Nicator himself, one of Alexander's generals and then successors. Whatever the actual circumstances of its founding, later in Dura's history, the people of the site repeatedly recorded their founder as King Seleucos Nicator.[7] The second-century CE relief of 159 (so, from Dura's Arsacid era) from the so-called temple of the Gaddé names Seleucos Nicator, a figure who wears Hellenistic military dress and a diadem indicative of his position, and is shown crowning the Fortune (Gad) of the city with a laurel wreath (Figure 2.2).[8] From this relief and from other late textual evidence, it seems clear that Seleucos Nicator was considered, at least by the inhabitants of Arsacid and Roman-era Dura, as the founder of the city.[9] It is notable, too, that this Hellenistic, Seleucid founder is crowning the Gad not of Europos (i.e. the supposed name of the original Greek colony) but of Dura. As is so often the case at Dura, we are reconstructing the site's early history from fragments of its later past: fragments which, as in the case of this relief, were deliberately made to express the past in terms of present identities and relationships, and which indeed use the past to construct these. In all likelihood, at least some aspects of early, Hellenistic, worship survived and were practiced in later Dura, but we lack indisputable evidence for their continuity.[10] Further complicating this picture is the fact that this relief bears an inscription in Palmyrene and was paired with a second relief depicting the Gad of Palmyra: this is, in many ways, an 'outsider' view of Dura's heritage, carved in limestone from Palmyra.[11]

The precise date of Dura's foundation is similarly hazy (and in any case, it did not spring fully formed into existence but came into being over a period of time); traditionally it is placed around 300 BCE, based on what we know of the settlement of Syria by the Seleucids.[12] It is worth pointing out, however, that the evidence from within Dura itself for the Hellenistic period is, as Rostovtzeff himself noted, very thin on the ground. Hellenistic Dura is attested, briefly, in documents which date to the period. The settlement of such a site as a small garrison or *phourion* by Macedonian settlers who would have been apportioned parcels of land, *kleroi*, is typical of the era, and there are mentions of such a *kleros* in P. Dura 15, a fragmentary second-century BCE deed of sale. The document was found by Cumont's team, redeposited in one of the city towers.[13] The Seleucid-era documents used the Seleucid calendar for dating, which reckoned from time in a royal era starting in the autumn of 312 BCE. The settlement was Seleucid royal land and did not, yet, have the status of a *polis*. All in all, from what little

Figure 2.2 Photograph of a relief from the temple of the Gaddé. In the centre is the personified fortune of the city (Gad), and Nicator on the right, crowning him. On the left stands the Palmyrene man Hairan, who dedicated the relief, wearing the hat typical of Palmyrene priests. The Palmyrene inscription reads, 'The Gad of Dura. Hairan, the son of Maliku, the son of Nasor, made (it) in the month of Nisan, of the year 470 [March/April 159 CE]'. YUAG y226/1938.5314.

survives, early Europos, as it seems to have been called in the Hellenistic period, was a rather typical Seleucid military settlement.[14]

The understanding of early Dura has nonetheless been transformed by the excavations of the *Mission Franco-Syrienne d'Europos-Doura* (MFSED), as it is now known, under the direction of Pierre Leriche. Leriche has shown that the earliest Hellenistic structures, probably that of the initial garrison, are in and around the citadel on the east side of the site (not in the agora near the centre of the site as had been thought), and that the road system was laid out later, long after the initial settlement, probably around 150 BCE based on his interpretation of the stratigraphy of the main street.[15] It is probably to this time that the fortifications of the city also mostly belong, built in the main of large ashlar blocks of limestone quarried in the *wadis* that form the boundaries on the north and south of the city, and those within the site itself. The quarries were key elements in the site's topography, and the volume of rock extracted from them has been estimated at half a million tonnes.[16] The citadel fortification and part of its palace also survive from the Hellenistic period, as do later elements of buildings built in the same ashlar masonry in the middle of the city, in what would come to be known as the agora. Only fragmentary elements of early phases of Hellenistic temples survive (the temples of Artemis and Zeus Megistos), within and beneath later structures, but even these are not securely dated.[17] What little there is, however, is of a different character to that which succeeded it, with the temple of Artemis including Doric features not seen in the later iterations of the temple.[18] Similarly, only fragmentary and re-used elements of Hellenistic houses are preserved.[19] The citadel palace, by the time of the excavations, had already partly fallen into the Euphrates valley, and so its plan was only partially preserved, with many of its features 'enigmatic', as has been noted by Susan Downey, who studied the archival records and conducted further work on site.[20] What was preserved were two phases of a Hellenistic building, which had a peristyle hall with narrow corridors around its open spaces; that is, it had elements 'typical' both of Eastern and Western traditions of palatial architecture.[21]

It is notable if not surprising that what is preserved of Hellenistic Seleucid Dura is already hybrid and not purely Hellenic in character. In light of the general dearth of excavated early architectural remains it is perhaps also unsurprising that there is no trace, as has often been remarked upon, of 'typically Greek' structures at Dura, such as a theatre or gymnasium.[22] As the site has not been fully excavated, and excavations often did not proceed to the deepest levels of the site, caution should be taken in basing too many assumptions on the lack of evidence. However, from available evidence, the picture of early Seleucid Dura is that of a small garrison community, who held small plots of land outside the city and lived around the base of the citadel, on which there was a palace from whence their commander could look out over the Euphrates and over the community itself.[23]

In addition to the fortifications enclosing about fifty-two hectares, the later Hellenistic period also saw, with the layout of the town's grid plan, civic buildings in its centre in what would be labelled by the Yale excavators the *agora* (marketplace) (Figure 2.3). Built using the same large cut-stone blocks as the fortifications, the walls of these buildings were preserved within the later structures of this, central, part of the city.[24] Here, a building which had been used as a records office was identified in block G3 (see location on Figure 2.3); pigeonholes for keeping documents were preserved; although this part of the structure seems to belong to a later period and is not itself Hellenistic.[25] Similarly, while the grid plan of the city, as has been shown by Leriche and his team, belongs to the mid-second century BCE, and the roads formed blocks, there is no evidence for the equal distribution of house plots within these blocks, nor an egalitarianism among the colonists, as has been previously postulated in reconstructions.[26] Dura was certainly a Seleucid foundation and settlement, but its existence as described since the 1920s is more of a scholarly edifice than an archaeological one. We must be careful to distinguish between securely dated evidence of the Seleucid period from later evidence at the site which testifies to earlier periods (such as the relief of Seleucus Nicator above), and consider the way that these fragments have been used to build a whole.[27]

Figure 2.3 Site plan including remains of all periods, showing block names. Plan adapted by author from plan of the *Mission Franco-Syrienne d'Europos-Doura*.

The Arsacid (Parthian) Period

The subjugation of Dura under Arsacid rule has traditionally been dated to 113 BCE, based on the reading of the coin evidence by Bellinger.[28] There is actually no secure evidence for the date at which the Arsacids took control of the site; instead, we can only presume this hegemony belongs to the late second or early first century BCE based on what is known of the general breakup of Seleucid control of the region.[29] Quite what the tenacity of the Arsacid grip was, however, is unclear, and while there are moments, attested in documents, at which they were certainly in control of the site, the situation on the Middle Euphrates was, like the river itself, constantly shifting. We have, for instance, an arch of Trajan just outside the city walls, testifying to a period of time, however brief, during which Rome controlled the site in the early second century, which is otherwise virtually unattested from evidence within the city.[30]

The recent recognition of three Roman marching camps north of the city and a likely battlefield marked by the aforementioned Trajanic arch demonstrates that Dura had a very precarious position between Parthia and Rome – one that we still do not fully understand.[31] While historical sources outside Dura are silent on Rome's intervention at the site under Trajan, a single Greek inscription tells us that it was not a quiet nor unnoticed handover: in 116/17 CE, the inscription records that a man called Alexander (he was also known as Ammaios, it reports), who was the son of one Epinicus, renovated the *naos* of a temple, as his father had, and that he replaced at his own expense the temple doors, the originals having been taken away by the Romans.[32] So, there was damage to the site (and the seizure of booty) by Roman forces, and the Romans were recorded by name as having desecrated a temple, all within Dura's Arsacid period; this was an explicit judgement against the Romans. Nonetheless, the coin evidence from Dura shows increasing numbers of Roman *denarii* around this time, from a range of mints, testifying to further connections between Dura and the Roman sphere in the early second century.[33] This is perhaps explicable in terms of Dura's relationship with Palmyra, as discussed below.

While precisely what, chronologically, constitutes Parthian-era Dura is complicated by power struggles between Rome and the Arsacids, the period from the late second century BCE to the late second century CE was nevertheless a time of expansion of the city and much building work. This is best attested by the temples and their inscriptions, upon which much of the material chronology of Dura is built. In the first century BCE there was work on both the temple of Zeus Megistos and that of Artemis (as well as the Palmyrene temple outside the city walls, on which more below). The temple of Artemis in block H4 was, at least by the time of the first dated inscription in 33/32 BCE, a 'major civic shrine', with a recorded dedication by one Seleukos, son of Lysias, who held official civic positions of *strategos* (general) and *genearches* (probably 'ruler of the tribes').[34] The first century CE saw continued temple building, including the construction of the temples of Azzanathkona (block E7 on Figure 2.3), Zeus Kyrios (against tower 16), Atargatis (H2), Bel (J7), and Aphlad (N8).[35] In the second century CE more temples were built, including those of Zeus Theos (B3), Adonis (L5), and the Gaddé (H1).

The names of the temples have become canonical from the expedition publications and subsequent scholarship, but the deities whose names were attributed to the sanctuaries are sometimes misleading. In some temples, for instance the temple of the Gaddé, the temple was named on the basis of subsidiary reliefs which flanked the central relief of a god which was found only in fragments. One of those reliefs was that depicting Seleucus Nicator, discussed earlier in this chapter, but the main deity was probably the Palmyrene god Malakbel.[36] The so-called 'necropolis temple' was given its misnomer because it was outside the gates of the city in the region of the necropolis, but from its dedicatory inscription, it is known that it was actually a temple for the Palmyrene gods Iarhibol and Bel.[37] In a number of cases, temples were given Greek names even when the deity was named in bilingual texts, giving a false sense of Hellenic cults predominating, for example that of Zeus Kyrios, when the Palmyrene part of the bilingual inscription names Baal-Shamin. In other instances, as that of Zeus Megistos, a number of deities were present within the sanctuary and no inscription records the dedication of the entire temple to a particular deity; there, we have also Baal-Shamin, Arsu, and Heracles within the same structure.[38] The consequence of this is that the character of the temples and religious practice within them is even more complicated than it might appear at first glance.

Further to such historiographical complications, the gods of Parthian Dura themselves often had multiple names and aspects. For instance, the goddess Artemis was worshipped in a temple which, like the others at Dura, was Mesopotamian in its form.[39] Heracles does not have his own temple that we know of, but his cult is attested by sculpture throughout the city, in both religious and domestic contexts; he was not simply a Classical hero but a Near Eastern nude hero, and probably had an apotropaic function (warding off evil) – and he seems to have been popular not just in Dura but regionally as well.[40] Also without his own temple, but represented at Dura in sculpture, is the Aramean storm god Hadad.[41] There are Syrian goddesses, including the great goddess Atargatis (Figure 2.4).[42] Others, like Azzanathkona, are known only from Dura. Some gods are those of particular localities, such as Aphlad, from the village of Anath, as a 54 CE inscription tells us (Azzanathkona might also have hailed from this place), and the gods of Palmyra as already mentioned. Some temples had portions of their structures paid for, and were perhaps even exclusively used by, particular elite families (e.g. the temples of Bel, Zeus Megistos, and Zeus Theos).[43] In simple terms, the number and diversity of cults is indicative of a certain diversity in the populace (e.g. in being built by or for specific groups, like that of Aphlad, the Gaddé, the so-called necropolis temple, and that of Zeus Kyrios), but the temples of Dura also share much in common, including their physical form and elements of religious practice.[44] Whatever the origin of Durene temples established by certain groups within the city, this does not necessarily mean they were exclusively for the use of those groups.[45]

The fragments of Doric capitals and other meagre evidence for Classical temples of the Seleucid era gave way in the Arsacid period to courtyard-based temples

Figure 2.4 A photograph of the relief of Atargatis and Hadad, taken in the field shortly after its discovery in the temple of Atargatis (block H2). On the right is the Great Syrian goddess Atargatis, flanked by lions, and on the left, her consort Hadad. Between them is a cult standard, a *semeion*. YUAG c144.

paralleled in Mesopotamia, within which was a central sanctuary unit, at a right angle to the entrance, with small rooms known as chapels around the perimeter, and often with a tower incorporated into their design.[46] While the fortifications of the city and its palaces were mostly built in stone, the temples were built of the same materials as the local houses, with wall foundations of limestone and plaster rubble, atop of which was mudbrick, which all received coats of plaster.[47] These materials, and the methods to build with them, remained in use at Dura from the Parthian period until the fall of the city.

The precise civic structure of Dura under the Arsacids is obscure, as is the administration of the Arsacid empire itself, which is generally interpreted through what is reported of it by Roman authors (whence comes the ethnic label of 'Arsacid' itself, and hence the preference here for 'Arsacid').[48] What is known at Dura of this administration is from the parchments and papyri recovered there, written in Greek. The place is in the Arsacid era referred to as a *polis*, and the preserved documents of the first century CE refer to it as 'Europos in Parapotamia'.[49] A *strategos kai epistates* (general and (royal) overseer/chief magistrate) of the city is known.[50] It seems that this elite position involved the extraction of taxation for the Arsacid king.[51] There were elite institutions, but no civic council is attested; officials in the city had Arsacid court ranks.[52] The royal Arsacid court was the ultimate authority, documents were held in a local record office at Dura, and prominent positions include titles such as heralds.[53] The question of whether these testify to the continuance of Greek administration of the town, as is usually argued, will be addressed in Chapter 4.[54] Nothing survives to attest direct Arsacid rule of the site. An at least nominally Greek hereditary elite, that is men with Greek names such as Seleucos, Lysias, and Heliodorus, who were members of a small number of families that seem to have held on to dynastic power throughout the period, constituted a local elite who acted as an 'interface with the royal administration' of the Arsacids.[55] We can link, perhaps, this ruling elite to the palatial structure known as the Redoubt or *Strategeion* in block C9, which overlooks the site from the edge of the interior wadi, although despite its moniker, there is nothing definitive to link it to the office of the *strategos*.[56] This building and the archives building in the agora are the only structures relating to civic administration during this period, although some temples also had a civic role. The documents of the period gave their date both in the reign of the Parthian king and that of the Parthian era, reckoned from 248 BCE, *and* according to the Seleucid era (' ... of the former reckoning', as is the formula in the parchments). Many of the excavated structures of Dura were built, or rebuilt, during this long post-Seleucid phase of the site. In addition to the building of temples, as already noted, houses filled the areas within the city walls, and the agora area was filled with shops. The dead were buried outside the city on the steppe in underground tombs.[57]

It is probably to this era that the painting of Conon, uncovered in 1920 and which sparked work at the site, belongs (Figure 2.5).[58] It was found in the temple of Bel, on the left wall of the *naos*, depicting an act of sacrifice, as do a number of Dura's surviving paintings.[59] The figures are identified by painted inscriptions.[60] In addition to showing the garments and jewellery of an elite Durene family in the Arsacid era (or at least an idealized version thereof), this demonstrates the importance of family within religious practice and the importance of lineages in the community.[61] The painting was a votive offering to the gods, but it was also a visual reminder of family power, one that was placed in the most sacred part of the temple and thus associated this important Durene family with the divine. The family is one usually considered part of Dura's 'Greek' elite, and from other documents, we know that they are among the *Europaioi*, people who claimed descent from the original Greco-Macedonian colonists of the site.[62] But, while the men bear Greek names like Conon and Patroclus, Conon's daughter is named Bithnanaia. She and the other women in the painting wear elaborate headdresses and jewellery, the men tunics, and the priests are in long-sleeved belted tunics and conical hats in the Near Eastern tradition.

During the Arsacid era, Dura seems to have been a regional capital of sorts for a stretch of territory along the Euphrates, controlling an agriculturally productive

Figure 2.5 Painting of Conon and his family from the temple of Bel, taken after it had been removed from the site in panels and re-installed in the National Museum in Damascus. From the left, the figures are the man usually identified as Conon, two priests recognizable from their distinctive conical hats and standing before altars, then Conon's daughter, Bithnanaia, wearing a headdress. To the right of Bithnanaia are four men, including one Patroclus, and his son, also named Conon, on the far right. In the foreground are three children, presumably more of Conon's descendants. YUAG Dam-157.

hinterland.[63] The nature of its economy, and its place in the ancient Near East, though, has been shaped by the notion it was a 'caravan city', a place whose economy was based on taxing and accommodating the caravan trade that moved through the site on the long-distance trade route to the East, the so-called Silk Road. The idea of the caravan city emerged in Rostovtzeff's writing before he began work at Dura and is mentioned when he first travelled in the region in 1928 on a reconnaissance trip to a number of sites in the region.[64] For Rostovtzeff, the characterization was largely a descriptive one which fitted into his 'modernizing' view of the ancient economy in which the ancient economy operated on a notionally rational basis. The description of ancient sites such as Palmyra and Dura as caravan cities also tied into contemporary notions of Eastern exoticism.[65] The status of Dura as a caravan city was cemented by Rostovtzeff's 1932 book of the same title.[66] In it, Rostovtzeff attributed Dura's growth to its place on Palmyra's caravan route.[67] It has since been shown that while long-distance trade and traders passed through many places, only Palmyra is truly deserving of the epithet, with the main caravan routes bypassing Dura, but the idea has been tenacious.[68] Dura, rather than being a caravan city, was a regional capital (as can be seen in the documents written in surrounding villages but lodged in Dura's archive building), and it produced and traded a broad range of goods including agricultural products.[69]

There was certainly a commercial relationship between Dura and Palmyra, and traders were present. While nothing directly testifies that Dura was a stop for Palmyrene caravans en route to the Persian gulf, it was noted by Rostovtzeff (and many others since) that Dura is the closest place that Palmyrene caravans could access the Euphrates for the downstream river journey southward; they would then return by a different route, leaving the Euphrates at Hit.[70] In all likelihood both local and caravan trade between Palmyra and Dura took place, but Dura's economy should not be defined by this.[71] The relationship between Palmyra and Dura is attested by a range of evidence at Dura itself, starting in the first century BCE, when a temple was dedicated by Palmyrenes of two different tribes just outside the city. This is the temple of Palmyrene gods Iarhibol and Bel outside the city walls known as the necropolis temple. From this time onward, the Palmyrenes documented at Dura can be traced by means of their names, their language, and their gods as recorded in inscriptions at the site: their presence was the subject of a comprehensive study by Lucinda Dirven, who has shown that the Palmyrenes at Dura were both soldiers and traders and that they were loyal to the gods of their home.[72] The exclusivity of their temples, both those of the Gaddé and of Iarhibol and Bel, testifies to a group which identified strongly with their place of origin and its gods.[73]

Increased amounts of trade and connectivity, of which the Palmyrenes were part, throughout the first two centuries CE seem to have played a role in Dura's growth in this period. Other major Durene events during this time included an earthquake. The earthquake which affected the site is known from a Greek inscription from the temple of Bel, which reads, 'The ninth day of the month of Dios about the fourth hour of the day, when the earthquake occurred throughout this region the *polis* set up this altar to the Zeus Megistos [the greatest Zeus]'.[74] That is, about ten in the morning on October 26th 160 CE, with the year given in the Seleucid calendar. No archaeological level of destruction and rebuilding has been securely associated with this earthquake, although this might be an issue of lack of precise stratigraphic excavation rather than lack of evidence (the partial collapse of the city wall in various places might have been a result of this earthquake).[75] In as much as we can define Arsacid Dura, the city was now regional capital and a node in long-distance trade networks. A group of elite citizens seems to have controlled the site administratively, economically, and perhaps even in terms of religion, and enacted the power of the Arsacid King of Kings. As will be seen in later chapters, which turn to the material culture of the city in detail, the nature of what it really meant to 'be Parthian' at Dura is a complex question.

The Roman Period

Just as the control of Dura fell from the Seleucids to Arsacids as the former dynasty itself entered terminal decline, so did Parthian Dura become Roman, as the Arsacids lost their grip on the Middle Euphrates. This is usually presumed to date to 165 CE, with the campaign of Lucius Verus against Parthia, and a Greek dedication to Lucius Verus was indeed found in the temple of Artemis at Dura.[76] The situation after 165 is blurry, and it is not certain that after this date the site was under direct Roman control.[77] Ted Kaizer has recently suggested that the territory may have been controlled not by Rome or Parthia but by Palmyra.[78] Nevertheless, the early years of Dura under Roman rule, perhaps starting as early as 165 or as late as the 190s, are not well attested. Specifically, they are not easily archaeologically isolated due to the nature of the excavations, although there are a number of dated inscriptions and parchments within the site which anchor particular structures and events. In either case, Dura would remain under Roman control for less than a century, but it is this, final, period of the site which is the most extensively excavated and studied archaeologically.

Some elements of civil administration continued as they were in this period; for instance, from 169/70 CE, from the temple of Zeus Megistos, there was a dedication made by one Seleucos, *strategos kai epistates* of the *polis*, who built parts of the temple 'to Zeus Megistos on behalf of his safety and that of his children in accord with a vow'.[79] There is no evidence that religious or other aspects of local life changed drastically immediately following the Roman seizure of control; nor would we necessarily expect there to be. The temple of Artemis also continued in use and was enlarged in the Roman period, as were the temples of Adonis and Bel.[80]

New introductions to the town included the Mithraeum, on the northwestern side of the site in block J7. The earliest dated inscription was preserved in its later rebuildings: a small relief of Mithras slaying the bull with a dedicatory inscription in Palmyrene, of 168 CE.[81] The inscription records the dedication by Atpeni the *strategos*, son of Zabdea, commander of the archers in Dura. A few years later, in 171/2, one Zenobius, an officer of the Palmyrene archers, as a Greek inscription records, dedicated another relief to Mithras.[82] These Palmyrene archers were now possibly at Dura as proxies for Roman imperial power. The cult of Mithras itself, while perhaps of Iranian origins, was very much a Roman imperial phenomenon.[83] On the main road through the site, in block M5 a small temple (probably another of Bel) was excavated starting in 1993 by the Franco-Syrian expedition, and a relief was found there with a Palmyrene inscription dedicated to the son of Shalman of *c*. 175 CE (still early in the possible period of Roman hegemony), which further testifies to the presence of Palmyrenes.[84]

A late-second-century parchment, *P. Dura* 17, preserves parts of four documents, as it was a registry roll of copies, dating to about 180 CE. These show us that at this time, it appears that Arsacid orders were still in use, there was still a *strategos kai epistates* of the city, and the magistrates who were archivists (*chreophylakes*, perhaps of the eponymous building identified in the agora) also continued. Dated to around the same time is *P. Dura* 25, a deed of sale of a slave, whose long opening gives a sense of the co-presence of different systems of dating and authority in use at the site during this time:

> In the consulship of Bruttius Praesens for the second time and of Julius Verus for the second time, in the twentieth year of the principate of Imperator Caesar Lucius Aurelius Commodus, Augusti, and 491 of the former reckoning, on the fourth of the month Peritius, in Europos toward Arabia. In the year when Lysanias, son of Zenodotus and grandson of Heliodorus was priest of Zeus; Theodorus, son of Athenodotus and grandson of Artemidorus, was priest of Apollo; Heliodorus, son of Diocles and grandson of Heliodorus was priest of the ancestors, and Danymus, son of Seleucus and grandson of Danymus, was priest of King Seleucus Nicator.

Starting with the consular and imperial dates typical of Roman documents, the month and year then follow in the Seleucid calendar ('of the former reckoning'). The year is then given by local, eponymous priesthoods, including one of King Seleucus Nicator, the supposed founder of the Hellenistic colony. It is likely that these priesthoods had been present at Dura from an early period.[85] All of these systems were perfectly compatible, and indeed necessary, in a legal document. Greek inscriptions and graffiti remained the norm throughout the Roman period but Latin also appears, occasionally in inscriptions, and less often in graffiti, and later in the wealth of military parchments and papyri. In 194, Dura fell within Emperor Septimius Severus' new province of Syria Coele.[86]

In third-century CE Dura, a *boule* or civic council is attested in an inscription discovered by the Franco-Syrian expedition in the *odeon* of the temple of Artemis.[87] Elements of Roman civic life appeared, including, probably, statues of the imperial family, such as that of Julia Domna, the Syrian wife of Septimius Severus, who was honoured by the *boule* of the city in that same temple.[88] From the third century also comes evidence of complex trade networks; this is evident from material culture, as will be discussed in later chapters, but also from texts, such as those scratched all over the house in block B8 known as the House of Nebuchelus. Near the centre of the site, the walls of the house recorded, among other things, transactions related to moneylending, trade, and agriculture.[89] From the parchments and graffiti, there is evidence of a range of crops, including barley, olives, lentils, and cabbage, as well as grapes for wine, fruit growing, and animal husbandry in a territory that stretched along the Euphrates.[90] Nebuchelus' walls also record more exotic items coming from further afield, attesting to Dura's place on long-distance networks. That Dura retained connections with regions outside the Roman empire is attested further by the presence of, for example, Hatrene inscriptions in the Aramaic of Hatra in upper Mesopotamia.[91]

In the late second or early third century the Roman military presence at Dura intensified, and not long after 210, substantial changes began to be made, particularly in the north half of the site.[92] The Mithraeum, first built by Palmyrenes, grew as the Roman garrison grew, and soldiers of Palmyrene origins joined the existing members of the Mithraeum.[93] The temple was rebuilt *c.* 209–211 CE, restored by vexillations of Legio XVI Flavia Firma and Legio IV Scythica, who recorded their work in a Latin inscription; the earlier cult reliefs were incorporated into the new structure.[94] It is probably about this time that a wall was built, partially enclosing the southern side of the Roman garrison which had taken over much of the north part of the site (marked as the southern boundary of the camp on Figure 2.3).[95] The north side of the site was transformed, with a range of new buildings constructed by and for the Roman military, and other existing buildings modified for their use, including those for accommodation of the soldiers and their commanders, as well as service buildings, baths, storehouses, and temples.[96] Around this time the *principia*, the headquarters building, was constructed.[97] In 216 CE, a Latin inscription records that soldiers of two legions, the Legio IV Scythica and III Cyrenaica, dedicated an amphitheatre.[98] Adding further to our knowledge of this period, from 208 CE and later, are the Latin military records of the *Cohors XX Palmyrenorum*, which were preserved at the site.

New building materials used in structures being built for use by the Roman military included fired brick, and features like hypocausts not previously present at Dura were used within otherwise traditional local forms of structures and building methods; even the headquarters building is in a plan which shares much with counterparts throughout the empire but is built with local building materials and techniques. What had been houses in blocks E4, E8, and elsewhere on the north side of the city were transformed for use by the military, for use as barracks and other purposes.[99] The Roman military presence was not limited to the north half of the city, though, and there is evidence for Roman military personnel throughout the site, including unsurprisingly in the Palmyrene gate, where many inscribed their names in graffiti scratched into the limestone of the fortifications. The agora area in the centre of the city was now full of shops, as well as entertainers and others associated with the wider military community.[100]

In addition to the *principia*, the amphitheatre, and many adapted structures, a new building of the Roman period is the large Roman palace in the northeast corner of the site, which is oriented not to the existing street grid but instead to the cliffs over the Euphrates.[101] The building has long been known as the Palace of the

Dux Ripae, based on the reading of a *dipinto* from the building which refers to one Domitius Pompeianus, who was said to be the 'pious and just commander of the river bank'.[102] Domitius is attested elsewhere in the building, without the title, but the title was used to hypothesize much about the rank and role of this commander of the river bank, the *Dux Ripae*.[103] The short Greek remembrance inscription painted on plaster which had fallen from one of the rooms of the palace, however, has borne too much weight: it is a short remembrance text made by an actor, not an official military communication or formal inscription.[104] Regardless of the identity and rank of the chief inhabitant of the building, however, it was nonetheless an important structure. Based around two large peristyle courtyards, the building was unlike the existing palatial structures at Dura, including as it did baths and apsidal rooms, and had a different orientation, taking its position from the cliff edge rather than the orthogonal plan of the town. The excavators postulated that the two courtyards related to the more public and private aspects of role of the dux, although there is little to indicate the function of the rooms other than their plan, and it has been suggested the building may have been a record office or otherwise relate to tax collection or administration of justice, either of which are certainly plausible.[105] The relatively shallow preservation on this side of the site meant there were few recorded artefacts which could help with identification, and a further problem is the collapse of the eastern side of the building over the cliff edge. The building did have a commanding view of the river bank, even if it had no commander.

A number of temples associated with the Roman military were also constructed, in addition to the Mithraeum, which had a longer history. Among the most famed of these is a small temple on the northeast side of the site in block X7, known as the Dolicheneum.[106] While Jupiter Dolichenus was worshipped at Dura, as is attested in a small altar dedicated by Antonius Valentinus, *centurio princeps* of two vexillations, the altar was actually found outside the temple and is not certainly associated with it.[107] Another small temple below the citadel in block A1 was connected with the military base.[108] Other temples, such as that of Azzanathkona on the north side of the site, were adapted during this period, and part of the temple of Azzanathkona was likely converted into the headquarters of the *Cohors XX Palmyrenorum*.[109] The temple of Azzanathkona, however, also remained in use for the civil population in the Roman period, so it seems some access was provided to this part of the city even when it was under Roman control.[110] The Mithraeum continued in use, being modified again, probably in the 240s.[111]

Not all of the religious structures of third century Dura were related to the Roman military, however, and it is during this period that both the synagogue and Christian building came into being, both being adapted from buildings which had been private houses, both on the western edge of the site. The synagogue, in block L7, is the most well known building at Dura, famed especially for the paintings which were discovered within it.[112] The synagogue as it is known to us is a rebuilding of the 240s CE; the precise date a building on this spot was first used as such is unknown, but it was likely the late second century CE. The rebuilding is better dated thanks to an Aramaic inscription from the building's ceiling tiles, which gives the date 244/5 CE, in the Seleucid era, the Roman regnal year, and the era of the synagogue leader.[113]

The paintings for which the synagogue is best known are spectacular, showing a variety of Hebrew Bible scenes in vibrant detail and colour. The paintings were made in a style preserved in other sanctuaries at the site, including the temple of Bel and Mithraeum, but which is not known from Roman era sanctuaries more broadly.[114] The painting of sacred space was a local phenomenon, executed in a local idiom seen throughout the site, including the use of frontal figures and in this case adapted for Jewish usage. The technique, too, is that used throughout the site which was not 'true' fresco, in wet plaster, but instead used tempera pigments on dry plaster. The paintings included an ornamental programme and a series of at least fifty-eight identified narrative biblical scenes made in registers of panels.[115] Less well known than the paintings but no less impressive or meaningful was the synagogue's ceiling, decorated with painted tiles, which also adapt local artistic and representational practices for specifically Jewish use.[116]

The Christian building in block M8 and its paintings were less well preserved than the synagogue, but this building, like the synagogue, has stood apart from other Durene monuments in scholarship.[117] A typical Durene house in plan, the main preserved adaptations which set the building apart were the small room converted for use as a baptistery, with the installation of a basin for use as a baptismal font, and the paintings which were found there.[118] The paintings were fragmentary when excavated, and their subject has been the topic of debate since that time, although their Christian significance has not been questioned, containing as they do a range of Christian imagery, including Christ walking on water.[119]

By the third century, the entire space within the city walls was filled with buildings, as can be seen on the results of geophysics at the site, which reveal unexcavated remains throughout the area inside the city walls (Figure 2.6). The northernmost part of the site became entirely a Roman military garrison, although inhabitants of Dura still had access to the temples, at least at some times, with access regulated by gates. The Roman military controlled not only the city but also its rhythms, patrolling the city's perimeter, manning its gates, changing the circulation of the street network. In the same temple, the temple of Bel, where the painting of Conon and his family was found in the *naos*, another painting was found in the *pronaos*, also recorded in brief by Breasted in his initial work at Dura, and now preserved at Yale.[120] This painting, probably painted in the late 230s, shows a similar scene of sacrifice, but in this case, it was being made by a man named by a painted Latin inscription as Julius Terentius, known from other evidence at the site to have been tribune of the *Cohors XX Palmyrenorum* (Figure 2.7).[121] He is accompanied by the soldiers of the cohort, in camp dress with their swords, who have raised their hands in worship, in the same manner as the family of Conon in the painting discussed above (Figure 2.5).[122] The soldiers of the Terentius paintings are worshipping figures on the upper left who are probably the gods of Palmyra.[123] The *Tychae* of Dura and Palmyra sit below these three gods, identified in Greek. There is a diversity of decoration in the temple; however, it is notable that while the

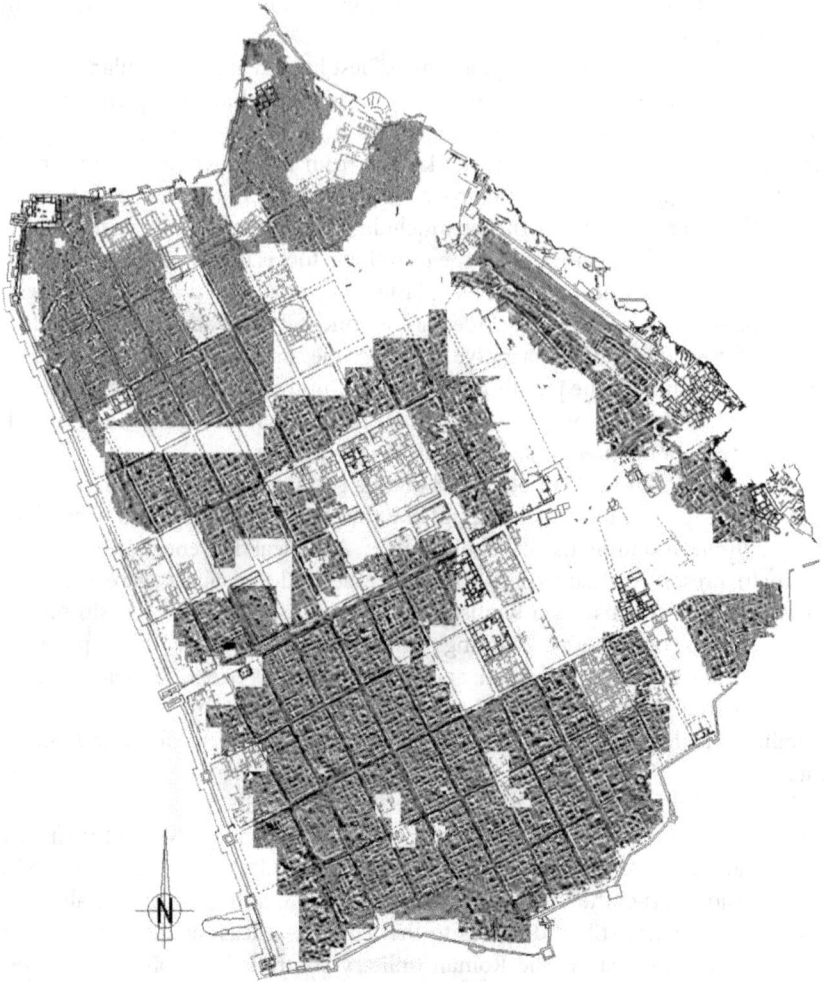

Figure 2.6 Image of geophysical results superimposed on excavated city plan. This image (by Ben Gourley, Kristian Strutt, Simon James, and author) combines the result of James, Baird, and Strutt 2013 with those of Benech 2003.

Conon and Terentius paintings depict two very different aspects of Dura's ruling groups at different points in the city's history (an elite family of the Arsacid era and the Roman military of the third century respectively), the two paintings coexisted until the time the temple went out of use and shared much of their style, form, and content.[124] Both paintings were similarly votive. In these paintings, as elsewhere at Dura, we see not only an acceptance of religious difference on the part of the Roman army for existing cults but also a compatibility between pre-Roman and Roman-era representations and practices.

Figure 2.7 Photograph of the restored painting of the Tribune of the twentieth Palmyrene cohort, Julius Terentius, and his soldiers (on the right) making a sacrifice to figures Roman emperors or Palmyrene deities (top left), 230s CE. At the bottom left are the Tyche of Dura and that of Palmyra: compare the Classical depiction of the Tyche of Dura in this context, female in form and wearing a mural crown, to the depiction of the Gad of Dura in the Gaddé relief of Figure 2.2. YUAG 1938.386.

Both the paintings of Conon and Terentius, and much else besides, including the synagogue, house church, Mithraeum, and many of the preserved documents, all owe their preservation to the building of a deep embankment within the city's walls, built in the very final years of Dura to shore up the western wall of the city against Sasanian attack. The construction of this embankment in *c.* 253 CE and later (dated by coins within the rampart) involved razing the eastern side of the blocks along wall street and using the resulting debris and material from elsewhere on the site, to fill in the remaining standing part of the buildings, as well as to fill the street between these blocks and the western wall (the so-called 'wall street').[125] The deep and deliberate deposits formed by this action, which also filled the city towers along this side of the site, created the permanently dry archaeological conditions which preserved textiles, parchments, wood, and other organic materials, which do not normally survive, even elsewhere on the site.

The precise sequence by which Dura fell in the 250s CE is problematic. It does seem, however, that there were probably two major Sasanian incursions, the latter of which was the end of Dura as a Roman site. The first of these seems to have happened *c.* 253, based on a number of hoards deposited around or before this time and some evidence for a Sasanid presence at Dura at this time.[126] By 254, the site was under Roman control and had the Roman status of a colony, as attested by *P. Dura* 32. This document attests to the complexity of the place at this time, recording the divorce of a Roman soldier, Julius Antiochus, of the fourth Scythian legion, from his wife Aurelia Amimma, a local woman who is said to be 'of Dura'; the place, however, is recorded as '*colonia Europaeorum*', the colony of the Europans. This document wasn't held for long in the archives, and it too ended up in the deep fill along the city wall.

In the final few years of Dura's existence, it seems that the Roman military had taken over all of the site, perhaps after the rest of the population had fled. Houses in the agora and elsewhere show evidence military presence in the form of small finds and fragments of scale armour.[127] Temples were deliberately desanctified, including the Mithraeum, the synagogue, the temple of Aphlad, and the Christian building, which were all partially destroyed and sealed beneath the rampart.[128] As part of this process, cult reliefs like that of Aphlad were put out of use by turning them around to face the wall before being sealed beneath the rampart: this may have been meant as a temporary measure, but, in the event, Aphlad's worshippers never returned to their *andron*.[129]

The traditional date of 256 CE for the fall of Dura was based on a single coin found on the person of a soldier who was buried hastily in the siege rampart.[130] While this is circumstantial, there is no evidence for Roman occupation after this date. From the preserved siege works, mines, and countermines, as well as evidence within the city, we know some of the specifics of Dura's final, gory, days, including the use of what amounted to poisonous gas in the siege mines.[131] By this time the site was no longer a functioning urban environment but entirely a Roman fortress at war. Temples, like the small temple of Bel in block M5, were used for storing ammunition, as was a room that had been part of the temple of Aphlad.[132] Bodies were left where they had fallen, wearing their armour, or were hastily covered in abandoned buildings.[133] Catapult bolts were found lying lined up in a street ready to be shot, inside the city, perhaps abandoned once the Sasanians had breached the walls.[134] Once the final battle occurred, many houses seem to have stood, empty, until their collapse; in some cases, their storerooms remained full of ceramics and other items too bulky to evacuate.[135] There is little material culture at Dura that would indicate a substantial occupation by Sasanian forces; for instance, the only Sasanian lamp, a stone example of a type not otherwise known at the site, comes from inside the siege mine.[136] There are some burials at the site, however, which may relate to a minor Sasanian presence at Dura after its fall, as do a handful of coins.[137]

This short overview of Dura's archaeological history shows that while the Roman period was the shortest, it was the most formative of the archaeological record of the site: much of what was excavated was from the final century, and even the final decades, of the site. The understanding of the form of Seleucid and Arsacid Dura is literally shaped by the third-century Roman occupation and the final destruction of the site. Until the recent Franco-Syrian project, little attention was paid to stratigraphy and much of what was known of the initial form of the site was an imagined topography. We now have a stronger idea of town's evolution, with the first structures in and around the citadel, the building of the city walls and later introduction of the town plan and focus on monumental structures near the centre of the town, and the gradual filling of space within the walls over the course of the Arsacid period. The later Roman period in the late second and early third century would eventually transform the northern side of the site into a Roman military environment, and in its final years, the entire site became a Roman fortress. Nonetheless, the periodization of the site and precisely when Dura moved between Seleucid, Arsacid, Roman, and perhaps even Palmyrene control is not known: not a single one of the conventional dates for these periods is secure.[138]

More than a century after the Roman military was defeated at Dura, in 363 CE, the Roman author Ammianus Marcellinus was with the emperor Julian on his Persian campaigns, and he later wrote that 'After making a march of two days … we approached the deserted city of Dura, situated on the river bank. Here so many herds of deer were found, some of which were slain with arrows, others knocked down with heavy oars, that all ate to satiety.' When Ammianus visited the site, deer may have been its only inhabitants, but the old name of the site, that known from the cuneiform tablet – Dura – had held on.[139]

Chapter 3

THE ARCHAEOLOGICAL ARCHIVE OF DURA-EUROPOS

It is often said that archaeology is a discipline of things, a study which has, at its core, a concern with objects. What are less remarked upon are the things that archaeology itself makes: the field notebooks, the photographs, the architectural plans, and the vast amount of material production that results from fieldwork. Archaeology is characterized as something which uncovers the past, but as it unearths, it transforms what it finds into something else: an archaeological archive.

The archive of Dura-Europos, held now mostly at Yale, is a necessary object of study for a number of reasons.[1] First, due to the incomplete or problematic publication of the excavations, it is often necessary to consult the archive directly for primary records. Second, the archive holds the history of the work itself, a disciplinary history of archaeology; archives can reveal much about why and how archaeology took place, including intellectual motivations, funding incentives, political stimuli, obstacles, and constraints. Third, and perhaps most importantly, the archive is both formative and revealing of the relationship between fieldwork, recording practices, and archaeological knowledge. That is, the narratives of archaeology emerge not from the ground but from a complex web of ancient remains, archaeological methods, and historical contexts. The Dura archive, in addition to all these things, also contains the archaeological assemblage of objects excavated at Dura that were brought to Yale in the *partage* which divided the material between Syria and America.

The first chapter gave an overview of the history of the excavations, and the second the archaeological site; this chapter will examine the practice and production of archaeology at Dura, both in the field and in the archive. This reveals both the potentials and limitations of archaeological data: how we know what we know about the site, and what it is possible to glean in the twenty-first century from 1920s to 1930s' fieldwork. It is crucial to examine the contexts of cultural production and the usually invisible way that archaeological field practices shape historical narratives.

Recording in the Field

For the excavations at Dura, only a few provisions were made regarding recording and archiving practices in the legal agreement between Yale and the Syrian government which permitted the work to take place. One has already been discussed, namely the arrangement of *partage* and the division of finds between Yale and Syria, relating to the ownership of archaeological finds. The only specified recording – records which the excavators were contractually obliged to keep – related to the objects: before they were divided, an inventory of the objects and a photographic dossier of these were to be submitted to the director of the Syrian antiquities service.[2] An inventory was necessary for *partage* and the photographs were understood from an early date to be useful as stand-in evidence for artefacts. All other recording was up to the excavators themselves: what they deemed intellectually relevant and proper for the (still nascent) discipline of archaeology, and what was required of them in terms of accountability to their superiors, both the scientific directors of the expedition and Angell, as president of Yale and unofficial proxy for the funders at the Rockefeller Foundation.

The initial field director, Maurice Pillet, was a problematic figure, and among the problems were his recording methodologies (or lack of them). For the first four seasons of work, there was very little in the way of attested systematic recording methodologies. Pillet likely had his own notebooks, but these were not deposited in the archive. Rather, for the early seasons, until 1931, the most comprehensive surviving documents are Pillet's formal reports to Yale and the letters he and other field staff wrote to Rostovtzeff and their superiors and colleagues at Yale. Pillet's contract specified that he produce a written and photographic record of the work done on site, that he was to cable Yale and the French Academy in the event of important discoveries, and that he was to submit a monthly 'written narrative statement concerning the excavations of that month illustrated by plans and photographs'.[3] These reports included an inventory of finds, but rather than being a contextual record, listing where the objects were found on the site, this enumerated what objects were packed in which crate: useful for insurance purposes, but much less so for archaeological context. These records noted some of the contexts in general terms (providing, for instance, a building where an object was found and the date it was found but no further detail).[4] Pillet's 1928 inventory of photographs listed seventy-six images, which were mostly of the monuments, but also included images of the workers during excavations and photographs of local people on the steppe.[5] The documents are broadly indicative of the priorities of the expedition, and Pillet's implementation of these, namely the collection of objects and recovery of monumental structures, is reflective of his Egyptological background.

The records that were produced generally went to Yale. This was true for the duration of the expedition, and the archive has been based there since, initially in the Classics Department and eventually in the Department of Ancient Art in the Yale University Art Gallery. There were of course exceptions to this. Some records were considered the personal property of individuals, and some members of the expedition also took archaeological finds, with the result being that known objects from Dura are not just in Damascus and Yale but also, via the Count Robert du Mesnil du Buisson, in Beirut, and via Cumont and Pillet, in the Louvre.[6] Other finds were left on site, including large ceramic vessels, because of problems around transport and lack of perceived value.[7] The detail and accuracy of records of any particular area of the excavation was for the most part down to the expertise, experience, and sometimes whims of the individual excavators, coupled with a range of factors from budgetary constraints (e.g. photography had a cost, and only a certain number of plates or films were available in any one season) to the weather, to the perceived importance of the part of the site being excavated.

The result was a wide range in the recording practices: Clark Hopkins kept a regular diary, but it related more to logistics than details of the excavation or archaeological evidence *per se*; Frank Brown was partial to recording on index cards, but only for monuments he found interesting; Robert du Mesnil du Buisson made detailed drawings, but from a visual perspective which might generously be called creative; and Henry Pearson and A. H. Detweiler had sharp eyes for architectural detail, which is evident in their plans, but they generally did not produce textual reports.[8] This differential approach to recording was a key factor in the lack of final publication reports from the site, as in the absence of thorough records, the ability to complete certain publications was dependent on the continued involvement of the staff members who had excavated particular areas. Timing was also crucial: the Second World War precipitated the scattering of and diversion of the field team and the severe decline of Rostovtzeff's mental health (and thus, the loss of Dura's twentieth-century *strategos*). For instance, the temple of Zeus Megistos remained unpublished because after the Second World War, Frank Brown's priorities were elsewhere (despite appeals from the Dura committee, which had by then formed at Yale), and the temple was published only when Susan Downey used Brown's archival photographs and other notes in conjunction with renewed fieldwork in the 1990s.[9]

When Hopkins took over as field director in the fifth season, there was an undeniable improvement in the quality of the excavation and its recording over the time of Pillet, testified by the proliferation of archived records. Hopkins stopped giving workers tips for good finds, as Pillet had done, and thus made the artefact recovery less biased towards inherently valuable objects.[10] The staff, including the architect, Henry Pearson, were also more specialized and skilled. From this period there was also a more systematic approach to photography, including a greater number of photographs and detailed photographic records, both of the monuments and of the objects. The latter satisfied not only the conditions of the agreement with Syria but served as records for Yale of the objects which remained in Damascus: that is, when the collection was divided, the objects not apportioned to Yale but to Damascus were replaced in the archive by photographs of those objects.

Archaeological Labours

Alongside the male Yale staff on site who were official and paid were a number of women, who were mostly unofficial and entirely unpaid. The most important of these for the purposes of understanding ancient Dura was Susan Hopkins, who usually accompanied her husband Clark to the site (Figure 3.1). Having trained extensively in Greek and Latin, Susan had met Clark Hopkins at the University of Wisconsin when they were both students of Classical Studies, and where they had first met Rostovtzeff.[11] Alongside the photographic records, the only other systematic approach to recording was Susan's work, which focused on the objects, what we would now call the 'small finds' of Dura; in her own letters she calls herself 'the cataloguer', a job she did not always relish as it tied her to the excavation house rather than the site.[12] Among the preserved records of Yale's archive are carefully made object registers, recording the find-spot of each object, even those deemed too mundane to photograph or draw, and including the date they were excavated, the field number, and a description. These documents, still not yet fully exploited, allow the reconstruction of contexts at Dura which were never published.[13] Because they were made in the field before the finds were divided between collections, they are the most complete and most accurate record of the artefacts of Dura that exists.[14] Susan Hopkins' work at Dura also included transcribing inscriptions, cleaning coins, organizing the camp (including the meals), and in later seasons, caring for her young daughter, Mary-Sue.[15]

The archive is revealing of other forms of labour which, like Susan Hopkins', was absolutely crucial to the excavation yet largely unrecognized. This includes the work of the Syrian men and boys who did all the actual excavation work: their work was often backbreaking labour involving the movement of massive quantities of earth on an almost industrial scale. Indeed, industrial methods and equipment were used, including a light-gauge Decauville mining railway which was set up at the site.[16] Along the tracks of the Decauville, carts were run, which allowed the workers to remove with relative speed massive quantities of excavated earth. This backdirt from the site was dumped over the exterior walls of the city into the *wadis* or the steppe, into the inner *wadis* of the city, or down onto the banks of the Euphrates itself. Archaeological work was considered a science by the foreign archaeologists, but for local workers their tools were the material culture of the hard labour of mining: picks, shovels, and tilting trams (see cover image).

While employing large teams of local workers was normal practice in the period, as was paying them 'local' rates of pay, the figures are nonetheless staggering. For instance, the budget for the first season of work allotted $3000 for Pillet's salary, plus travel and living expenses. The budget for the workers, 110 men for 150 days, was $3450. Dividing this into a daily wage, Pillet would earn twenty dollars daily, and each worker would earn twenty-one cents.[17] In the second season, Pillet reduced the wage without forewarning the workers, which was contentious with his American colleagues, because it caused trouble with recruitment.[18] Local labour was always a factor in the budgets, but was otherwise very little remarked upon, although Pillet complained of their 'ignorance' in his report.[19] His views of local peoples were neither unique nor unrelated to the archaeological results. The implicit paternalistic attitude towards Syrian peoples on the part of the expedition members would find its way into the interpretations of ancient Dura, as will be discussed below.

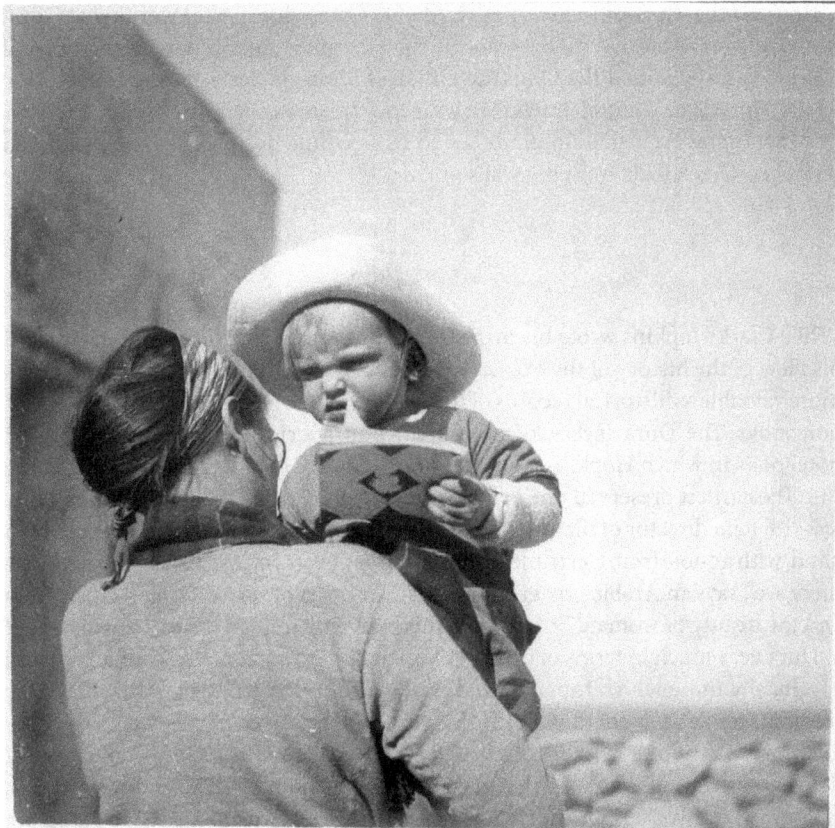

Figure 3.1 Susan Hopkins carrying her daughter in the courtyard of the excavation house in the early 1930s. Here, as in most of the photographs of her in the Dura archive, she turns her back to the camera. YUAG.

Another of those who was, like Susan Hopkins, unpaid was the graduate student Margaret Crosby. Crosby worked on the graffiti and decorated ceiling tiles at the site during her time there, and was also responsible for the photographic catalogue.[20] Unlike the male graduate assistants, Crosby had to pay her own travel to the site and received no salary, in what Hopkins later called an 'an experiment in having a woman in her own right in the camp'.[21] Rostovtzeff, in his letter to Clark saying that she would be going to Dura, was more positive about her abilities: 'She's a fine scholar, an excellent worker, does her job thoroughly and with intelligence ... I regard her as the best possible assistant for Dura. Though she looks thin and not very strong, she is very strong and able to stand all sorts of hardships. Besides, as you know, she has some means of her own.'[22] Her personal means were not only financial; her father, John Crosby, was 'an old friend' of the American secretary of state, Henry Stimson.[23] He ensured that she was equipped with letters of introduction to American diplomatic and consular officials throughout the region and that their offices were advised of her presence.²⁴ After working at Dura, she would excavate for many years in the Athenian Agora; during the Second World War, she joined the OSS (the Office of Strategic Services, the predecessor of the American Central Intelligence Agency). Among her work with the OSS was cryptography, a skill no doubt aided by her time deciphering the weathered scratched Greek texts from the walls of Dura.²⁵

Durene Days

While Clark Hopkins wrote his own story of adventure which retrospectively told his view of the history of the excavations, *The Discovery of Dura-Europos*, perhaps more valuable as historical records of the work in which he was involved are his field notebooks. The 'Dura daybooks' of the archive are a series of small lined and bound notebooks in which Hopkins, and later Frank Brown, recorded an overview of the site. The earliest preserved one is that made by Hopkins in 1928/1929, when Pillet was still field director of the site. The very first page was inscribed, in Hopkins' own hand, with a quote from Gertrude Bell's *Syria: The Desert and the Sown*: "'Three things there are", says an Arabic proverb, "that ease the heart of sorrow: water, green grass and the beauty of women."'²⁶ Hopkins thus explicitly framed his own involvement at Dura very much in terms of existing Western experiences of the Middle East and specifically those which romanticized Arab culture. The daybooks also show how the archaeologists spent their days: The next page begins on Thursday, 25 October 1928, with the six a.m. roll call of eighty-seven men and twenty-eight boys. It details the working hours, which were six–twelve and two–five, and the day was spent with the workers clearing rocks from the citadel to make space for the camp; 'Joe' (Jotham Johnson) was in the gate (the Palmyrene gate), and Hopkins was with him there for a couple of hours. Pillet was with 'the contractor' (probably the one responsible for building the excavation house), and other workers were laying rail tracks. He closed the half-page entry by writing that it had been 'A wonderful day. No dust, cool morning and evening, hot at midday'.²⁷

The entries in Hopkins' daybooks are generally, like that of his first day, relatively brief – usually less than a page for a day, noting the disposition of the supervisors in the site and details of the weather. Attempts at poetic descriptions, for instance of the sunrise or clouds, show that this was not an archaeological record in the way that we might now think of it (although scientific reports were being made for submission to the institution), but rather a hybrid of a travel journal, archaeological notebook, and sketchbook. These daybooks give a sense of what was occupying the time and minds of the staff on site, and what was being prioritized: their content is a combination of personal issues, the logistics of running the excavation, first interpretations of the archaeology that was being recovered, particular finds that caught their eye, and observations on the foreign lands and peoples they encountered.²⁸ In terms of archaeological recording, there is an interestingly haphazard and unsystematic approach; Hopkins for instance repeatedly gives measurements of objects or of depths in the earth of finds but without reference to an object number or drawing or points from which depth is measured, so these are not useful, except in a general or relative way. This is to say that it is as though Hopkins has a sense of the type of information which should be collected (and by this time, archaeological field manuals had been published, even if they had not come to his attention), but he nonetheless used the daybook in a fairly casual way. Like many archaeologists at the time, he had little formal field training, although he and Susan had been to Olynthos, in Greece, at the American excavations there.[29] For instance, about a month after starting the daybook, Hopkins begins a list titled 'Catalogue of finds up to Nov 21 (many of which should have been entered before in this book)'. He then enumerates twenty-one objects, an inconceivably tiny number of finds given the immense amount of earth that has been cleared from the citadel, and these are therefore clearly a selection: all are ceramics, although his other entries in the daybook have already noted a number of other finds in passing. No inventory numbers are given, but there are short descriptions, some measurements, and some find-spots. After twenty-one objects, he tires of the exercise and lists, simply, 'other finds': 'coins. Skeletons. Fibula … '.[30]

These notebooks fill in a great many details which were not included in the published accounts: for instance, in the 1929 daybook, Hopkins gives what is basically a stratigraphic account of the finds in the citadel, including late burials found there. There are also many details on specifics, including workers, visitors to the site, and the minutiae of daily life on the excavation. Methodologies are revealed, for instance the way in which each excavation of a block of the city was excavated by first chasing the walls with trenches along the perimeter, a method that allowed them to quickly reveal particular types of buildings and the scale of those structures, but made it very difficult to examine (e.g.) the stratigraphic relationships between the streets and the buildings or identify ground levels (Figure 3.2).[31] But the greatest value of the notebooks, particularly in Hopkins' accounts, perhaps lies in the fact that they give a sense of what it meant to be an archaeologist at Dura in the 1920s and 1930s: regular illnesses, problems of procuring supplies, a sometimes troublesome relationship with the workforce of labourers, having to supervise teams on multiple parts of the site simultaneously, a reliance on the French and Syrian military for safety and logistical assistance, and the need to produce work which satisfied Rostovtzeff and Angell back at Yale. These were very serious pressures on fieldwork.

Like the daybooks kept on site, the regular correspondence between the field staff and those at Yale (most importantly, Angell and Rostovtzeff) is useful for a number of reasons. They record and report finds as they were made, sometimes giving detail that was not, for various reasons, published. They also elucidate priorities set and problems encountered, including many issues that were glossed over by the time the publications were made. For instance, excavations were begun in some parts of the city and then abandoned and not published when they proved not to be of interest. This is the case of some Roman-era houses which were partially excavated in block D2 – the houses themselves were partially constructed from re-used ashlar masonry. These were later included on the overall map of the

Figure 3.2 Yale supervisors (facing camera) and local workers excavating the arch in the centre of the city, between blocks C7 and B8. Photograph taken in 1930–1931. YUAG d108.

site, but otherwise go unremarked in the publications; from one of Hopkins' letters to Rostovtzeff we learn that these excavations were 'just to see if what looked like a wall of cut stone was a public building or a house'.[32] That is, the ashlar masonry was tempting in case it was a public building; as soon as the building was seen to be an average house, its excavation was abandoned. Other letters are among the only record of excavation of particular structures, such as Alan Little's description of the houses in block D5 in a letter to Rostovtzeff, which includes a note that human remains were found interred in a jar in a house; the sketch plan he made shows that when excavating, they did not realize that they had dug through the floor level and revealed foundations of earlier levels, as these are marked on the sketch as 'ledges' in a room.[33] The letters also make clear that the large workforce and large areas being cleared meant that the expedition members were spread very thin and not always able to study the archaeology to the level they would have liked, as was the price of such a large-scale operation. The consequence and restraints of the pressures of the excavation under which they were operating had a real impact on the nature of the excavations themselves. For example, Frank Brown, in a letter to Rostovtzeff, wrote, 'It is hard to do much toward studying the walls [of the city] while actual excavation is in progress. With 360 workmen Hopkins, du Mesnil, and I are continually on the run.'[34]

While the letters of the excavators were always, in many ways, official and have been retained by the archive, other correspondence of a less formal nature is also revealing of the situation on the site. These include the letters that Susan Hopkins wrote to her family, which were privately held but have now been published.[35] These letters, unguarded in their gossip about the people at the site and unworried about institutional politics, report much that would have been inappropriate in the official letters, including details of the camp setup (for instance the use of one of the citadel towers as a makeshift kitchen, which would have left its own archaeological traces) and the people she found troublesome on site: Pillet in particular, but also the Rostovtzeffs, on the occasions that they visited.[36] While Pillet's unpleasant manner is remarked upon by Clark Hopkins and others, it is only in Susan's letters that, for instance, it becomes clear the magnitude of the problems, including that Pillet had been telling other archaeologists working in the region that Jotham Johnson had been carving inscriptions in the Palmyrene gate himself, in order to get the acclaim of publishing them.[37]

Jotham Johnson had in fact carefully recorded the inscriptions of the Palmyrene gate. This would eventually lead to his work reconstructing the genealogies of Durene families, on the basis of attested individuals in inscriptions at the site.[38] Like Hopkins, Johnson was both a serious scholar of the ancient world and deeply in thrall to the romance of working in the Middle East: he wrote of his experience for his *alma mater*, Princeton, in the 1929 *Princeton Alumni Weekly*: 'The Outer World believes that archaeology is a profession of romance, of stately caravans in far-off lands, of exciting discoveries, of leisurely study. The Outer World is not far wrong.'[39] His attitude towards the workmen, too, while normal at the time, would now be recognized as deeply problematic. In his words, 'Managing the workmen is remarkably like taming lions or running slum kids at a fresh air camp. The medium is the same, a four-foot switch, and equally uncountenanced by authority.'[40] In Johnson's travel writing there is a clear sense of the elision of ancient Dura and modern Syria, with the ancient city being socially stratified in the same way the site was in the 1920s: 'He [Seleucos] called it [the site] Europos, and the inhabitants were Europeans; the natives – it seems they had them, even in those days – called it simply *Doura*, the Castle.'[41] In Johnson's description, then, the ancient site had been occupied, on the one hand, by Greeks, Europeans (here, it seems, both in the sense of being 'of Europos' and 'from Europe') and, on the other hand, by 'natives'. Johnson saw this mirrored in his own time, and he identified, naturally, with the former. In this reading, the expedition members were Greeks and thus inheritors of the territory; the local workers were subordinate.

Visualising Ancient Dura

Of all archaeological recording techniques, perhaps the one that was the most entrenched by the late 1920s was the making of architectural plans of excavated structures. The ability to draw a plan was considered a key ability of field archaeologists, and indeed it was enumerated amongst Pillet's skills when he was hired as field director: he is described as an 'architect and engineer'.[42] The other field directors, Hopkins and Brown, also drew plans. The recognition of the importance of the plans is evident in the employment of specialized architects, including Henry Pearson from the Yale School of Fine Art, and A. H. Detweiler, who would go on to be the dean of the College of Architecture at Cornell and president of the American Schools of Oriental Research. Detweiler was responsible for the site plan which remains the most accurate and detailed published plan to emanate from the Yale expedition (Figure 1).

The survey of the site which formed the basis for Detweiler's plan is the only record of a number of structures, as he recorded all exposed architecture, including that which had been uncovered by clandestine digs. This involved superimposing a grid on the site and making plans of all exposed architecture within each square, whether or not it was the Yale expedition which had excavated it; eventually these detailed plans were reduced in size and reproduced together, being redrawn as an overall plan. Detweiler's methods were refined in the field at sites including Dura and later published in his *Manual of Archaeological Surveying*, which uses Dura as an example, including reproducing pages from his own surveying notebook made in the field.[43] Despite the importance of his plan of the site (and the studies on which he based them), one of the problems that nonetheless arises is that it treats the site as though it is made up of a single phase.[44] This is partly an issue of the conventions of contemporary draftsmanship, as the solid black lines that were used to represent the walls of each structure do not show the relationships between walls (e.g. where they abut or superimpose). While reconstructions were made of what Dura looked like in its Hellenistic and later phases, there is no phased plan of the remains of the site itself.

Some of Detweiler's reconstruction drawings showed the extant remains against restored projections. Detweiler's drawings demonstrate his impressive knowledge of Durene architecture, and they are convincing in re-creating the lost parts of the buildings. They also show the way in which the visualizations of the site elide contemporary local workers with ancient inhabitants (Figure 3.3). Figures wearing the long contemporary garments and headcovering hold the scale in the drawing of the 'present' state of remains, mirrored by shadowy robed figures in the same position in the restoration of the ancient structure.[45] In a typescript amongst his papers, Detweiler, like Johnson and others, compares the local workers to the labourers at home: 'The strangely clad figures at work in the dusty excavation site become as natural as a road-gang at work with steam-rollers and tarring apparatus.'[46] Such class distinctions were clearly another facet to the relationship between the Yale team and the local workforce. Reflecting on his drawing of isometric reconstructions, Detweiler stated, 'If properly presented, the atmosphere of the period can be recreated for the layman as successfully as if photographs were available from the period being studied.'[47] Such drawings then were not only to understand and communicate the technical details of architecture but were meant to evoke a sense of place, a place that was considered to be an authentic past by its makers.

As Detweiler alluded, perhaps nothing was more evocative for the understanding of the past than a photograph. Photographs were, by the 1920s, an integral part of archaeology, and as already noted, the systematic record of photographs taken was

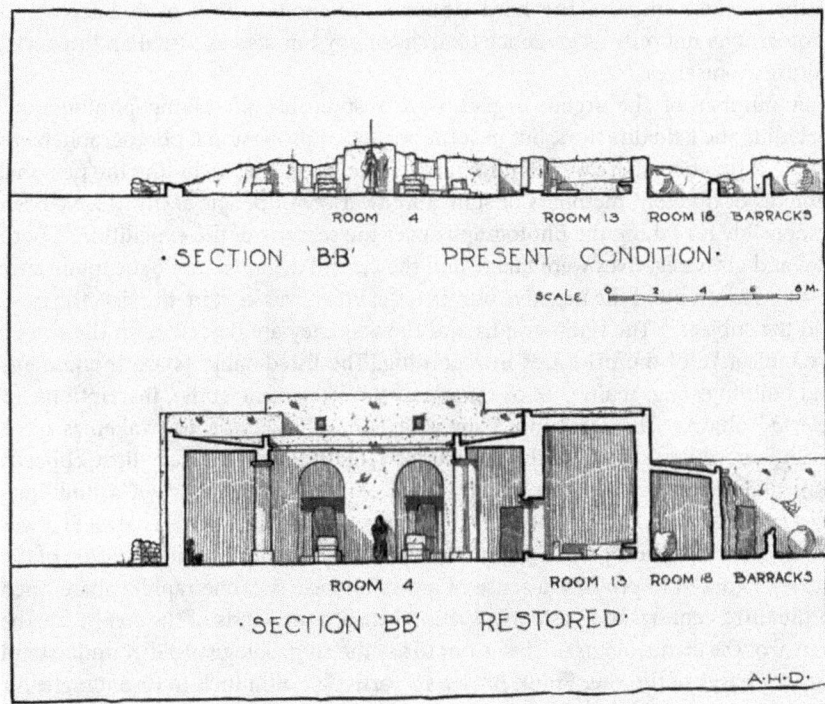

Figure 3.3 Detweiler's drawing of extant remains in block X7 (at top) and his restoration of the superstructure beneath. Note the person in local dress holding the scale rod in the middle of the upper drawing, and the shadowy figure in the same position in the lower drawing. YUAG Y597b.

one of the most important forms of recording at the site. Some developing was even done on site, in tents, before the excavation house was built, such was the importance of the prints. Many were sent with the correspondence back to Yale, as evidence of the work that was being carried out in the field and proof that the expedition was giving a return on the investment: not only in terms of scientific or intellectual value but in terms of inscriptions and objects for the collections of the Department of Classics and the Yale Art Gallery.[48] Photographs of objects guaranteed their authenticity, their antiquity, and acted as a 'virtual witness' for those not in the field.[49]

This evidentiary quality was one of the key reasons photographs were taken, but it would be a mistake to think of archaeological photographs purely as evidence of that which was excavated on site. Rather, photographs serve a range of purposes, including visually constructing the ancient site and the nature of the modern intervention there, and fixing the relationships of different people to the site – for instance in the case of female archaeologists like Margaret Crosby, who was photographed scrubbing the Roman mosaic floors, or the depictions of the workers undertaking hard labour.[50] We should think of archaeological photographs not only as evidence of archaeology but also as visual and material culture themselves.

A number of the archaeologists were responsible for taking photographs, including the field directors, but in some seasons, a professional photographer was hired. In practice, there were a number of cameras on site, including the personal cameras of different members of staff, and a variety of people seem to have been responsible for taking the photographs over the seasons of the expedition.[51] Both film and glass negatives were taken, and the careful negative catalogue made later in New Haven listed the negative number, the box it was kept in, the size, the type, and the subject.[52] The photographs and the way they are described in the record are indicative of the priorities in recording. The listed subjects are monuments and buildings (e.g. main gate or temple of the Palmyrene gods), inscriptions, or selected objects. The direction from which the photograph was taken is often given, but while there is a concern with orientation, there is very little concern with phasing or levels: the photographs are generally taken when a building's excavation was complete, which usually meant excavated to the floor level, if it was recognized. The photographs, like the site plan, erased much of the duration of the site and worked to produce a sense of a single-phase site, one rapidly abandoned in the third century and patiently waiting beneath the sands of the steppe for the arrival of the archaeologists. This is not to say the archaeologists didn't understand earlier phases of the site: Frank Brown in particular did much to disentangle, for instance, the earlier periods of the agora. Rather, it is an issue with archaeological photography and recording more broadly, which seeks to capture a particular architectural view of archaeological remains, devoid of objects or inhabitation.[53] Particularly at Classical sites like Dura, there was almost a desire to capture the building as art object, leading to different photographic attempts to aestheticize Dura's buildings, which, being built mostly of mudbrick and plaster, did not sit easily alongside the Classical canon. Photographs worked to make the site more monumental than it was, more Classical, and hence more important. Within Classical Archaeology, the boundary between scientific and aesthetic images was always blurry.[54] This is not because Classical archaeologists did not think of their enterprise as being amongst emerging scientific fields – they did – but the artistic value they sought in the objects consistently transcended any notional scientific objectives.

While a human presence is invisible in the catalogue description of the photographs, the images themselves are populated with many figures (Figure 3.4). These are generally the workers of the site, posed as human scale against the architecture, in the same way that human figures were used in the drawings of Detweiler, discussed above. Also unremarked in the catalogue descriptions of photographs, and unpublished in the reports, were photographs which included the realities of archaeological labour, including the use of mining equipment (Figure 3.5). Nonetheless such photographs were taken (and photographic materials were at a premium), perhaps as a way of helping the photographers reinforce the difference between themselves and the local workers.

Figure 3.4 Photograph of worker posed inside bock M8, 1934–1935. YUAG h306.

The contemporary world of the archaeologists became the ancient world they were excavating, in some cases, by means of the local people employed as labourers. The careful staging of romanticized scenes was meant to conjure a timeless East, one that both let the viewer place the local people in the past and

Dura-Europos

Figure 3.5 Photograph showing workers excavating along wall street with picks, shovels, baskets, and trams. To the left is the inside of the western city wall, to the right, block L7. YUAG fxIII93.

which peopled the Roman period. That such conceptions entered the archaeology is clear at Dura for instance in the way in which Roman houses are labelled as having *harems* (the women's area of an Islamic house) and *diwans* (reception rooms in Islamic architecture).[55] Just as Johnson's description of local 'natives' for his Princeton classmates elided the ancient and modern, so did the photographs. The Syrian men and boys were depicted as being 'of the past', but the past wasn't theirs to possess or study. Rather, they are scale and cipher, signifying an Other: photography created 'the Orient as European canvas'.[56] The publications which resulted from the excavation usually used photographs of monuments without any human figure in them. These carefully cleaned-up images served to position archaeology as a science, and the science of archaeology demanded tidy sites in its photographs. As carefully manicured stage sets, they also presented the buildings as blank canvases onto which archaeology's narratives could be projected (Figure 3.6).[57] The situation at Dura was not unique: in the same period, in the sky above Syria, Antoine Poidebard was taking photographs that would be published as *Le Trace de Rome*, using photographs to create a connection between Roman and French civilizations in the Mandate zone (that many of the monuments he photographed were not actually Roman in date hardly mattered).[58]

The way in which the human figure used in photographs is reflective and constitutive of particular values can be seen in the contrast with portraits of archaeologists. While the workers appear either as scale or *en masse* as part of the great movement of earth, the portraits of archaeologists are generally singular, focused on individuals, and show them as active participants in the archaeological project: making notes, pointing at features, or triumphantly posed atop the architecture as a hunter atop a carcass, or Du Mesnil always in official French military dress.[59] These serve to legitimize archaeological control of the site and naturalize the authority of the archaeologist over it.

From the time of the spectacular discovery of the synagogue, one of the central demands made consistently by the Yale team to the field team was for photographs of the paintings. When the paintings of Dura didn't fulfil the desires of the Yale committee for clean, crisp Pompeian paintings, it was assumed the photographs

Figure 3.6 Photograph of archives building in block G3, from the south, following excavation, probably taken in 1931–1932. YUAG e303.

were the problem. Initial photographs of paintings were considered out of focus by the Dura committee at Yale, and this resulted in hiring of a professional photographer.[60] They were still disappointed with the results, and it would be some time before they understood that it was in part the paintings themselves that were not fulfilling their expectations.

In the photographic archive, there are many photographs of Dura's synagogue, and in large part, these tell a story of the spectacular failure of photography to adequately record the remains. Both the expedition directors and the professional photographer tried to capture Dura's paintings, but on the whole, they failed. There was not enough space in the excavated room to get full views, there was not enough light under the corrugated cover that had been installed to protect the paintings, and the camera was just not the right tool to capture the large colour paintings from within an enclosed space. The photographs of Dura's synagogue taken in Syria in the 1930s, together with the painted reproductions of the original paintings made by Herbert Gute, became a substitute for the paintings which remained in Syria and were inaccessible to most Western scholars. In scholarship on these and other paintings from the site, the lack of good legible colour photographs has resulted in decades of scholarly disputes about their content and meaning.[61] It is perhaps also one reason the reading of them is so beholden to textual sources.[62] The images of the paintings which were included in the final report, when it was finally published in 1956, were from those taken after the paintings had been removed from the building and reconstructed in the museum in Damascus.[63]

Images like Figure 3.7, catching the moment of the day when a shaft of light fell under the corrugated field cover onto a face of the painting of Moses, show the way that the photographs tried to grasp at something more fleeting. Such images attest to the way that the photographic beauty attainable with the camera was used to compensate for other shortcomings. It was not just the synagogue paintings that photography failed to adequately record (to the standards of the time) but the paintings throughout the site. For many of the paintings, the only surviving version of them as a whole comes from modern reconstruction paintings. These paintings were sometimes made in New Haven, by people who had never seen the original paintings in person, but worked from photographs and other records.

The Production of the Archive

The archive was not static once the expedition ended, even with the disjuncture caused by the Second World War, but transformed and moved a number of times. It was also added to, for instance, by many more photographs that were taken, of objects, of plans, and drawings, for publication and other purposes.[64] The prints themselves, of photographs taken throughout the expedition, continued to have a life in the archive long after the expedition ended. A series of annotations in different hands and different media shows the history of different sequences of images that

Figure 3.7 Photograph of painting of Moses from the synagogue, while *in situ* during excavation, beneath a temporary awning YUAG FI77.

were made. They sometimes reveal the changing interpretations of different parts of the site, for instance changing the name of monuments.[65] The photographs also, of course, captured material that the photographer had no intention to record, and thus allow alternate interpretations and readings of the site.

At Dura as elsewhere the people who wrote the reports were very often not those who had worked at the site, and the photographs, like the daybooks, became sites of translation between the field and the archive.[66] Other parts of the site moved and could be encountered in other contexts; the synagogue paintings and ceiling tiles moved to Damascus, where the paintings were re-installed in a purpose-built reconstruction, and the paintings of the Christian building and Mithraeum to Yale. The most mobile part of Dura, however, were its artefacts.

The field object registers compiled largely by Susan Hopkins, as discussed already, are the most complete record of the objects excavated, because they were made before the objects were divided amongst museums, although they cover only the fifth through tenth seasons of the expedition. These recorded thousands of objects, describing them briefly in textual lists. Objects were also recorded in drawings and photographs, and photographs *of* the drawings of objects. In the field, almost 40 per cent of the photographs taken were of objects. The photographic record was a means of reproduction and of sending information back to Yale, but it was also a way of holding on to material that stayed in Syria after the *partage*.[67] The photographic record as a whole was a responsibility of the *accord* (i.e. photographs of all objects were to be given to Syria), but it is unclear if this actually happened in practice. Indeed, given that Nicholas Toll (of the Kondakov Institute in Prague, who was responsible for the excavation of the necropolis) found it necessary to photograph all the Dura material in Damascus, it seems this might not have consistently happened in practice (Figure 3.8). The photographs of objects were also a way that the excavators could retain material that stayed in Damascus, and for the objects that went in the *partage* to Damascus (when the collection was divided between Syria and America), the photographs essentially *became the objects*, as the Damascus collections were not accessible to the Western scholars who continued to work on the Dura material. This was problematic, because the objects chosen to be photographed were those which were valued in particular ways: priorities were placed on Greek or Roman material (especially imports) to the detriment of locally produced forms (of ceramics, lamps, and other objects), even though the latter made up a larger proportion of the assemblage.[68]

The way that objects were photographed is also revealing about where value was placed. At Dura, the objects were positioned in arrangements that sometimes are indistinguishable from, for instance, still life painting. These objects were very rarely photographed in context, but rather removed from the structures and strata in which they were found, arranged according to the way in which they were understood (typologically and by material, rather than as assemblages), and photographed as *objets d'art* rather than artefacts. In part, this was because they were a different category of archaeological evidence than the architecture, which itself demanded buildings be swept clean of objects. The exclusion of human agency from object photos and the desire to make them authorless is further underscored by the manipulation of the negatives: in a pre-photoshop world, this involved altering the negatives to eliminate the background by physically painting it out.[69] This separation between find (ideally isolated against a blank backdrop) and context (architecture cleaned of all finds) in the photography is broadly

Figure 3.8 Photograph by Nicholas Toll of a green-glazed vase and commonware jug from the temple of Azzanathkona, taken in Damascus in 1946. Dam-177, YUAG.

indicative of the approaches of the time, and this disassociation not surprising given the nature of archaeology in this period, as archaeology was supplementary to philology or history.[70]

One of the forces shaping the archaeological interpretations made about Dura was an analogy drawn between ancient and modern peoples of the Euphrates valley, and between ancient and modern 'Oriental' people broadly. In an unpublished manuscript from Clark Hopkins' personal papers entitled 'The Old and the New on the Syrian Euphrates', Hopkins explicitly draws out what he sees as the links between the ancient inhabitants of the site and the modern people there, including the workers, simultaneously making a direct equation between the two, and implying the contemporary people couldn't possibly understand the ancient (the study must be, by implication, made by foreigners):

The nomad Arabs dig for us on the banks of the Euphrates. They understand some of the domestic arrangements in the modern houses; they cannot comprehend the significance of the paintings nor the meaning of the parchments and papyri. They live apart their simple primitive lives, looking a little contemptuously at modern politics, preferring the free, easy life of the desert. On moonlight nights they dance in the Turkish manner, singing to the accompaniment of the Rhababa, the single string stretched over sheepskin, and to the double flute made from the long bones of eagle wings. I like best the song the camel troops sing as they move out into the solitude. It is guided by the sound of the tom-tom and rises and falls monotonously along the line of camels. It seems to express, however, a life unchanging and wild; and even after the caravan has disappeared into the desert, that tune seems to echo through the desert spaces. It is the song of a region that goes on from age to age while kingdoms rise and fall, while men come and go unnoticed.[71]

The conflation of ancient and modern peoples, as already seen in Johnson's travel writing, in Detweiler's reconstruction drawings, in the excavation photographs, and here in Hopkins' description of an unchanging (if also romanticising) primitivism, is also a recurring theme. The relationship between the local workers and the Yale excavators became part of the interpretation of archaeology. We see this implicitly in photographs and explicitly in Hopkins' manuscript. The language of subjugation, of local populations described as naive 'minors' under the hegemony of a justified overlord that had their best interests at heart, was not only the terms for understanding the ancient peoples of the Euphrates under the Romans; it was the language used by France and America to describe the peoples of Syria under the mandate. Hopkins' words are the language of the League of Nations.[72] The pervasiveness of this world view perhaps meant such interpretations were almost inevitable in Hopkins' context. Their geography, too, compressed the ancient and modern worlds, expressing one in terms of the other (as for example in Gute's map of the region, Figure 1.3).

After the Expedition

C. Bradford Welles, Frank Brown, and Alfred Bellinger, all Rostovtzeff's students who worked extensively on Dura material, remained at Yale and made important contributions to archaeology and ancient history after the war.[73] All would also have long scholarly genealogies, training their own students at Yale and the American Academy at Rome. Archaeology and archaeologists would remain deeply entwined with the State Department and the war effort. Welles was also head of Counter Espionage section of the OSS during the war, in Cairo.[74] With Robert O. Fink and J. Frank Gilliam, he produced the final report on the parchments and papyri in the 1950s; it appeared in 1959 and remains the landmark publication of the Dura documents. Frank Brown was also part of the OSS, as was Margaret Crosby.

Little is currently known about what happened at the site itself between Yale ceasing work in the late 1930s and the Franco-Syrian expedition beginning in the 1980s.[75] Throughout the 1950s and 1960s the publications programme continued, depending heavily on the generosity of individual private donors.[76] In the 1960s, Welles, still at Yale, and Detweiler, then in the College of Architecture at Cornell University, tried to complete the publication of the material, including putting in a request to the American Council of Learned Societies for funding, for volumes that would cover the temple of Zeus Megistos and the House of Lysias, among others.[77] However, as Brown (then at the American Academy at Rome) was the excavator, they needed his cooperation and, as Welles wrote to Detweiler, the situation with Brown was 'delicate and amorphous'.[78] It eventually became clear that Brown was not eager to be involved.[79] It was a situation that was not resolved, and it ended with the deaths of Welles in 1969 and Detweiler in 1970.[80] Welles' death also meant the final publication on the inscriptions of Dura was not completed, and this remains the case almost fifty years later.

For many years the collections, including objects and archives, were held by the Classics Department of Yale. Ann Perkins, an art historian, was responsible for their care before they were transferred to the Yale Art Gallery in 1975. Perkins took over care of the Dura material at Yale in 1957, including editing a number of the final reports, and she wrote *The Art of Dura Europos* based on her experience with the archive and objects.[81] Published in 1973, this was the first general book on the site since Rostovtzeff's own *Dura-Europos and Its Art*. Perkins also wrote a short summary of the archive, as it existed when she worked with it, which was still the document supplied to scholars working in the archive in the early 2000s.[82] The sets of files she enumerated included the photographic negative catalogue and the field object catalogues already mentioned, as well as a card file which was meant to supplement the photographic catalogue (but was incomplete), locus files, which collated loose material on particular part of the site, and an object catalogue.

This object catalogue was another series of cards, which collated all information about each object from the site. While it was incomplete, the attempt at comprehensiveness is notable, as is the way they were organized, that is, typologically: the primary piece of data used to organize it was not the accession number but the object type. It is also interesting that Perkins did much to try and update the archive into something that was more workable, for instance updating photographic labels from general terms such as 'architectural view' to something more specific, and updating the terminology where the name of a monument had changed in light of more recent finds or research.[83] The cards and prints within the archive contain the material history of these interventions, as the series of corrections and additions in different hands is visible on the records.[84] From these changes, it is possible to observe some of the ways in which archaeological archives impose an order on the records of the excavation which they didn't have in the field. This work was key in making the records accessible to new scholarship (and continues to be), but in some ways, this made the archaeology seem more systematic than it had been. The typological classification of the finds was to be mirrored in the reports which would be produced by Yale students and graduates, including Dyson's 1968 work on the commonware pottery, Downey's 1969 report on the Heracles sculpture and subsequent 1977 report on the stone and plaster sculpture, all published within the official series, and other unpublished ones including the 1971 report on the leatherwork.[85] Perkins' organization of the archive marked a major transformation in the shape of the surviving material and the way it was encountered by users of the archive, one that changed again decades later when the information was digitized.

After the death of Welles, much of the Dura publication programme remained incomplete. In 1970 Harald Ingoldt, Ramsey McMullen, and J. J. Pollitt, the 'Dura Committee' of the Yale Classics department wrote a report on the state of affairs at Dura which survives in the papers of the later acting president of Yale, Hannah Holborn Grey. Among the points made by the scholars is that the programme of publication ought not to be abandoned, on the basis of continued scholarly interest in Dura and issues raised by the Dura material; it also points out that the Rostovtzeff's estate, willed to the Classics department, was meant to be used to further research in the fields of archaeology and ancient history, and that Dura, of course, was close to his heart.[86] Further, the committee raised the question of the 'moral obligation' to publish, given that Dura was financed by outside funds (i.e. Rockefeller), and pointed out the archaeological obligation was also imperative: 'An unpublished, or only partly published excavation is worse than no excavation at all.'[87] In addition to this ethical obligation, written long before most archaeological organizations had thought to codify such things, the committee pointed out that the most interesting material from Dura was not the imported material culture 'of Hellenistic or Roman origin' that had so interested the initial excavators, but the material that was unique to Dura, 'those made by the native, Semitic population, or by the neighbouring Iranians'.[88] The interest in this material marks an important change in focus and priorities, recognizing that 'non-Classical' nature of Dura was in fact its strength as a body of data.[89]

The Dura committee was also cognisant of the fact some material (including the parchments and papyri) should have been returned to Syria as their final publication was completed, as was the contractual obligation to the government of Syria.[90] They closed their letter with a quote from Rostovtzeff, who, in his application for funds to complete the final three seasons at Yale, had written thus: 'In uncovering the important monuments to which I have alluded, we have not only increased the fame of America in the learned world, but at the same time incurred obligations. We are expected to bring our work to a reasonable conclusion, and we are also expected to publish adequately the results so far attained and to be attained in the future.'[91] Unfortunately, the plans they suggested – publishing a volume on the painting, and another on the architecture and town planning (which they reported Brown to have now abandoned due to his obligations in Italy at the American Academy), as well as the inscriptions, the Mithraeum, the history, and the cults – did not come to fruition.[92]

In the meantime, the Conon painting and the synagogue paintings remained safely in the National Museum in Damascus, where Pearson helped build and install the rebuilt synagogue in 1936.[93] There, they were protected and did not suffer any of the well-intentioned but ill-fated conservation issues that happened to some of the paintings at Yale.[94] Rather, the problem was lack of access to good reproductions, specifically photographs and permission to reproduce them, and scholars as a result continued to (with few exceptions, up to the present day) work from the relatively poor quality reproductions made by the original expedition or the paintings made by Gute (Figure 3.9).

Until 1975 the bulk of the Dura collection (then enumerated at 8,000 objects) had its home in Yale's Classics Department; its curator was a member of the department. In 1975, the collection was passed to the Yale Art Gallery and the

Figure 3.9 Photograph, dated June 1959, of Gute's reproduction of one of the synagogue painting panels as installed in the Classical collection at Yale, above vitrines containing material from Gerasa and Dura. YUAG Yale-2200.

curatorship of Susan Matheson.[95] In 1982, the Dura material was the focus of the exhibition *Life in an Eastern Province: The Roman Fortress at Dura-Europos*. The accompanying checklist for the exhibit shows that the full range of Dura's material culture was included, not only the paintings and inscriptions but also ceramics and small finds.[96]

The continued stewardship, under Susan Matheson (now the Moly and Walter Bareiss curator of Ancient Art) and now also Lisa Brody (associate curator of Ancient Art), and the preservation of the objects of Dura and its archive have allowed a new installation of a permanent gallery in Yale University Art Gallery. The *Mary and James Ottaway Gallery of Dura-Europos* opened in 2014, after some of its material was displayed in New York and Boston during an extensive refurbishment of the art gallery.[97] The continued preservation has also allowed the study and publication of material excavated by the original expedition, including the arms and armour, the terracottas, the houses, and the Christian building, which would have been otherwise impossible.[98] Digitization projects undertaken using the archive mean that much of the Dura material is now available online, including all the objects accessioned to the Yale University Art Gallery and the Dura photographs.[99] The digitization – largely of images – marks another major transformation in the way that archaeological information is encountered and used. The new gallery, which includes the freshly conserved Christian paintings and paintings from the Mithraeum, displays a full range of the type of objects recovered at the site and parses their relevance to its religion and society. The most recent status of the Dura material held in Damascus is that they too remain safe, although the situation is precarious.

Archaeological archival material tends to take on an epistemological status of 'the site itself', rather than being recognized as representations and interpretations.[100] Archaeological work doesn't stop with the end of the field project. Rather there is an act of translation, between field records in the archive and published accounts, which is usually invisible. As can be seen from all aspects of archaeological practice at Dura, the intellectual production of Dura's history was tied to the recording methods and especially to the attitudes of the archaeologists towards Syrians and local workers. These attitudes were not separate from the production of the archaeological interpretation but were part of it, as their relationship with their workers and with the Middle East more broadly was transposed onto their archaeological drawings, photographs, and writings.

The metanarrative, in the way local people were represented in photographs, in drawings, and in the writing of the archaeologists, is that of an ancient occupation of the Middle East by Europeans. In this way, the past of the region was constructed as an object for study by the West, and while the contemporary people of the region might be 'living in the past', the past was not considered to be theirs.

The paternalistic attitude of archaeologists working in the Middle East in the 1920s through the 1940s (of which Dura is only one example) was reflected in the practice, and interpretation of archaeology, and this is not an issue only for the history of archaeology, nor only for the historiography of the site. It is relevant, for example, to current discussions of 'World' heritage and the protection of Syrian sites in the present conflict. Modern archaeological practice, particularly that by 'foreigners', needs to be reflective about the legacy of such practices and to recognize that archaeological knowledge isn't something which emerges as an independent science from the Syrian sand.

Chapter 4

THE TEXTS OF DURA-EUROPOS

One of the chief motivations of the excavations at Dura was the search for documents. Yale was already acquiring papyri before work at the site had begun, and by the early 1930s had amassed an impressive collection.[1] Dura obliged, producing a significant collection of parchments, papyri, inscriptions, and graffiti, even more valuable because it was from a secure archaeological context, unlike earlier parts of Yale's collection, which had been purchased and secured by other means. Languages found at Dura included Greek, Latin, Persian, Palmyrenean, Safaitic, Hatrean, and Hebrew. These were preserved in a range of media, including the parchments and papyri of official records, a variety of stone inscriptions, as well as scratched graffiti and painted texts. Of these, only the parchments and papyri received a full publication (the texts published in this series were numbered in a sequence abbreviated as *P. Dura*).[2] The inscriptions and graffiti were mostly published in preliminary form, but the planned final report on these did not appear, as discussed in the previous chapter, and most are not included in the scholarly corpora whose volumes form the starting point for epigraphers: for these reasons, the textual evidence of Dura has perhaps not received as much attention as it has deserved.[3] This chapter aims to give a survey of this evidence and to trace and unpack the main narratives that have arisen from the surviving texts. Chief among these is the nature of Durene identity, between the Hellenic, Arsacid, and Roman worlds.

Durene Documents

While it is not unusual for inscriptions carved into stone to survive, the preservation of parchments and papyri is rarer, enabled by particular archaeological conditions. At Dura, it was the desiccated environment created by the deep mounds of earth used to reinforce the city's walls and towers against Sasanian invaders which allowed their preservation. Most of the preserved documents of Dura were found in this destruction fill used along the interior of the city. Documents which had been held in the local archives of Dura for centuries were preserved by the act of their discard and by the site's destruction.

From the textual remains unearthed by excavations at the site, much emerges about the life of Dura. There is evidence for legal practices and the administration of the city, particularly in the parchments. The parchments and papyri of the military archives of Roman Dura are amongst the most extensive found anywhere in the empire.[4] In the inscriptions, many of which are religious dedications, there is a rich documentation concerning the religious life. Graffiti scratched into the stone and plaster surfaces of the walls attest to more informal activities, from shopping lists and inventories to short remembrances of individuals, their quantity vastly outnumbering the formal texts. Other types of texts, like *ostraca*, texts made on sherds of pottery, are known from a very small number of examples.[5] The small number, however, is probably a result of lack of attention to individual potsherds during the excavations.[6] The linguistic diversity is matched by a diversity of materials and forms, from the formal Latin inscription carved into the arch of Trajan, to Greek marriage contracts on parchment, to painted Persian texts on the decorated walls of the synagogue, to a Hatrean graffito scratched into wall plaster.

As discussed in Chapter 2, very little survives from Dura's Hellenistic period. Yet, the city is generally classified as a Greek one due in part to the perhaps unwarranted primacy given to language in ascribing culture. Just as is the case with the physical form of early Hellenistic Dura discussed in Chapter 2, because of the absence of early evidence, there is a general necessity to project backwards from later, richer, evidence. Indeed, the firm evidence not only of texts but for archives themselves comes from the Arsacid (Parthian) era and later: The archives office of the Chreophylakion for example is mentioned in a third-century CE (Roman) copy of an early succession law, *P. Dura* 12. Overwhelmingly, the surviving textual evidence from Dura belongs to the periods of Arsacid and Roman rule: just two parchments are dated before this time.[7] Similarly, there are no preserved inscriptions at Dura, Greek or otherwise, until the first century BCE. In addition to the many chronological complexities of Dura's evidence, there is also a need to exercise caution when equating language with culture. This is a particular problem because Dura's largely Greek written records have been long used to argue for its fundamentally 'Greek' character, but those written records in Greek are almost entirely products of the Arsacid and Roman eras, and are records of particular types, being mostly civic documents or religious inscriptions. There is, however, evidence of connectivity to a wider Greek literary world, and in addition to civic documents, a fragment of Herodotus was also found.[8]

The earliest preserved inscriptions are actually from the second half of the first century BCE. While it is possible that this late date for the earliest inscription is an accident of recovery, the lack of early Greek inscriptions from excavations that sometimes went as deep as bedrock in the vicinity of the citadel and agora, where the Hellenistic occupation was focused, would apparently indicate that there was not a substantial epigraphic habit in Dura until rather late in its existence. As noted in Chapter 2, even the precise nature of the rule of the city, its administration, and its periodization from Seleucid, to Arsacid, to Roman rule are not entirely clear. From an early inscription found in the temple of Artemis, dated to 31 BCE, there is mention of a *strategos* and *genearch* (probably meaning something like 'general and ruler of tribes').[9] This title does not recur, but the inscription hints at the organization of the city on a tribal basis in the Arsacid era, which is otherwise obscure. In the late first century CE, *P. Dura* 16 records the *strategos kai epistates*, 'general and overseer', of the city, but the document is a registry roll of copies and may preserve an earlier, rather than contemporary, title. A *strategos* in a Hellenistic city would typically be the chief official of the city (in Egypt, where there is more detailed documentation for this period, they were responsible for the *klerouchoi*, the land allotments given to settlers, such as we know existed also at Dura), and an *epistates* an intermediary for the king.[10] Under Arsacid rule, the same title is used for governors of provinces. The *strategos* of Dura, then, was a position which likely started off as a military one under the Seleucids and became a title of civic authority. The *strategos* continues to be attested throughout the Arsacid period and into the Roman one. In Arsacid Dura, it is likely that this local *strategos kai epistates* would have served as an imperial official and had a role in collecting money for Arsacid rulers.[11] An unnamed *strategos kai epistates* is documented as a witness, for example in a late-first-century parchment, and later *strategoi* are regularly honoured in dedications within sanctuaries.[12] Throughout the Arsacid period and even when the Roman military came to dominate the scene, there is an absence of records which indicate anyone other than a *strategos* as leader of the city. There are also records of functionaries of the Arsacid royal court, bailiffs, and collectors; for example two late-first-century CE parchments both have among their witnesses 'Seleucus and Adaeus, members of the panel of royal judges, and of the order of first and chiefly-honored friends and bodyguards; Pausanias, bailiff and collector, member of the order of bodyguards'.[13]

A relatively small corpus of surviving Arsacid-era parchments (only seven, *P. Dura* 18–24, are securely dated) is nonetheless suggestive about the administrative and social history of Dura. Interestingly, the Seleucid calendar continues to be relevant and is used alongside the Arsacid one in documents, indicating that the Seleucid reckoning of time had been relevant in earlier Dura, and was probably the dating system which people knew and understood in their daily lives. These documents give a suggestion of the ways in which elites could use their economic power as a means of securing their position in both social and economic terms. For instance, parchment *P. Dura* 20, dated to 121 CE, is a document which records an antichretic loan; it was found amongst the fill in a tower of the Palmyrene gate. An antichretic loan is a loan in which a good or service is provided in lieu of interest on a principle amount. In this case, the borrower named Baarlas provided his own labour in addition to mortgaging his property as a security on a loan he had taken out. His menial services repaid the interest, but not the principle, on four hundred drachmae of Tyrian silver he had borrowed from Phraates the eunuch (the penalty for Baarlas missing a day's labour is one drachma, so the total loan was probably about the equivalent of at least a year's wages for a labourer). Among other things, the document stipulates the penalties for breaking the contract and that the contract had to be renewed in the record office in Dura (it was written elsewhere, in the 'village of Peliga of the subdistrict about Iardas', so Dura was evidently something of a regional capital, with its record office).

Only part of this 'double document' was preserved; it is a type of document in which the same text was repeated twice, with the copy on the lower half of the parchment sealed so that it could be used to verify the unsealed copy above, effectively making the text consultable but tamper-proof (Figure 4.1). The form of a double document implies that it is an active text: not only to be lodged in an archive but to be used. *P. Dura* 20 records a number of interesting fragments of Dura's Arsacid-era administration. The place itself is referred to only as Europos. The lender, Phraates the eunuch, bears the title *arkapet*, and is described as 'one of the people of Manesus son of Phraates, member of the order of the *batesa* and of the Freemen, tax collector and *strategos* of Mesopotamia and Parapotamia and ruler of the Arabs'. It is possible that the *strategos* of the Arsacid province of Mesopotamia and Parapotamia and that of Dura were one in the same, but we lack explicit confirmation of this.[14] In any case, while this is a Greek-language legal document, it operates within Arsacid royal administration, opening as it does 'In the reign of the King of Kings Arsaces, benefactor, just, manifest god, and friend of the Greeks'; Phraates' title *Arkapet* is a transliterated Iranian designation. One of the penalties for breaking the contract was a payment to the Arsacid royal treasury, and further, with the document being lodged with the archives office in Arsacid Dura, the regime is also acting as the guarantor and authenticator of legal documents and enforcer of legal agreements.[15] The Arsacids inherited a Greek legal and administrative framework from their Seleucid predecessors, but there was no question that power was in the hands of the new King of Kings even if the language used to enact that power was Greek.

Family and Civic Relationships

From the documents, we know that property moved through the male line of the family and that the naming pattern of the male heirs was one in which the first son was usually named for the paternal grandfather.[16] It is such elite men, with a relatively small number of Greek personal names, who are best attested (and best studied) throughout the site, usually in inscriptions they themselves put up, for example when dedicating part of a religious building, or which were put up in their honour. As already noted, these men held civic office and were probably the means by which the Arsacids enacted their rule over the site. The Arsacid-era inscription of 135/6 CE recorded by Cumont records the *strategos kai epistates* Lysias, son of Lysanias and grandson of Seleucus; Lysias also has an Arsacid court rank.[17]

It appears that the title of *strategos* was maintained (if not inherited) within an elite family or families of Dura, families with Greco-Macedonian male names, including Seleucos, Lysias, and Lysanias. Problematically, a small number of names were common amongst these families, and it is not always possible to distinguish between them.[18] The women of the same family to whom these Seleucos, Lysias, and others were married had both Greek and non-Greek names, however, and this is true over multiple generations, so it is not a simple case of early Greek or Macedonian colonists marrying local women and a subsequent 'Hellenized' population, but a rather more complicated picture. Indeed, there is no evidence that is actually Hellenistic in date which demonstrates these families had been

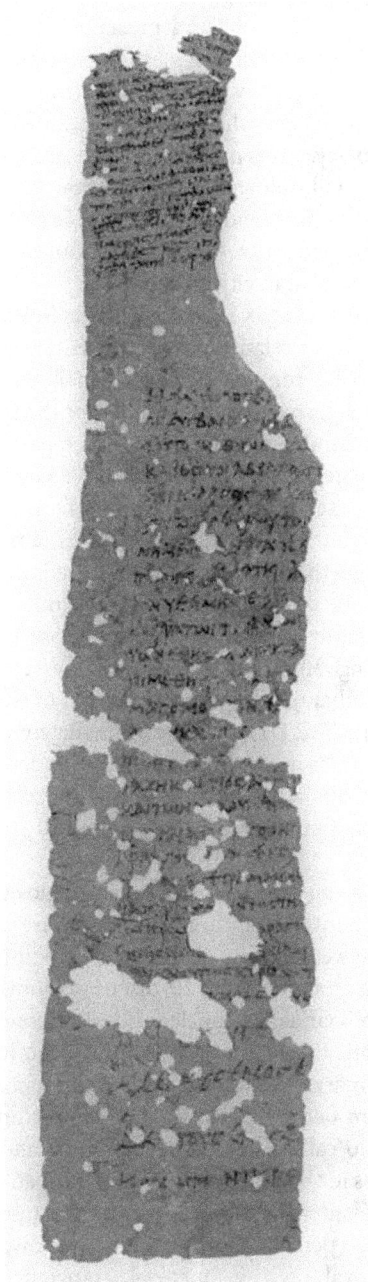

Figure 4.1 Photograph of *P. Dura* 24, a double document of 159/160 CE. One version of the text is written at the top in a smaller hand than the more generously spaced text below. The document records a debt of one Conon, son of Nicostratus, to Cronides, son of Damonicus. YUAG.

amongst Dura's initial settlers: it is generally presumed that was so, but that is because the Arsacid-era families of Dura presented it as such, by designating themselves *Europaioi*, those 'of Europos'. Amongst these families, inscriptions testify to a relatively high frequency of endogamy (marriage within the family), including brother-sister marriage, which likely functioned to insure the retention of family power and property.[19] This marriage may or may not have been biological siblings, as marrying adopted siblings would also allow the retention of property.[20] Throughout the inscriptions it is evident that lineages are important, not only to identify the family to whom an individual belonged but to demonstrate legitimacy as well as, probably, entitlement to citizenship.

Among the cults of Dura, too, we see not only dedications which honour the *strategos* of the city, which are relatively frequent, but also a strong tendency for particular sanctuaries to be connected with a small number of elite families. Whether the cults were exclusive to those families, or the families were patrons of the cults, or if there were familial associations between particular elite families and particular cults in a more general way is unclear.[21] We know of these relationships from a range of media, for example the painting of the family of Conon in the temple of Bel (discussed in Chapter 2); women from Conon's family are also recorded in the temple of Artemis.[22] Further, from *graffiti* (scratched texts) and *dipinti* (painted texts) found on the remains of what was probably a similar painting to that in the temple of Bel in the 'temple of Zeus Theos' were those that recorded names of the people in the painting, among whom is also a Lysias.[23] More circumstantial evidence, for instance, is that of topographic position of wealthy domicile known as the House of Lysias (in block D1), with the immediately adjacent temple of Zeus Megistos (in block C4). Their main entrances were just across the road from each other, which is also perhaps an indication of a close relationship between elite families (and indeed elite families with the position of *strategos*) and particular cults within the city.[24]

These same families seem also to have been in a position to lend money to others at the site. We cannot be certain about the nature of the patronage, but it is relatively clear that the wealthy elite of Dura gave credit to others on terms that were beneficial to the lenders. In *P. Dura* 20, discussed above, in which the eunuch Phraates loaned silver to Baarlas, it is unclear how someone such as Baarlas could ever escape from beneath the loan made to him, if he is not paying back the principle (whether this marks his descent into permanent servitude or if Baarlas was making a short-term hedge against his turning fortunes, we do not know). Phraates had the right to call in the loan at any time after the initial term had elapsed, and the penalties for breaking the terms of the loan were high: for example if the loan was not repaid after the initial year and the contract not renewed at the record office in Europos, a penalty of 400 drachma was owed not only to Phraates but also to the Arsacid royal treasury. Financial arrangements such as this are also evident in other documents, for example *P. Dura* 17C, an antichretic loan in which one Conon, of Europos, loaned money to a number of unrelated men who were also apparently citizens, *Europaioi*, presumably members of an association. These asymmetrical monetary arrangements would have solidified social hierarchies at

Dura.[25] It is notable here that the borrowers in *P. Dura* 17C were also (despite the superficial evidence of their 'Semitic', non Greek, names) explicitly designated as *Europaioi*. In addition to those people in the antichretic loans who had effectively become debt-slaves, slaves are attested at Dura in a number of documents referring to servile labour inside the city, on agricultural land, and later, as part of the military community.[26]

A number of documents from Arsacid Dura preserve the practice of people with both Greek and Semitic names (the editors of the parchments called these *aliases*, but this has a pejorative quality which is not in the documents themselves).[27] The significance of this practice of 'double naming' is not well understood. 'Semitic' at Dura has been used as a shorthand for the non-Classical linguistic background of the names rather than an indicator of the use of a Semitic language or ethnicity, and these names are themselves diverse, being Aramaic, Arabic, and Persian. For example the first-century CE document *P. Dura* 19 (another 'double document') records the division of a house amongst four brothers upon the death of their father. The father is recorded as having the Greek name Polemocrates (his own father and grandfather also bearing the names Demetrius and Polemocrates, respectively), and amongst the younger Polemocrates' sons, all had both Greek *and* Aramaic names, for instance Demetrius, also known as Nabusamus. The document records the concern with noting patrilineal descent – descent along the male line – and a pattern of sons taking the Greek name of their grandfathers. They are described as *Europaioi*, 'of Europos', a designation of place which, as seen above, is generally assumed to indicate citizen status.[28] As also noted above, there is virtually no contemporary evidence from Seleucid Dura, but the use of *Europaios* as a designation in Arsacid-era documents suggests that the elite of Parthian Dura leveraged claims of continuity via descent from the earlier Hellenic (Seleucid) era as a means of reinforcing their status. This continuity may have been entirely fictive or strategic, and it should not be assumed that it is indicative of any biological descent from the 'original' settlers of Europos, only that such claims were seen to be relevant to the inhabitants of later, Arsacid, Dura (which is not to say that they wouldn't have believed such claims to be true).[29]

During the probably brief Roman occupation of Dura under Trajan, the Romans reportedly stole the doors to a shrine 'of Epinicus and Alexander', which we know of only from inscriptions. No associated building has been identified, but the inscriptions were found near the Mithraeum, so it was possibly in that part of the city.[30] The name refers to the men who paid for the building of the temple, but to which god or gods it was dedicated is not recorded. Among these three Greek inscriptions is one on a stone stele which records the restoration of the doors of the temple, *c.* 116–117 CE, by the son of the man who had built the first temple. It reads as follows:

Year 428 [116/117 CE]. I, Alexander the son of Epinicus, renovated this *naos* which my father built for himself long ago, and I added five cubits to it in front, and the original doors were taken away by the Romans, and after their departure

from the city I made anew other doors for the same *naos* at my own expense, and
outer doors also. May Ammaios, who is the same Alexander, priest of the god
and herald of the city, be remembered before the same god.[31]

Again in this text we see the practice of using both Greek and Semitic personal
names, with the son describing himself *both* as Alexander son of Epinicus *and*
as Ammaios in the same inscription. This man, 'Ammaios, who is the same
Alexander', was 'priest of the god and herald of the city': a person of significant –
and we can assume given those titles, citizen – standing. Onomastics are of course
problematic, and should not be taken as a simple proxy for ethnic identity. Yet,
the use of multiple names of different types for the same individual did have some
significance for people at Dura.

The inscription of Ammios/Alexander would have meant to have been read, at
least, by others within the sanctuary, as would have an inscription in the temple
of Azzanathkona which had been above a door lintel (although it was eventually
plastered over): at the time it was made in 153 CE, it recorded one 'Heliodoros son of
Theodorus, called Samsbanas, son of Abidisomos'.[32] The use of such double naming,
then, is appropriate both in civic legal documents and in religious epigraphic ones.
Why, in both civic and religious contexts in Arsacid Dura, would these relatively
wealthy male citizens find it necessary or desirable to have both Greek and Semitic
names, in addition to patronymics (i.e. designations by the names of their fathers)?
We cannot be certain, but it does seem that the relationship between Greek names
and status was not straightforward. If a Greek name was simply a marker of status
because of the privileged status of Hellenism, the inclusion of a non-Greek name
would surely dilute this. It is possible that names were used in a contextual way:
for instance in the case of Alexander who is also known as Ammaios, Alexander
was appropriate in his civic role as herald, but Ammaios was more suitable for his
role as a priest of a local cult.[33] While double naming is not the standard practice
in preserved inscriptions, it could be under-represented due to the contextual use
of different names. Regardless, its use in Arsacid-era Dura demonstrates that the
population cannot be easily divided into a Greco-Macedonian elite, on the one
hand, and a native Semitic population, on the other, as has usually been assumed
to be the case.[34] It seems also that naming practices even within a family were
gendered, so while the male family members on the paintings of the temples of Bel
and Zeus Theos all had Greek names (like Conon, Nikostratus, Patroclus, Lysias),
the women had Semitic ones, such as Baribonnea and Bithnania. The evidence of
names and naming practices at Dura is thus complex, and no simple equations
between names and cultural affiliations can be made.

Religious Relationships

Gods and goddesses, as well as men and women, had complex identities in Arsacid
Dura. These included 'syncretized' gods and those of foreign origin. In addition
to gods who are named in multiple languages such as Zeus Kyrios/Baalshamin

(named in Greek and Palmyrenean, respectively) are those who themselves have multiple names, for instance in a Greek inscription: 'Artemis, the goddess called Azzanathkona' found within her temple (on the north edge of the site in block E7).[35] In this latter case, a part of a temple is erected by Barnabous, son of Zabidkonos, son of Rhaeibelos, 'on behalf of the safety of himself and his children'. The goddess, like some of the men with both Greek and Semitic names discussed above, is explicitly said to have multiple names within the same text: she is both Artemis and Azzanathkona. The goddess Azzanathkona is only known from Dura and was perhaps the goddess of a place called Anath, on the Euphrates, as was the god Aphlad attested in inscriptions elsewhere at the site. As with the men with double names, it is not clear what the significance is of the gods and goddesses known by both Greek and non-Greek names in Greek inscriptions. But, given the complexity of their cults, it is not a simple case of translating gods into different languages, nor of simple 'syncretism' when two deities from different backgrounds with similar aspects are merged into one. For example, the temple of Artemis/Azzanathkona is itself a form which has more in common with Mesopotamian than Classical temples, but the cult relief looks similar to that which would be found in Roman relief sculpture, and the appropriate language for religious inscriptions was Greek. The temples, their gods, and perhaps even their religious practices were hybrid local forms.

Also within the temple of Artemis/Azzanathkona, as in the temple of Artemis (in block H4, referred to in one text as Artemis Nanaia), was a 'room with steps' (*salle à gradins*) that functioned as seats or benches and which bore inscriptions of names.[36] In Artemis/Azzanathkona, these date from the early first century CE until about a century later, and like those in the temple of Artemis, the names inscribed are mostly female names, including some members of the same families attested in the temple of Artemis.[37] Seats in the temple went from a woman to her daughters, so while property moved along the male line of the family, in this religious context female lineage within elite families was also visible and important, even if it was another means of reinforcing the bonds of the same family.

From another temple, that of Aphlad in the southwest corner of the site in block N8, comes a Arsacid-era Greek inscription to the god of another place, in whose name the temple is founded:

> This foundation of the sanctuary of Aphlad, called god of the village of Anath on the Euphrates, Adadiabos, the son of Zabdibolos, son of Silloi, erected as his vow on behalf of the safety of himself and his children and his entire house.[38]

The inscription accompanies a relief showing Adadiabos as he makes his vow. Smoke rises from the altar at which he has sacrificed (Figure 4.2). The depiction of the god Aphlad shows him as wearing Persian military dress like the Mesopotamian god Bel and bearded like Baal-Shamin, Semitic lord of the heavens, standing on top of griffins, not unlike Jupiter Dolichenus atop his bull.[39] So, from this corner of Dura in a temple, we have a locally produced stone relief, with a Greek inscription describing a Semitic dedicant to the god Aphlad, depicted with attributes from

Figure 4.2 Photograph of Aphlad relief taken shortly after its excavation. Adadiabos, wearing the conical hat of a priest, is shown on the left; to the right, the god Aphlad stands upon two griffins; *c.* 54 CE. YUAG e103.

Mesopotamia, Syria, and beyond, himself god of a place called Anath on the Euphrates.[40] The religious vow itself in the inscription is made in typical Greco-Roman formulaic language, but the request for personal well-being or salvation (here, *soteria*, but other inscriptions use *hygieia*) was deeply embedded in Near

Eastern religious practice, a vow for the safety of the dedicant and his house.[41] Although the inscription is written in Greek, the idea of making a vow to the gods for personal salvation exists not only in Greek religious practice but in Near Eastern ones as well and these conceptual commonalities between (what had been) different practices perhaps explains why there is a prevalence of dedications of this type in the Near East.[42]

A contemporary inscription from within the same structure records the setting up of an *andron* (this translates directly as 'men's room', but probably can be more broadly understood as a meeting place or banqueting room) to Aphlad by members of an association for 'the safety of the *strategos* Seleucos, of themselves and of their children'.[43] The names and patronyms (fathers' names) of the members of the association are almost all Aramaic or Arabic (Zabdibolos, Rachimnaios, Phalazzacheis, etc), except for one Greek name, Theogenes. The graffiti in the sanctuary are in Greek, but within them are men with Greek names (including those with the status of *Europaioi*) and men with non-Greek ones; they are of the remembrance graffiti type that occurs throughout the site and are found even on the cult relief itself.[44] The texts from the temple of Aphlad then give an impression of one Arsacid-era cult: within it, a group of men formed an association together to worship the god of another place (Anath on the Euphrates), but they did so within the terms of Dura, for the local *strategos*, gathered in a particular room. Whether the cult was exclusive (i.e. only those from Anath worshipped there) or not (i.e. others from Dura worshipped or at least saw the relief, too, as seems to be implied by the specificity with which the god is described), their presentation of the god is based in and normative within the broader community, and there is no reason to suspect the sanctuary denied entrance to people who were not of Anathene origin (indeed, the graffiti testify to their presence).[45] All of this tells a story of Dura that is not a linear progression of a Greek colony slowly becoming more Syro-Mesopotamian, nor a local Syrian population becoming Hellenized (the two narratives prevalent in scholarship on the Greco-Roman Near East), but rather a complicated interaction of a number of cultural, religious, and linguistic practices which had long been deeply entangled, to the point of being inextricable from one another.

Arsacid-era Dura had other sanctuaries based around cults of 'foreign' origin.[46] Amongst the earliest inscriptions at Dura is one set up by two men from Palmyra when they founded a temple to the Palmyrene deities Iarhibol and Bel (the temple outside the city walls, misleadingly known as the necropolis temple). Unlike the inscription of the Aphlad relief, this inscription, dated to 33 BCE, was not in Greek but in Palmyrene.[47] The occurrence of these two deities together in the dedication being offered by members of two different Palmyrene tribes is distinct from anything that occurs at Palmyra itself; the 'expatriate' Palmyrenes of first-century Dura found that their common origin and language were grounds on which a Palmyrene identity could coalesce, surmounting the distinctions that would have been relevant at Palmyra itself.[48]

While that temple, outside the city walls in the necropolis, was founded for Palmyrene gods and for Palmyrene worshippers, others had inscriptions which probably had worshippers from multiple Durene communities, and not only expatriates of Palmyra itself. From 31 CE, a relief dedicated to Zeus Kyrios-Baalshamin (Figure 4.3), against tower 16 on the west side of the site, has a bilingual inscription in Greek and Palmyrene, perhaps indicative of worshippers from both Durene and Palmyrene communities (although it should be noted that Greek-Palmyrene bilingual texts are common at Palmyra itself).[49] The inscription reads, 'Seleucos, the son of Leukios and his son Ababouis dedicated this image to Zeus Kyrios, in the month of Apellaios of the year 343 [31 CE]. May [the sculptor] Iaraios be remembered'.[50] The god wears a mantle and long-sleeved tunic and is bearded, and this depiction echoes his Phoenician origins and Palmyrene depiction, rather than an origin in the Euphrates region.[51] The stone from which it is carved is local limestone, but both the style of the carving and the named sculptor indicate that artists were probably among Dura's Palmyrene population.[52] The excavators used this relief to name the sanctuary within which it was found, but the inscription notes only the dedication of this image so it is possible other gods were worshipped there, too.

Palmyrene texts are found elsewhere in the city as well, including later in the second century, in the sanctuary in block H1 known as the temple of the Gaddé or the personified fortunes of both Dura and Palmyra. The sanctuary included a number of Palmyrene deities, including Malakbel and Iarhibol.[53] The main inscriptions on the cult reliefs were Palmyrene, but graffiti in Greek, and later, Latin, were also recorded. While there are people worshipping gods from Palmyra and writing in Palmyrenean Aramaic at Dura, it has recently been questioned whether these people should truly be considered foreigners at Dura or whether Palmyrenean should be considered a regional dialect that is in use at both Palmyra and Dura, by Palmyrenes and Durenes.[54]

The 'foreigners' of Dura were not just from Palmyra or Anath but also Hatra, the famed city of the sun god in Mesopotamia, now northern Iraq. Someone from Hatra put up dedication to their god Shamash in the temple of Atargatis; a few graffiti in Hatrene were found elsewhere at the site.[55] It's unclear whether there were many people capable of reading the Hatrene texts at Dura, but one graffito was accompanied by a Greek translation of the Hatrene sun god Shamash, as Helios. But what is more clear is that the gods of Hatra were compatible with a Durene sanctuary and that Hatrenes seem to have been present within those sanctuaries.[56]

Within the Roman era at Dura, initially at least, much of the existing civic infrastructure seems to have continued. In 180 CE, a deed of sale is written in Greek, but the opening date indicates Roman administration, as it is given as 'In the consulship of Bruttius Praesens for the second time and of Julius Verus for the second time, in the twentieth year of the principate of Imperator Caesar Marcus Aurelius Antoninus'.[57] That is, using standard Roman formulae followed by the Seleucid-era date given by the eponymous priests including that of Seleucos Nicator, the place is called 'Europos toward Arabia'.[58] The deed records the sale of a slave named Achabous and part of a vineyard by one Lysias, son of Lysias, grandson of Heliodorus and great-grandson of Aristonicus, who are *Europaioi* and resident in the village of Nabagath. Among the document's

Figure 4.3 Photograph of Zeus Kyrios-Baalshamin relief, while still *in situ* in the western desert wall of the city, tower 16, against which was built the sanctuary known as the temple of Zeus Kyrios. The god sits on the right, holding a sceptre and a bouquet of grain and fruit, and is crowned with a *polos*. The dedicant Seleucos stands to the left, holding a ram. Beneath them, the Greek inscription is at the right, the Palmyrene at the left, and at the top margin above the relief are the labels 'Seleukos son of Leuckios' and 'Zeus', both in Greek. The Greek inscription below the relief notes that Seleukos son of Leuckios gave this sculpture as an offering to Zeus Kyrios, along with his son Ababouis. Seleukos is known by another name in the Palmyrene which names the god not as Zeus but Baalshamin, and the dedicant 'Bar['at]eh the son of Leuq[a], and his son Ababuhi'. YUAG g1112a.

witnesses are one Heliodorus, the *strategos kai epistates* of the city, and Theomnestus, Theodotus, and Athenodorus, who are *Chreophylakes*. So, it seems at least initially under Roman power, civic institutions including the registry office (*Chreophyakeion*) continued, *Europaioi* remained a meaningful designation, and the office of *strategos kai epistates* continued. The names of the men involved in the transaction are of the same group of Greek names the elites of Dura have drawn on for centuries under Arsacid rule; the cash part of the transaction is reckoned in Tyrian silver *drachmae* (Tyrian silver is also specifically mentioned in Arsacid documents). The precise nature of the relationship of existing civic structures to Roman rule is unclear, but while there is no doubt the ruling polity is Rome, it seems, unsurprisingly, there is much continuity with the Arsacid era, with Roman power being grafted onto existing infrastructure, as was normal Roman practice.

The major Roman transformation of the site was later, as seen in Chapter 2, most notably with the building programme which probably took place in the late second and early third century CE that adapted much of the north side of the site for use by the Roman military garrison. Dates for this building programme are known mostly from or by association with a small number of inscriptions. From the headquarters building, the *principia*, the building's dedicatory inscription, was for the emperor Caracalla.[59] Latin inscriptions also included one that adorned the amphitheatre but misspelled the building *anpytaeatrum*.[60] While the carver of that inscription may have not had the best command of Latin, elsewhere on the site were those who knew (or at least knew a pretence of) Vergil, as lines from the *Aeneid* were scratched into plaster walls in military buildings.[61] Members of the Roman military also made dedications in Latin for the salvation of the emperor, as earlier Greek inscriptions at Dura had for the salvation of families. Such inscriptions, made by members of the military, were not only to gods like Jupiter Optimus Maximus Dolichenus typical of other military sites but also for local ones, like Azzanathkona, for the salvation of the emperor.[62]

The third century saw the continuation and growth of some cults including the Mithraeum, the foundation of others (including, probably, both the Christian and Jewish dedicated religious structures), and the transformation of others. The building of the 'temple of Azzanathkona' on the north edge of the site for example was partially taken over for use by the Roman military, although it seems likely that access to some parts of it for the local population was maintained.[63] The temple of Bel, too, was within this zone, and there the Roman military installed a painting in the same tradition as that of Conon, continuing to use at least part of the space for religious practice, but showing a sacrifice not by an elite Durene man and his family but a parallel one by a Roman tribune, Julius Terentius, and men of his cohort (Figures 2.5 and 2.7).

The third-century Jewish synagogue is a useful example of the way in which a community which was quite defined in religious terms was quite diverse in linguistic ones. While a fragment of a Hebrew prayer was found in redeposited fill near the synagogue (*P. Dura* 11), and one of the paintings was labelled in Hebrew, the preserved languages of the synagogue were predominantly Aramaic and Greek.[64] Greek and Aramaic in the synagogue included that found on painted inscriptions on walls and ceiling tiles, as well as scratched graffiti. Long Persian inscriptions were also painted onto the figural wall paintings, but unlike the Greek and Aramaic labels, they were made later than the wall paintings themselves.[65] Aramaic is perhaps the most significant within the building, as the longer and more detailed texts are Aramaic, not Greek.[66] As a whole the Aramaic, Greek, Persian, and Hebrew of the synagogue are one facet of the diversity evident in the Jewish community at Dura.[67] Texts associated with Dura's Christian community are also known, including graffiti from within the house church, as well as a parchment, part of what is thought to be Tatian's *Diatesseron*, a gospel harmony which may demonstrate that the Durene Christian community practised a particular doctrine.[68] The spelling of the painted inscriptions on the Christian painting of David and Goliath implies access to Syriac Christian texts, and indeed the presence of biblical scenes indicates the participation of Durenes in a broader Christian community.[69] Outside the Christian building itself, there is virtually no direct evidence for Christians at Dura, unless we count the acrostic Rotas-Sator square which can be rearranged to read *Pater Noster* and has hence been interpreted by some as (cryptic) Christian text.[70]

Complex and Contextual Relationships

As noted already with reference to the synagogue, the use of languages was in some ways contextual.[71] Overwhelmingly, the civic documents of Dura are in Greek, as would be expected in a place with Greek civic administration, and indeed subsequently a Arsacid one. Civil documents continued to be in Greek even under Roman administration, although all formal army matters were conducted in Latin, the soldiers themselves nonetheless used Greek when making graffiti or writing private letters (e.g. *P. Dura* 46). There were, alongside this, some Aramaic parchments, which are fragmentary legal documents (*P. Dura* 151, 152),[72] as well as Parthian and Persian parchments (*P. Dura* 153 and 154), the Hebrew prayer already mentioned (*P. Dura* 11), and a Syriac deed of sale (*P. Dura* 28), all of which are seemingly third century in date.[73] Aramaic appears in written form at Dura only in the third century CE (Palmyrene being the only Semitic language extensively preserved from Arsacid era Dura), although the nature of the bulk of the preserved records, being religious inscriptions and civic documents whose form in some ways necessitated Greek, perhaps belies the more common use of spoken Aramaic, which we can only suppose. That a written form of Aramaic was in use even for some legal transactions may indicate that it was a written representation of the 'underlying native language'.[74]

A third-century Greek document (204 CE), *P. Dura* 31, records a divorce in the village of Ossa. Again in this text are complicated names and lineages; rather than double naming, instead we have Semitic names for people whose parentage is recorded as people with Greco-Macedonian ones: 'Nabusamaus, son of Conon, and Acozzis, daughter of Seleucus'.[75] Dates are reckoned in both Seleucid and Roman eras, and the penalty for breaking the contract is to be made in *drachmae* but paid to a *fiscus*. Amongst the witnesses is the Roman veteran Julius Germanus.

In the second quarter of the third century, *P. Dura* 27, a deed of sale, records the signatures of witnesses to the document, amongst whom are three decurions of Dura (*bouletai Douranoi*): those whose names are partially preserved are a son of Rhechomnaeus and a son of Antoninus. Evidently, some of the elite of the site have taken up Roman names, but Rhechomnaeus is neither Greek nor Roman. Caution needs to be taken, as their entire names are not preserved, but it seems that by this time, the civic council (*boule*) was made up not only of those whose names indicated their links to a perceived Greco-Macedonian heritage (i.e. the elite who had been in control during the Arsacid era), or that those who had found it useful to have a Greco-Macedonian name under Arsacid rule no longer found this to be the case under Roman hegemony.

While it has usually been argued, following Welles, that the Greco-Macedonian elite at Dura broke down and succumbed to local 'native' peoples in the Roman era (indicated in the documents by the use of Greek names becoming less frequent and the use of Aramaic, Arabic, and Persian names becoming more common), the actual situation is much less clear. First, as has been seen, there are non-Greek names in the Arascid era, including double names for people otherwise known by Greek ones. Aramaic names are more frequent in the third century, but the Greek names do not disappear. Was this due to a conscious resistance to the old aristocratic Greek traditions (perhaps surprising in the context of the second Sophistic) or other 'cultural cleavages'?[76] It could be that the increased prevalence of non-Greek names in the Roman period reflects a different selection of information for inclusion in documents (i.e. that people were not explicitly recording the Greek 'alias' that had been recorded in the Arsacid era). Perhaps 'Greek' names had lost the political clout they had under the Arsacids, particularly after citizenship was extended broadly by the Antonine constitution. Indeed, in some cases it seems the traditional aristocracy was leveraging their position to act in concert with or on behalf of the Romans. For example in the north tower of the Palmyrene gate was found a Latin text painted in white on a wooden *tabella ansata* (Figure 4.4).[77] It records that early in the third century, there was still a *strategos* in Dura, and in addition to the typical name of Lysias, the *strategos* of Dura also had the name Septimius and was being honoured by members of a Roman cohort. 'Septimius' can be safely presumed to have been adopted from the Roman emperor Septimius Severus, presumably indicating the recent assumption of Roman citizenship. One of his sons bears the Iranian name Thiridates. So, we have Lysias, a *strategos*, taking on a Roman name but who has given one of his sons an Iranian name, being honoured in a Latin inscription. The use of Greek, Roman, and Iranian names here seems less about ethnic affiliation and more about political expedience and the careful negotiation of personal place in relation to power.

Similarly, a Greek inscription excavated by the Franco-Syrian expedition in 1999 in the temple of Artemis further attests to the existing elite of Dura taking up

Figure 4.4 Wooden plaque with painted Latin inscription to Septimius Lysias. The Latin reads, 'To Septimius Lysias *Strategos* of Dura and the wife of the one mentioned above, Nathis, and their children Lysanius and Mecannaea and Apollophanes and Thiridates, From the *Beneficiarii* and *Decurions* of the Cohort'. Excavated in the Palmyrene gate. YUAG 1929.370; YUAG y468.

Roman names, recording one 'Septimius Aurelios Lysias, *strategos kai epistates*'.[78] The use of 'Aurelios' here indicates it is probably later than the wooden inscription, as it would have been likely such a name was taken after the Antonine constitution and would indicate citizenship, when the emperor Caracalla extended Roman citizenship to all free (i.e. non-slave) subjects in 211 CE.[79] But, while at least some of the families that had previously leveraged a perceived Greek heritage continued to hold positions of power in the city, a wide range of names (i.e. not only Greek) is found in the *boule* within the temple of Artemis. Again, whether this marks a shift towards a wider portion of the population able to participate in civic life or whether people are differently self-identifying, we cannot know from the current evidence.

There is much in the textual evidence also which elucidates the economy of Dura's Roman period. This includes the extensive graffiti records from the House of Nebuchelus in block B8, also called the House of the Archive on account of the large amount of texts found on its walls.[80] Among these texts were the remembrance graffiti found throughout the site, and horoscopes, as well as many relating to commercial transactions, testifying to involvement in agriculture, trade, and money-lending.[81] Specific transactions recorded on the walls of this house included, for example, trans-shipment of consignments of wine.[82] Papyri further fill in this picture, testifying to wine production, fruit growing, and a range of agricultural activities, as well as a number of merchants within the city, including bakers, builders, and barbers.[83] While there is little evidence that Dura relied on the caravan trade from Palmyra for its economy, nor was it fully reliant on the Roman military even in the third century, having its own production in agriculture and crafts, as well as participating in regional and long-distance trade.[84] Dura seems to have acted as something of a regional capital, with its territory extending as far as the Khabur river, as is attested in documents relating to villages within its territory but lodged in the archives at Dura itself.[85]

Military Relationships

Like the parchments preserved under the embankment of the western city wall, the Roman military records owe their preservation to the city's destruction. The military archive of Dura, belonging to roughly the first half of the third century CE, is one of the most important collections preserved anywhere in the Roman empire.[86] Among the documents is the group of parchment and papyrus records which were part of the archive of the twentieth Palmyrene Cohort, found under the embankment against the city wall on the north edge of the site in what had been part of the temple of Azzanathkona before it had been partially taken over by the cohort. There are also official correspondence, a number of texts called 'morning reports' (the term used by historians, due to their similarity to documents in the modern American army) and unit journals which detail personnel movements and the daily operations of the cohort, as well as long rosters detailing personnel and administrative roles.[87]

Famously, amongst the military documents is the *Feriale Duranum* (*P. Dura* 54), a Latin religious calendar listing the festivals that were part of official military life, and the most important source for these that survives from antiquity.[88] There is no material evidence for its enactment at Dura, but the document itself was consulted frequently enough in antiquity to have needed repairs.[89] The calendar may have been one example of a 'standard' military calendar, of which no other examples exist, but it does not necessarily follow that it was put into practice in a uniform way, and who among the Durene population participated in which of its festivals is not known.[90] Texts also testify to more quotidian Roman military practices, including those that followed local Durene traditions, for example in making remembrance graffiti in the formula of the Greek word *mnesthe* plus a name, which roughly translates as 'may so-and-so be remembered': many Roman soldiers inscribed themselves onto Dura's fortifications in this way (Figure 4.5). Of course, there were also cults of Mithras and Jupiter Dolichenus, already mentioned, among those practiced by the Roman military at Dura, and it seems that local traditions happened alongside other communal practices, like that of Mithras, and more official imperial ones of the *feriale*. Roman soldiers were also worshipping other gods: an altar to Zeus Betylos was dedicated by a member of the fourth Scythian legion within the temple of Bel, and from the Palmryene gate was found a relief dedicated by in Greek and Palmyrene by Julius Aurelius Malochus in 228 CE to the goddess Nemesis.[91]

Preserved military rosters from Dura include names of soldiers and their assignments. The 'great' rosters were *P. Dura* 100 and 101, two sides of one long papyrus roll: its original length was probably about five and a half meters, each side listing more than one thousand individual men. The first of these

Figure 4.5 Photograph of interior of Palmyrene gate after excavation showing altars on left and scratched inscriptions carved into the stone blocks. YUAG b108.

documents (*P. Dura* 100) was a roster of the twentieth Palmyrene cohort, and it included remains of forty-four columns of text written in the same hand; each column contained names and ranks of members of the military and where they were stationed with notations which probably relate to movement, indicating that these were active, working, documents.[92] It lists almost the complete cohort: the personnel of six *centuries* and five *turmae* by the year in which they enlisted in the army, headed by the name of the *centurion* or *decurion* in charge and his lieutenants.[93] From the handwriting, it appears that one clerk prepared the entire document, but that the notations were later added to and changed by other people, so it seems it was in use over a period of time.[94] The same clerk, probably for ease of writing the document, gave every single soldier in *P. Dura 100* the *nomen* Aurelius, which would have been typical after the Antonine constitution.[95]

The so-called morning reports of the twentieth Palmyrene Cohort (e.g. *P. Dura* 82) generally give the date by day and month, and the number of men, listing separately the number of *centurions* and lieutenants, the *dromedarii* (camel-riding auxiliaries) and their officers, as well as other specialized military men. Each day's entry also records the official name of the cohort, the name of the tribune in charge, the daily password, departures or returns of particular people or units, the orders of the day, and the name and ranks of that day's guard of honour (the ritual guarding of the Roman military standards), amongst other details. There are also preserved monthly summaries (e.g. *P. Dura* 92).

The documents provide many minutiae on the workings of the Roman army, particularly the structures and bureaucracies. As a group, the documents also hint at the impact that this Roman military presence would have had on the local community at Dura, bringing not only a new local authority but also its large number of personnel, its broader military community, and its infrastructure. Latin is the language of Roman military administration, but not, probably, the language of daily use: casual graffiti by the military are often in Greek, and many of the troops were of eastern extraction.[96] Latin was the language used for official documents, which was the language of power but also simply expedient within the larger Roman military machine.[97]

From the documents of Dura, we know not only of Dura's active military but also veterans. *P. Dura* 26 records a veteran buying local land in a village called Sachare, by paying 175 *denarii* in the year 227 CE. Witnesses to the document include active soldiers who sign in Latin in this otherwise Greek-language document; another veteran writes on behalf of the illiterate man Otarnaeus, son of Abadabus, who has sold the land. The veteran purchasing it, Julius Demetrius, is part of the military community, but now he is buying land from a local person to add to his existing land, producing wine and fruits. The land in question is near the Khabur river but Julius is living elsewhere, at a place called Raquqeta, so he seems to have been of sufficient means to have slaves or others cultivate the land for him.[98] While Julius Demetrius is only one individual, we can imagine this situation being replicated many times, and the impact this might have had on the regional landscape.

Another Greek civil text, amongst the latest dated examples from the site, is a divorce document of 254 CE, *P. Dura* 32. The document records the divorce of Julius Antiochus, soldier of the fourth Scythian legion, from a local woman named Aurelia Amimma. Aurelia Amimma is recorded to be of Dura (not Europos), as is one of the witnesses with the very Roman name Aurelius Valentinus, son of Antoninus, and another, with the partially preserved name Julius, who signs in Latin. While Aurelia Amimma is 'of Dura', the place name given in the opening of the document is, however, *the colony of Europos*, which has gained a number of honorific titles, now being the colony of Europos, the holy and inviolate and autonomous. What this means, in terms of the name used for the site in the Roman period, is unclear. It could be that the local name of Dura was re-invigorated under Roman rule, paralleling the increase in use of Aramaic personal names in the third century; this document demonstrates that the names used for the site and the names used for its people were not a simple matter of chronology (i.e. it is not the case the site was exclusively called 'Dura' in the Roman period). What can be seen from *P. Dura* 32 and other documents, from the divorce of Aurelia Amimma of Dura from her husband Julius Antiochus of the Scythian legion, to the veteran Julius Demetrius' growing ownership of cultivatable land in *P. Dura* 26, as well as in the archaeological evidence, is that the military community was not a strictly bounded one but came to pervade and transform many aspects of local life.

Scholarly Relationships

The wealth and complexity of the documents from Dura means that any short account is necessarily incomplete and selective. The texts used to construct the assessment above give a view from the perspective of an archaeological approach to the documents: it is contextual, material, and chronological, and it foregrounds the complexity and fragmentary nature of the material. Very different stories have been, and will continue to be, told with this material. Many of the existing accounts of the site for example hinge on the nature of what is, or isn't, considered to be 'Classical' and hence recognizable to the scholars who approached the site, who were largely trained in the Classical tradition: language, gods, and personal names chief among these. That which was not Classical was Other. As seen in previous chapters, this Other was an elision of ancient and modern categories.

The characterization of Dura's population has long hinged on C. B. Welles' interpretations and those of the other Yale excavators. These interpretations were based on a close reading of the textual sources, but also deeply intertwined with contemporary relationships with the Middle East and wider attitudes towards race. The formative piece is Welles' 1951 chapter *The Population of Roman Dura*, written before the final edition of the parchments and papyri was published.[99] This remains widely cited despite the fact Welles explicitly grounds his study in the concept of race: in it he describes how language and especially how *onomastics* (personal names) can be used to understand racial origins – for Welles the onomastic was racial.[100] More recent scholarship tends to accept his interpretations of the population while turning a blind eye to the deeply problematic principles on which it is based, namely that the personal names are a direct link to race, which was at the time Welles was writing considered to be a meaningful biological category with an (at least implicit) hierarchy.

These two facets of the scholarship, the historical and the racist, are, however, inextricable. Welles' approach was one that conceptualized populations as monolithic, in which the 'Greco-Macedonian aristocracy', which for him formed the key element of Dura's population until the late Roman period, was not only an onomastic group but a cultural and biological one.[101] These are the people with Greek personal names in the documents and who are described as *Europaioi*, the people of Europos. They were contrasted with people of Aramaic or Arabic or Iranian names, the 'natives' (the quotations are Welles' own).[102] When the documents record something which disrupts this narrative – as when people with Iranian or Semitic names are recorded as *Europaioi*, as they are in a document of 180 CE – it is considered 'ominous' and a threat; if men with Greek names have parents with Aramaic names, they were to Welles 'half-breeds'.[103] Welles saw the gradual disappearance of what he considered proper Greco-Macedonian names under Roman rule and the replacement by a great variety of name types (Iranian, Palmyrene, Arabic, Latin, etc) as a tragedy brought on by Rome.[104]

Rostovtzeff, too, had seen the Macedonian inhabitants of early Dura as the lone citizens and rulers of the place, *Europaioi*, who 'tried to resist the semitization of their families'.[105] The Parthian period, for Rostovtzeff, was a time of 'orientalization' but one during which the 'Macedonians remained what they were before, comparatively rich landowners, and that a number of Greeks and many natives were among the other owners of the land'.[106] For Rostovtzeff the Roman era was also an unhappy one – in his case, this was partially due not to the increasing arrival of foreigners but due to the fact that it was no longer a caravan city.[107] Rostovtzeff, too, saw the Roman era as one of decline from a period of wealthy Macedonian ruling families under Parthian rule: for him, 'Dura was dying before the Sasanians killed it.'[108] Rostovtzeff, perhaps because of his attention to art as well as to documents, did not interpret the population of the city in the way that Welles had (in which personal names were the guide to 'race') but saw the population as a more complex group, different facets of which had been differently impacted upon by Parthian and Roman rule.

Among Rostovtzeff's papers held in the archives of Yale University was an essay by Frank Brown entitled 'Orientalization', in which he responds to Welles' (then unpublished) ideas about 'The Survival of Hellenism', and the inherent and continued Greek character of Dura and its people.[109] This was apparently part of a seminar series on Dura held at Yale, probably the same one which saw some of its papers become sections of the *Preliminary Reports* series.[110] In Brown's essay, he questions the textually driven definition of Greekness, based on names and language, and instead asks whether the community 'acted like Greeks, were Greek in spirit'.[111] While Brown also saw (as Welles did) a strong contrast between the Macedonians and 'natives', he looked to the material evidence, including the architecture, for evidence of Greekness and found very little: instead, for Brown, even 'the most hellenized Durene breathed a spiritual atmosphere totally unhellenic, his physical life to the last detail was no less "barbarian"'.[112] In his reading, the most indicative measure was the transformation of the centre of the city from a Hellenistic *agora* into the oriental *bazaar*. The term *bazaar* of course was a way Brown could connect the people he saw as barbarians in ancient and modern times; he compared Dura directly to contemporary cities, as well, writing that 'it was as surely an oriental city as modern Baghdad or Aleppo'.[113] And just as this analogy between ancient and modern helped Brown and his colleagues explain the character of Dura, it helped them explain to themselves their own presence in the region. They were the new Greeks, attempting to impose order on a troublesome local population.

Rostovtzeff thought that the place of Dura between East and West was the chief answer to the question of 'Why have we spent so much time and money to excavate such an insignificant and short-lived city, far away from the great and active centres of the ancient Greek and Oriental world?'[114] For him, it was 'the problem of the hellenization of the East and the orientalization of the Western conquerors', a process which 'began in the time after the conquest of the East by Alexander, *and is still going on*'.[115] The outbreak of the Second World War apparently precipitated the steep decline in Rostovtzeff's mental health; by 1944 he was no longer writing and he would not be able to publish the parchments and papyri which had first drawn him to Dura – he died in 1952. Given his work on 'bottom-up' social history and the masterful way in which he had integrated different forms of evidence, the version of Dura which emerged from those documents might have looked very different had he been the one writing it.[116]

Throughout these works and into twenty-first-century scholarship on Dura-Europos, there is a dichotomy between Greco-Macedonian, citizen, '*Europaioi*', on the one hand, and native, local, 'Durenes', on the other. Underlying this (explicitly or implicitly) is the notion that Greek culture was racial: Hellenism was thought to have been something that ran in the blood of the colonists of Dura. Both sides of the equation were treated monolithically, with 'Semitic-speaking natives ... formed in an ancient Oriental cultural tradition going back through millennia to the days of Mari'.[117] Both Welles and Brown sought what they hoped would be Hellenism at Dura (in texts and archaeology, respectively), and both were disappointed. At the heart of it, Brown and Welles differed only on the specifics of how Hellenism was diluted and corrupted over time.

Jotham Johnson, whose colonial travel writing was discussed in the previous chapter, is the only one who systematically attempted to demonstrate that the office of the *strategos* was hereditary (and thus evidence of a ruling elite ruling through at least nominal descent), but he too could not conceive of this material as other than troubling. Instead he conceptualized Dura as an oriental city under a veneer of Hellenism, writing that 'Dura, in spite of its Greek speech and its pseudo-Greek worship – and barbarous they must have been – is a native community ruled by a sheikh, who masquerades under a Greek title and by right of birth is the city's chief magistrate'.[118] Despite this assessment, Johnson like Welles made a strong distinction between Greeks and 'natives' at Dura, viewing the endogamy he uncovered in drawing up lineages as 'astonishing attempts to ward off the rabble'.[119]

Even on its own terms, the dichotomy between 'Greek' and 'Semitic' at Dura breaks down in face of the evidence. That is, there is no clear line between 'Greco-Macedonian', on the one hand, and 'native' or Semitic, on the other. As we have seen, the Hellenistic period at Dura provides us with virtually no primary evidence on which to judge the situation, nor to judge how much the later periods were a marked change from it.[120] It is difficult to argue, for instance, that *the introduction of Greek inscriptions under the Arsacids can be seen as a decline in Hellenism*. Under Arsacid rule, there are practices of double naming (using both Greek and Aramaic names, for example) in both parchments and inscriptions *including* amongst the citizenry, and the women of elite families are given non-Greek names over generations. The continued presence of non-Greek names, but in higher frequency in the Roman period, need not be read as a tragic loss of a Greek aristocracy, as Welles envisaged it. This is not only because some families certainly continued, and even took up Roman names, as did the *strategos* Lysias, who had become also Septimius, but also because this shift (if indeed it is a real one and not just an outcome of a partial documentary record) is much more complicated than the decline of a single group of people under Roman rule. Full publication of all the inscriptions found at Dura and new studies looking at not only the Greek but other languages will undoubtedly further clarify this picture.

Overwhelmingly, the evidence from Dura gives a picture of incredible diversity. The different names for the city and for its inhabitants (Dura or Europos, Durenes, and *Europaioi*), the co-presence of multiple schemes of dating (the Seleucid calendar, Parthian regnal years, eponymous priesthoods, and Roman consular dates), the phenomenon of double naming, the variety of languages, and much besides all attest to an extremely complex cultural and political situation, on the edge of two empires (and sometimes, as in its final phases, even as the interface between these empires). The question that arises from the evidence is not whether Dura was fundamentally a Greek or Parthian or Roman city but to what extent facets of each of those were locally relevant at different times, and the way the interaction of these contributed to a hybrid local culture.

Chapter 5

THE BUILDINGS OF DURA-EUROPOS

Dura-Europos was a city built of materials which were of its place in the Euphrates valley: stone carved from the plateau, mudbrick of river water and earth dried in the sun, and plaster made primarily from local gypsum.[1] The architecture of the city, including its fortification walls, its religious buildings, its houses, civic structures, and eventually even many of the Roman military buildings, were all made of these fabrics, which could be obtained in the immediate vicinity of the site. Perhaps due to the relatively humble nature of the materials – this was not a city of stone columns or marble like others in the Roman Middle East – contemporary reviews remarked that Dura was 'a grim looking site: its most striking features are the west wall on the desert side and the citadel above the Euphrates, both built of dull grey gypsum blocks: between them stretches a waste of mud brick walls'.[2]

Amongst that mudbrick wasteland, however, was one of the most extensively preserved and excavated urban environments from the ancient world, including more than a hundred houses and at least nineteen religious buildings, as well as shops, baths, and other structures. Despite this wealth, Dura has often been characterized by what it lacks – for instance, there is no trace, yet, of a gymnasium or theatre – thus it was perceived to be without the 'essential components' of a typical Greek city.[3] The Othering of the site as a 'humble' place was one function of the Orientalist discourse within which the site was initially interpreted.[4] Similarly, the perceived lack of Greek buildings is a function of the focus on the Hellenistic origin of the site to the detriment of the Arsacid and Roman eras, for which there is much more abundant evidence (and, as we have seen, to which most of the Greek-language textual remains actually date).[5] Rather than focusing on what is not there, however, this chapter surveys the physical character of the site, examining its architecture, and asking what that evidence can add to our understanding of religion, culture, and society at Dura.

Houses

By the time of Dura's fall to the Sasanians in the mid-third century CE, houses filled the space inside the city walls, the full extent of which can be seen on the geophysical survey of the site (see Figure 2.6). The excavated houses of the site were largely those that were standing in the third century, when the site was under Roman rule, but many of these had been built in the Arsacid era and were maintained, modified, and inhabited until the fall of the city *c.* 256 CE. Virtually nothing that can be securely dated to the Hellenistic period is known of Dura's domestic architecture, although it is likely that any Hellenistic houses would have been in the immediate vicinity of the citadel.[6]

There is much diversity in the extant remains of Dura's houses, but several features are shared throughout each of them in both building materials and architectural form. The houses were built of mudbrick superstructures atop bases of plaster and stone rubble, which was plastered to a smooth finish. The plaster used to cover the mudbrick walls, both on the interior and exterior, protected them from water. Thresholds of doors and the doorframes and lintels above were generally gypsum and were often carved with a decorative profile.[7] Roofs were made with woven reed matting laid over wooden beams, which was plastered; of this, usually only fragments of reed-impressed plaster survive. The extent to which houses and other buildings were preserved differed greatly across the site, depending on a range of factors, including erosion (particularly on the Euphrates side), exposure to the elements, destruction or preservation in antiquity during the building of the ramparts within the city walls, and proximity to an early-modern road which ran through the site. Of some houses, we have only partial foundations; of others, the superstructure is preserved several metres in height. Only those terraced into the hillside in block C3 preserve much above the ground-floor level.[8]

The houses were built within city blocks delimited by the grid of roads, which was probably set out in the second half of the second century BCE. Within those blocks, houses shared space with other houses as well as religious buildings and shops. Each block was twice as long as it was wide, about thirty-five by seventy metres, and the number of houses within each block varied: the biggest house took up an entire city block, but other blocks could have ten or more houses within them (Figure 5.1). Where houses were on slopes, they were terraced along the roads, as in block C5, although where the topography was most steep, the houses are irregularly placed so as to best exploit this terrain, as in block C3, where some houses utilize the exposed rock faces of the old quarries as walls and where they are built directly into the hillside.

Each house had an entrance which opened directly off the street outside, but it was not possible to see into the core of the house from the road, as a short vestibule at a right angle to the interior courtyard created a buffer between the house and the world outside. Every house, even the smallest, included at least three rooms: a vestibule shielding the house from the street, an open-air courtyard around which the house was focused, and a 'principal room', which may have been called an *andron* or 'men's room' and which served as a reception room, amongst other functions.[9] These rooms often had a central entrance off the courtyard hung with double doors, and some had a low plaster bench around the perimeter of the room, on which couches were probably placed. The concern with privacy and access to the house and the naming in texts of a

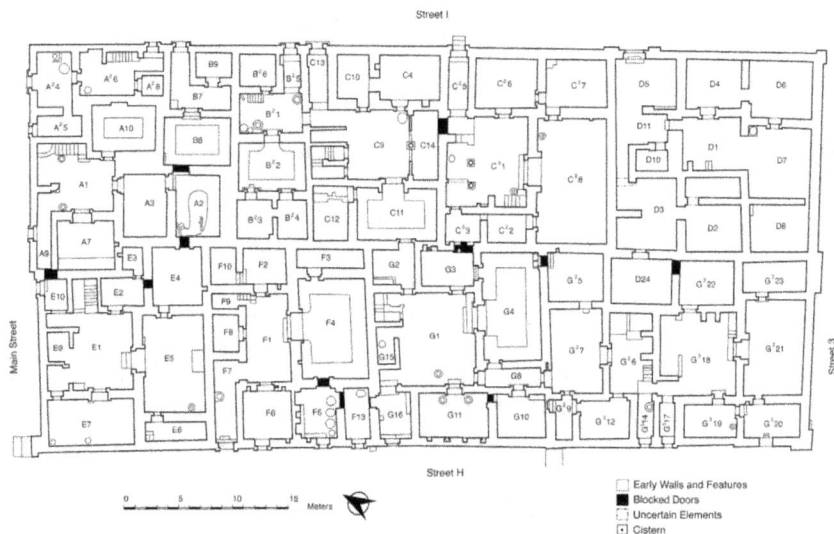

Figure 5.1 Plan of block C7, comprised of a number of houses. Blocked doors indicate where the interior arrangement of house plans has been modified or relationships between different houses have changed. Plan by author based on plan by H. Pearson.

room as an *andron* perhaps reflect that the house functioned to regulate gender relations and the visibility of women and spatially isolate the family unit as a distinct entity.

The courtyard of most houses included a cistern in its centre, which enabled the household to have some access to its own water supply. There is no evidence for a municipal water supply for houses, so it is likely rainwater was collected when possible; there is also evidence of water carriers who perhaps made a business of bringing water from the Euphrates up the steep climb to the city.[10] The courtyard brought light, air, and water into the house and also linked the other parts of the house. Stairways to upper storeys and flat roofs also led up from the courtyard, making it a node through which much household traffic had to pass. The houses did not have 'kitchens', but many did have ovens, also in the courtyard, or portable braziers for cooking.[11]

In addition to the shape of the entrance, the exterior of the houses also presented a blank façade to the street outside; there was little elaboration on the exterior of houses, and windows were high and narrow. Privacy from the public world of the street was valued, as was physical security, and many thresholds and door frames bear the marks of systems of heavy bolts for locking the external doors.[12] However, we know little of the upper storeys of Durene houses, but some houses seemed to have had them, and most houses had staircases which would have at led if not to upper storeys then to flat roofs, which would have provided additional space. Upper storeys are clearly attested in at least some houses in the documentary evidence, as discussed below.

Houses were sometimes decorated with paintings, but more frequent was moulded plasterwork.[13] While such extensive use of plaster decoration is found at other Arsacid sites, the houses of Dura do not have the *iwan*, the barrel-vaulted room open on one end which characterize elite houses at Arsacid settlements including Nippur and Assur.[14] Similarly, houses had some 'Hellenic' elements, including the use of columns within courtyards which the documents of Dura seem to call *stoa*, but the houses were not fundamentally Greek, either. Rather, the houses were a local vernacular type, specific to the site, but drawing on many traditions, including Babylonian and Seleucid, but not conforming neatly to either category. In addition to plasterwork and paintings, pictorial and textual graffiti were also found within houses. Houses frequently had graffiti on their walls, including lists or inventories, short messages of remembrance, horoscopes, or even receipts for business conducted within them, as noted in the previous chapter.[15]

The forms of the houses, and how the houses relate to each other (many were internally connected to other houses), seem to relate directly to kinship at the site. Houses were amongst the property that moved via inheritance along the male line within a family, and houses were modified to accommodate the changing shape of their inhabitants' kin groups, for example when a house was divided among heirs. It is possible to trace some of the changes made to houses through the alterations that were made to them over time which are archaeologically visible: doors were blocked up with mudbrick and plaster, new walls added (evident where they abut earlier ones), features were plastered over, or rooms fell out of use. An Arsacid-era document, *P. Dura* 19, gives an idea of how the houses would be transformed. In it, the text records the division of property amongst four brothers at the time of their father's death. The property comprised two houses, one of which had come to the father Polemocrates (presumed to be a citizen as he is referred to as *Europaios*) when it was divided with his brother, presumably on the death of their own father. Polemocrates' sons divide the houses between themselves by making a number of physical changes in the structure: they share an entrance and courtyard, but each brother (and presumably their families if they had them) had an otherwise self-contained suite of rooms. The rooms of each brother were vertically contiguous, so that each brother owned the upper-floor room above the ground-floor rooms they owned in the two-storey building. Each brother's space was also delimited by changing the circulation of the house: doors that had connected adjacent rooms which were allotted to different brothers were blocked. Thus, we see that what appears to be physically a single house unit might comprise multiple family units, sharing communal spaces like entrances and courtyards, but each with their own suite of rooms.[16]

P. Dura 19 has a number of implications for the understanding of houses. It shows that each house might not contain a single 'nuclear' family but could also hold other forms of household including, as in this case, a multiple family unit or 'joint' family, with multiple family groups of the same generation living together. This also means that the density of occupation within the city might have been quite high; previous estimations have given a population in the region of 5–6,000 for Dura, but by late second century we might as much as double this.[17] Further, the document implies that one reason houses were physically modified relates directly to the transformation of the household within it (in this case, the houses seem to have been divided between the brothers at the time of the father's death, although this is not explicitly stated). Of course, houses or parts of houses could also be bought or sold, and this is also textually attested, including in *P. Dura* 19 which notes that Polemocrates had purchased part of the property, in addition to inheriting part of it, which eventually passed to his sons.

The relationship between houses and families is also evident in one of the largest structures of Dura, the so-called 'House of Lysias', which occupies the entire block of D1 (Figure 5.2). Graffiti give the house its name, linking the structure to an elite family of the site, who are also known from documents and inscriptions as being amongst the holders of the title *strategos*. As noted in the previous chapters, such families were sometimes apparently endogamous, marrying within the family, and this was likely a strategy for holding on to and consolidating property.[18] As a result, while the house was modified over time, it was not divided into smaller units as would happen if partible inheritance, when property is split between heirs, was practiced along the male line over a long period. The house had multiple courtyards and a number of decorative features not found in other houses at the site, including exterior columns, elaborating its main entrance.[19] Some of the objects found within it were also exceptional for houses, including a number of portable altars that were found in its courtyard, and numerous pieces of sculpture.

In addition to the large House of Lysias, Dura also had a number of palaces: the Roman military palace in the northeast corner of the site (discussed below, in

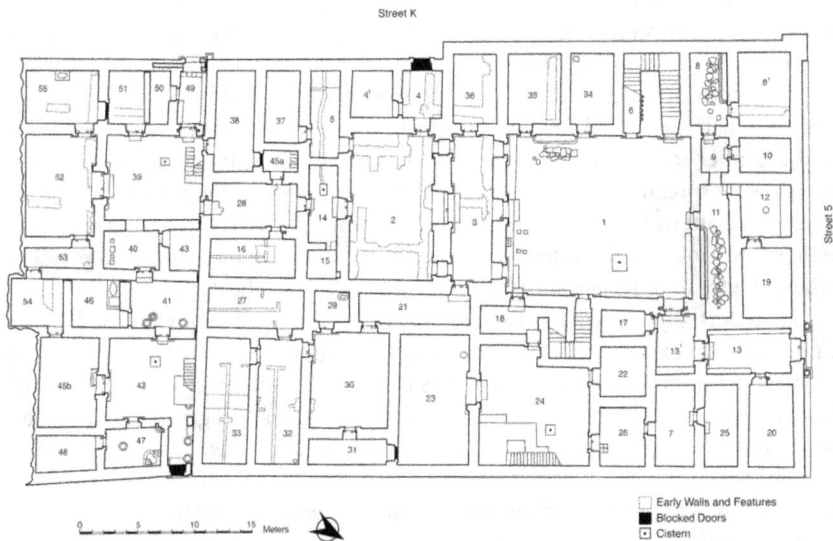

Figure 5.2 Plan of the House of Lysias in block D1. Plan by author after plans by N. C. Andrews in YUAG Archive.

relation to Roman military structures), the palace on the citadel, and the 'strategeion' or 'redoubt' palace.[20] The citadel palace is only partially preserved; much of it has disappeared over the cliff into the Euphrates valley below, and its plan was heavily, and not uncontroversially, restored. Nonetheless, from what remains, it seems to have contained both Hellenic and Achaemenid Persian architectural elements, as would be expected of an elite Seleucid administrative building. Holding a commanding place at the high point of the city and overlooking the Euphrates and Mesopotamia, the structure was in an important position atop the citadel which likely formed the nucleus of the initial Hellenistic settlement. It seems to have been organized around two courtyards, including a southern Doric peristyle courtyard with a residential character and a northern one of more public function.[21]

The citadel palace seems to have gone out of use in the Arsacid period, perhaps due to collapse of the cliffside. Its administrative function may have been replaced in part by the palace on the edge of the southern plateau, the 'redoubt' or 'strategeion' in block C9.[22] Like the palace within the walled citadel, the building had a defensive character, commanding a high point in the settlement and with a view beyond it and built of limestone ashlars, the huge walls of which were remain visible throughout the north side of the settlement.[23] The building, like the citadel palace, had residential and public aspects, but despite its name, nothing definitively links it to the men that held the office of *strategos* at Dura other than its palatial character.

Tombs

Outside the city walls, the necropolis of Dura was partially excavated on the steppe to the west. Poor preservation on the wind-whipped plain has meant little standing architecture has survived. The Yale expedition excavated a number of *hypogea*, or chamber tombs, which had been carved into the earth outside the city.[24] Toll, who was responsible for much of this work and for the necropolis publication, estimated 950 chamber tombs were visible, as well as uncertain number of single graves, which were spread over the space surrounding the city on the plateau; he did not discern a pattern to their placement.[25] The tombs were visible on the ground as either low mounds, the remains of tumuli or built structures, or as depressions where the tomb or its entrance had partially or completely collapsed.

Six reportedly Hellenistic tombs have been more recently excavated by the Franco-Syrian expedition, in a low tell on the steppe to the west outside the city, on a site with inhabitation apparently as early as the Neolithic. Of these, only the human remains have been published, and they were so fragmentary that likely sex and age were determinable for only one individual, a woman of about sixty years old. A number of the skeletons did preserve evidence for growth defects and trauma, testifying to the difficult lives of whoever was interred there.[26]

Most of the existing knowledge concerning the funerary landscape of Dura-Europos, however, comes from the chamber tombs excavated by the Yale expedition. These were cut into the stone of the plateau and usually consisted of a large central chamber with individual niches into which bodies could be placed. At least some of the tombs also had a built structure above them on the surface of the plateau as well.[27] Many of the tombs were disturbed, in antiquity and later, and the human remains were not retained for study, with many so poorly preserved that they 'fell to dust at the slightest contact'.[28] The focus of excavations was tombs that were covered under a mound of debris opposite the main (Palmyrene) gate, presumed to have been a dump from the city. The mound was not well dated, but the latest coin found within the tombs beneath it was Trajanic, and a huge range of material was found within them, including coins ranging from Hellenistic to Roman.[29] Fifty-two chamber tombs were excavated in this part of the necropolis, of which only two were fully intact, and just a handful of which were only partially disturbed.[30]

The rock-cut chamber tombs were entered by a stairway from the surface, into a central chamber which was sometimes supported by a central pillar. The tombs were usually sealed with a vertical stone slab at the bottom of the stairway.[31] Off the central chamber *loculi* (niches) were cut large enough for single or double inhumations. The niches often had arched entrances, with the ceiling cut either flat, curved like a barrel vault, or peaked like a triangular gable.[32] The simplest of these tombs were built for a single individual.[33] Some tombs had internal benches sixty to eighty centimetres high; unlike the low plaster benches of the houses, these were not only for supporting built furniture, and funerary objects were sometimes found placed on these.[34] Some tombs were plastered, and even painted. No inscriptions were found, however, except for one first century date scratched into a tomb wall, and two names in another (all in Greek).[35] Both men and women were interred within the chamber tombs, as well as children, who sometimes accompanied women together in single niches. Some were interred only in shrouds, but the remains of wooden coffins were found in many tombs. Undisturbed remains were found placed with their heads towards the open end of the niche. This type of tomb was apparently in use for a long time at Dura, which is evident from the chronology of the tombs constructed from their relative positions, some even cutting accidentally into others during their construction.[36]

In addition to the chamber tombs, single inhumations were noted as having been placed into the mound of earth above the chamber tombs, which was softer than the surrounding limestone of the plateau. These were assumed to have belonged to the poor of the city, as they were without accompanying grave goods.[37] Even less well understood are the poorly recovered deposits of disarticulated human remains within the mound, including what appears to have been a mass grave or tomb clearance, a pit which contained at least thirty-three human skulls.[38]

The other type of tomb at Dura, alongside single graves and rock-cut chamber tombs, were tower tombs. Several of these were located outside the main area of the necropolis, along a presumed ancient route which also passed the arch of Trajan (Figure 5.3). Others were found within the necropolis, including two near the main gate to the city, with eight in total being identified. The tower tombs had stepped bases built of stone, and had been plastered, but little of their

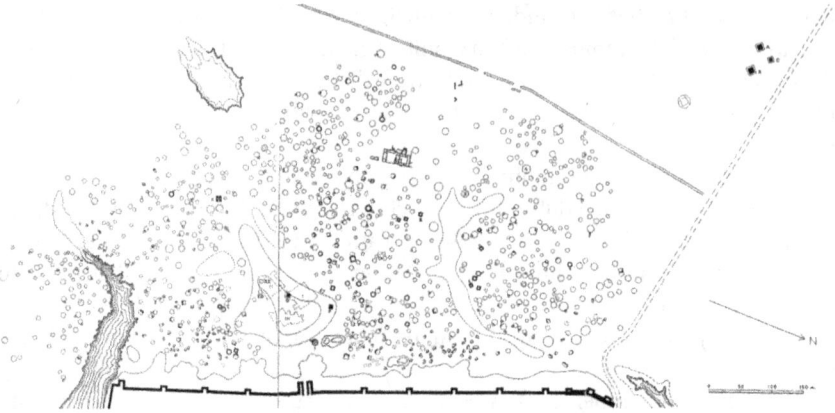

Figure 5.3 Plan of Necropolis. The western city wall of the site is at the bottom of the plan; the building indicated is the 'necropolis' temple. The tombs labelled with letters are tower tombs. YUAG y24.

superstructures survived. Their niches were apparently plastered shut once their occupants were interred.[39]

All of the burials at Dura were inhumations, save for three cremations which were found interred in commonware jars; two of these are associated with a particular tower tomb.[40] While the wood coffins did not survive, bronze corner fittings were preserved, as well as indentations in the earth showing the shape and size of the boards, and the painted plaster which had covered some examples.[41] Only a handful of tombs contained ceramic coffins rather than wooden ones; the ceramic examples were dated to about the second century CE based on their position, but without further secure evidence for dating it is difficult to be certain that, as the excavators presumed, these marked a late shift away from wooden coffins due to increasing Mesopotamian influences.[42] A glazed sarcophagus with a moulded relief of a head discovered in fragments was the only example of its type at Dura.[43]

Most of the tombs had four or more niches on each side of its square central chamber (some had many more – tomb 55 for example had 31 niches which could have held at least that number of individuals). The original excavators did not notice anything sealing the individual niches, but it is possible there were wooden coverings that were not preserved. The grouping of individuals within tombs presumably relates, like the form of the houses, to kinship at the site and reflects the patrilocal joint families of Dura. That is, from what we know of Durene society, these were probably family tombs used over generations, although there is little besides the form of the tombs containing as they do groups of people to confirm this. In the absence of clear evidence, however, it is possible that the groups, or some of them, were related to other factors such as origins or associations.[44] It is notable that at Dura, little in the way of funerary inscriptions or portraiture has been found, in great contrast to other Eastern cities including Palmyra.[45] Many of

Figure 5.4 Photograph of interior of chamber tomb 55 in the necropolis taken in 1935–1936. YUAG k250a.

the individual chambers of the tombs were re-used over time, and the remains of the previous occupants were sometimes simply swept to one end of the chamber or dumped elsewhere in the tomb: the amount of decomposition necessary for this latter (Figure 5.4) option indicates generations passed before such events happened.

While most of the tombs were disturbed in antiquity, many objects were found, some *in situ*. These comprised both grave goods interred with individuals and the apparent remains of funerary rituals within the central chamber. Ceramics, some with the remains of food in them, were found placed on the benches of the chambers. Amongst the ceramics, the most common in the tombs was the fine ware of Dura, the green-glazed pottery.[46] Wooden vessels were found by the excavators but did not survive the process of excavation; much glassware was found, amongst which were a number of vessels which the excavators thought to have been deliberately broken during the funerary rituals, as they could be completely reconstructed.[47] On the occupants of the tombs themselves, and particularly the women, were found a range of objects, including jewellery, and leaves made of thin gold which were found arranged as if they had been worn as crowns; perforated gold disks were found, in some cases, over their eyes. The jewellery is like that found within the city and depicted in paintings at the site, with the exception of the gold leaf crowns and disks which occur only in the city of the dead.[48]

Human remains were also discovered inside the city, but these individuals relate to the fall of the city and subsequent reoccupation, and it was not normal practice to inter people within the city walls. Those bodies that were found included members of the Roman military, like the one buried in the city embankment, a number of graves made by hastily cutting into the plaster floors of 'Dolicheneum', and a body still wearing its armour and lying directly on the floor was found in block E8.[49] Later internments were found in the citadel and in block C11, which post-date the fall of the site.[50] The only human remains found inside the city which are not clearly linked to the fall or post-abandonment phases of the city were found sealed beneath the floor of a room of the House of Lysias in D1, similar remains in D5, and two burials in ceramic sarcophagi beneath the city walls.[51]

Religious Buildings

The religious buildings were one of the foci of the Yale-French Academy expedition, both because of an interest in ancient religion, particularly by Cumont and Rostovtzeff, and because of the wealth of archaeological finds: the associated inscriptions, sculptures, and paintings which tended to be found within them. Religious structures were scattered throughout the city, built of the same limestone, mudbrick, and plaster as the houses, and the search for religious structures was one of the reasons so many houses were excavated, incidentally recovered during the search.[52]

The nineteen religious buildings that were excavated, like the houses, do not fit easily into existing typologies and understandings of Classical and Near Eastern temples. As the deities attested within them, the structures were complicated forms, drawing on Mesopotamian, Syrian, and Classical traditions.[53] As noted in earlier chapters, the inscriptions from Dura's religious buildings provide much of the secure dating for the building sequence at the site. Very little is known of the Hellenistic period, although the temple of Artemis and the temple of Zeus Megistos, both on the plateau, may have had Hellenistic phases which were fragmentarily preserved in later rebuildings of those structures.[54] The most recent excavations in the temple of Zeus Megistos, however, seem to indicate that there was no positively identifiable temple on the site in the Hellenistic period.[55] Most of Dura's religious buildings were built under Arsacid rule, in two 'bursts' of temple building, known from the dates on inscriptions found within them: from the mid-first century BCE to the mid-first century CE, and then in the mid-second century CE following the earthquake in 160.[56]

Care needs to be taken with the terminology used for the religious buildings at Dura, which is a combination of terms taken from ancient sources (both at Dura and elsewhere), terms taken from more recent religious buildings, and modern coinages. Each of the religious buildings were labelled 'temples' by the original excavators, although they do not comprise of a temple structure within a sanctuary, a larger demarcated area or *temenos*: at Dura, the term 'temple' was used to refer to the entire religious structure as a whole. The term 'sanctuary', or the more generic 'religious building', is perhaps preferable.[57] Just as the terminology used to refer to the different parts of the religious buildings of Dura needs to be used with caution, so too the names that were assigned to the 'temples' are also problematic, as noted in Chapter 2. These are sometimes misleading, privileging the Greek deity over the Near Eastern one even when the inscriptions are bilingual (e.g. the temple of Zeus Kyrios rather than that of Zeus Kyrios/Baal-Shamin), or giving it a single name when multiple deities were present (e.g. a number of deities were recorded in the 'temple of Zeus Megistos' and the 'temple of Bel'), or naming it for a subsidiary deity when the central one was not identified (e.g. the temple of the Gaddé probably had Malakbel as its principal deity).[58] In this chapter, the labels the excavators gave each structure are used (e.g. 'the temple of Zeus Megistos') to avoid confusion and allow easy reference to other publications, but with the caveat that such labels are sometimes problematic.

The religious buildings of Arsacid Dura, most of which continued in use into the Roman period, shared a number of features. They were typically entered directly from the street into a courtyard, via a monumentalized entrance flanked by buttresses and sometimes with a small gateway or porch formed by columns. The religious buildings were based around large courtyards, usually surrounded by small rooms generally called 'chapels', with the central sanctuary unit on one end or side. This 'sanctuary unit', as it is sometimes referred to by the excavators, generally consists of the central room of the building, which the excavators referred to as the *naos*, with a preceding room, the *pronaos*, and sometimes skirted by subsidiary anterooms to the sides referred to as 'sacristies', which were perhaps treasuries (as with 'chapel', 'sacristy' was a term anachronistically borrowed from later Christian architecture). The axis of the *naos* and its *pronaos*, and any adjoining rooms, usually faced east and was perpendicular to the axis of the courtyard.

There were a number of variations on this overall plan, with some having a street entrance that aligned with the sanctuary unit, as the temples of Zeus Theos (Figure 5.5), Azzanathkona, and Artemis. Others had a sanctuary unit which was offset from the axis of the entrance; the temple of Adonis (Figure 5.6) had a 'bent axis' plan, in which the sanctuary unit was perpendicular to the entrance. Towers were a frequent feature of Durene religious architecture, with a number of religious structures incorporating towers of the city wall, such as the temples of Zeus Kyrios, Aphlad, Azzanathkona, and Bel. Others had staircases leading to the roof or other raised part of the structure, including the temples of Zeus Megistos, Adonis, and Atargatis, although the superstructure is not well-preserved enough to say precisely what form this took, and it might have been a tower, terrace, or roof space.[59] Several temples, those of Artemis, Atargatis, the Gaddé, and Azzanathkona, had rooms with stepped benches known by the French term *salle à gradins*.[60] Some of the larger temples took up entire city blocks, such as that of Artemis, but others, like Adonis, shared blocks with houses. The precinct known as the temple of Zeus Kyrios is unusually small, without any 'chapels', its main feature being the cult relief set into tower 16 of the city wall, with a small enclosure beneath.[61]

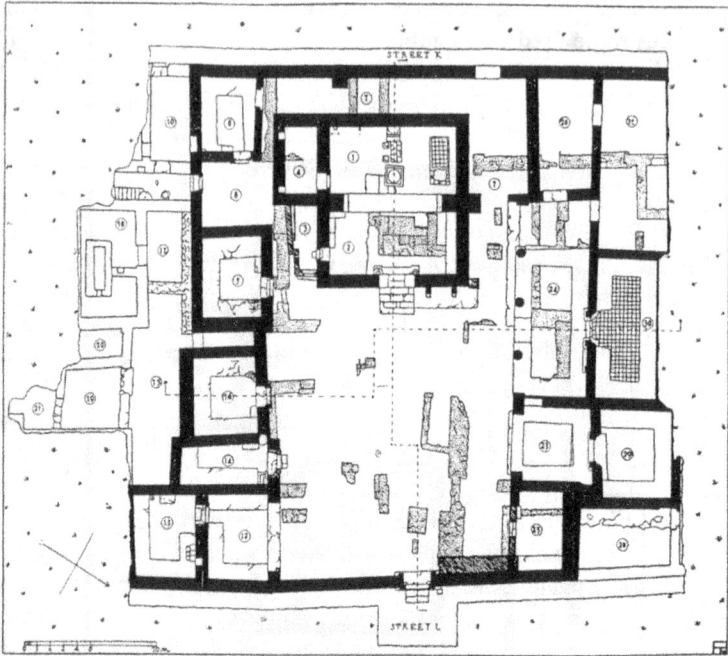

Figure 5.5 Plan of the temple of Zeus Theos in block B3, by Henry Pearson. The *naos* in which paintings were found is room 1, room 2 was the *pronaos*, and room 4 the 'sacristy'. The stippled walls denote walls of underlying structures. YUAG.

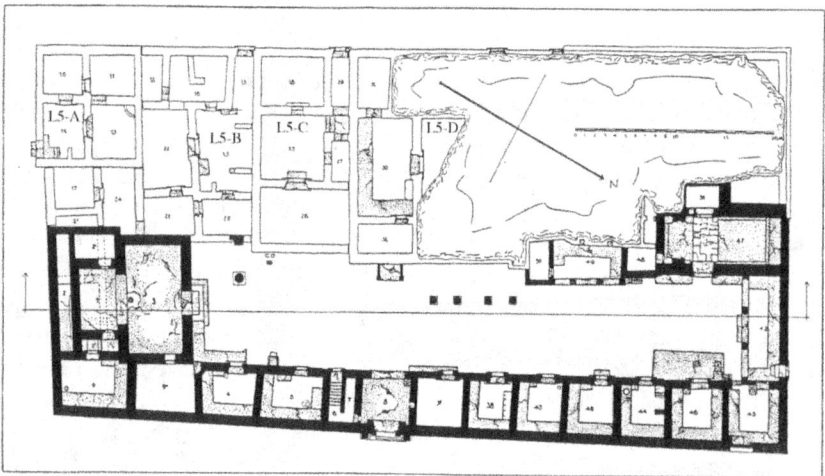

Figure 5.6 Plan of block L5, by Frank Brown. North is at right of the plan. At the bottom of the plan, with the walls coloured black, is the temple of Adonis, with the *naos* and *pronaos* on the left (south) side; on the top of the plan are a series of private houses and an unexcavated area. YUAG.

The street entrance into the courtyard of a temple was sometimes monumentalized or had a built gateway. Occasionally these were perhaps adorned with inscriptions, as for instance the dedicatory inscription found on the lintel of the secondary doorway to the temple of Zeus Theos.[62] The temple of Aphlad (Figure 5.7) had no enclosure and so did not have a formal entrance on its open (eastern) side, unusually, but other sanctuaries, such as the temple of Bel (Figure 5.8), had entrances made of columned porches, or the temple of the Gaddé which had buttresses on either side of the entrance, with columns set in front of them forming a small covered porch.[63]

The open courtyards of Durene temples held altars, both monumental built structures and smaller portable types. The monumental altars were sometimes aligned with the centre of the *naos* unit.[64] Smaller built altars were also found, often against the walls of courtyards, as well as portable ones carved from stone, or made from copper alloy or clay.[65] Some courtyards, such as that of Aphlad, contained a variety of built altars on different orientations (Figure 5.7).[66] Courtyards of religious buildings also contained staircases which led to roofs or terraces (as can be seen in the temple of Adonis, Figure 5.6 above). Courtyards often also had covered areas on their perimeter made by columns (such as in the temples of Bel, Gaddé, Megistos, and Adonis), as well as entrances to the 'chapels' around the courtyard's edge. Beneath the temples, there was sometimes evidence of a foundation deposit; contents included animal bones in the temple of Artemis, 21 amulets in the temple of the Gaddé, and human finger bones beneath the synagogue.[67]

As noted already, the term *naos* is used by the archaeologists at Dura to refer to the main room of the sanctuary. The word *naos* is also used in inscriptions at Dura, for instance that of an otherwise unknown religious structure at Dura, recorded to have been built by the herald Epinicus, and then renovated by his son after its destruction by the Romans (See p.69-70).[68] It is not clear, however, what the Greek word *naos* refers to in an architectural sense at Dura, particularly as this inscription is not certainly associated with any specific architectural remains. Here, the term could have referred to the entire religious building or only its central rooms, although the description of Alexander/Ammaios, Epinicus' son, as extending the *naos* by five cubits and replacing its doors does at least confirm this is a physical space and not a more generalized religious place or area.[69] *Naos* is used in this chapter following the archaeological usage by the excavators for the main interior room of a temple and the *pronaos* the room by which it is entered, again with the caveat that this terminology does not necessarily map neatly onto the ancient usage of the word.[70]

The sanctuary unit formed by the *naos, pronaos*, and any adjoining 'sacristies' was often raised above the level of the courtyard and other rooms and accessed by steps.[71] The unit was sometimes isolated from the exterior walls of the sanctuary with a corridor space which has been likened to the 'isolating corridor' of Mesopotamian temples.[72] In the *naos*, the most commonly found representation of the deity was not in sculpture, but in painting, where it seems the main deity was

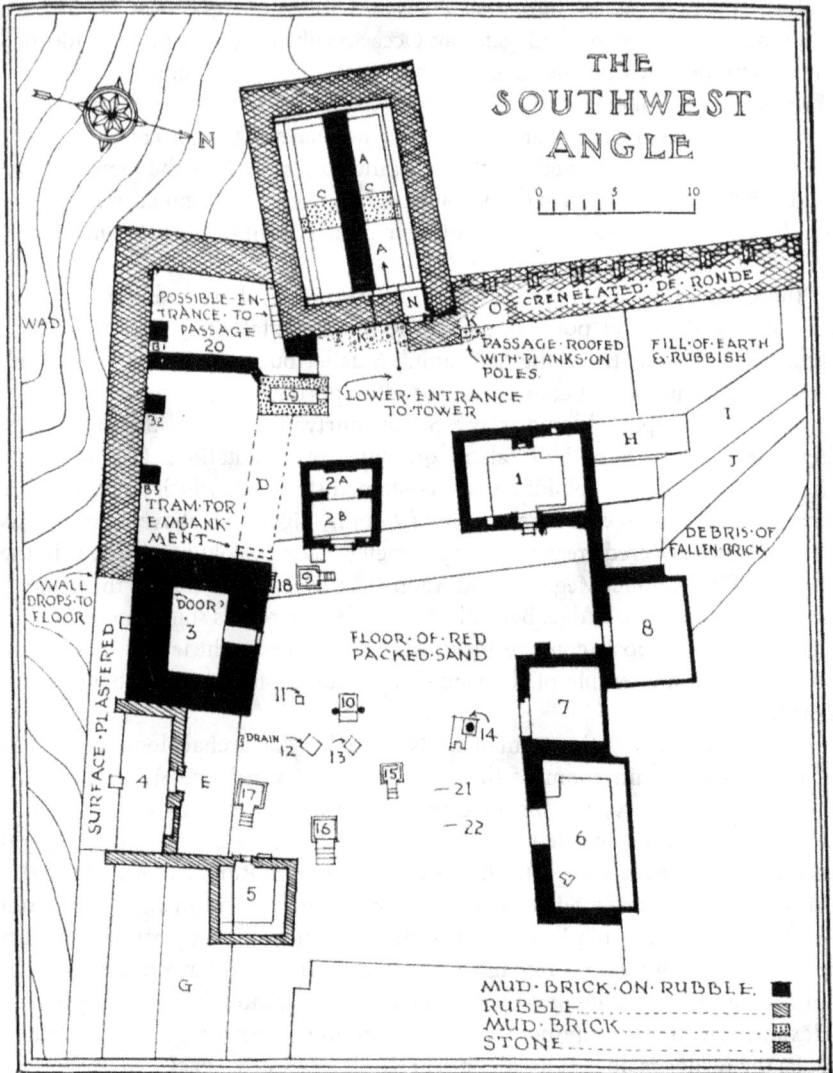

Figure 5.7 Henry Pearson's plan of the southwest corner of the site including the temple of Aphlad, originally published in Dura P. R. 5: 98–130 and plate 1. The cult relief of Aphlad was found in room 1, as was the *andron* inscription; the room identified *naos* is room 2a, the *pronaos* 2b. The temple lacks an enclosure on the east side (at the bottom of the plan), although the surrounding area was not fully excavated. The area between the rear of room 1 and the city wall was also left open. Built altars are indicated throughout the courtyard, nos. 9, 15, 16, 17, and 18; 12 and 13 were bases, 21 and 22 were fragmentary bases, probably also of altars (not all were in contemporary use). The areas I and J indicate phases of the embankment along the city wall. YUAG.

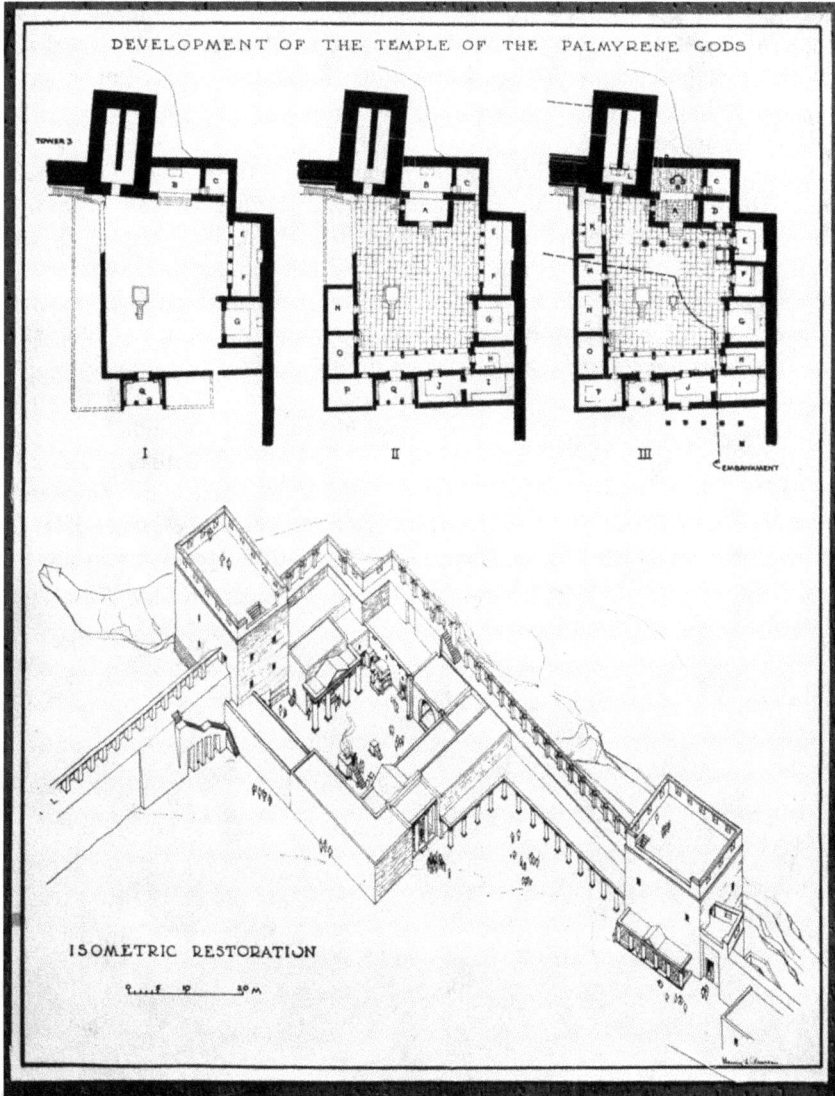

Figure 5.8 Phased plan and reconstruction of the temple of Bel by Henry Pearson. North is at the right of the plan. The *naos* is room B at the top of the plan. YUAG.

generally painted on the rear wall of the room. Problematically, however, while there is evidence of paintings in many of the *naoi* of Durene temples, paintings from the main, rear, wall have only been preserved in very fragmentary states. Such fragmentary paintings are nonetheless known from the temples of Atargatis, Azzanathkona, Aphlad, Adonis, Bel, and Zeus Theos.[73] Perhaps the best preserved of these – still very fragmentary – was found on the rear wall of the *naos* of the temple of Zeus Theos, which contained an over-life-size representation of the deity, with his foot (one of the preserved fragments) resting on a three-dimensional stone plinth built against the *naos* wall, perhaps meant to show him as if he were a statue (Figure 5.9).[74]

On the side walls of the *naos* and in the *pronaos*, where there is more extensively preserved paintings, these often depicted scenes of sacrifice, as the paintings of Conon and Julius Terentius in the temple of Bel, which also both include the depiction of incense offerings which is fairly typical in Durene images of sacrifice (Figures 2.5 and 2.7).[75] Both the temples of Bel and Zeus Theos partially preserve images of the chief deity on the rear wall of the *naos* of the sanctuary unit and scenes of worshippers making offerings on the side walls. In the temple of Bel, priests are shown making sacrifices of wine and incense, perhaps in preparation for animal sacrifice.[76] The cult relief of Azzanathkona may also indicate animal sacrifice as having taken place, depicting as it does a bull.[77] Similarly, a ram is depicted on the relief of Zeus Kyrios, and remains of a sacrificed bird were found on the altar within the temple.[78] Other types of offerings include evidence of burnt oil, which was recorded as having been found in cup-like depressions on altars.[79]

Figure 5.9 Frank Brown's reconstruction of the *naos* of the temple of Zeus Theos. The physical plinth on which the god stands is recorded, but the paintings were recovered in a very fragmentary condition. YUAG y-39.

Paintings often show priests with leaf-covered branches and vessels for washing them, suggesting that incense, wine, and fruit were normal offerings.[80] While the deities to whom sacrifice is being offered are both male and female, priests are male in all attested evidence from Dura, including both inscriptions and the paintings, in which they wear distinctive conical hats.[81]

There is relatively little evidence for the precise nature of religious activities within buildings, although in addition to religious sculpture and paintings, there are some preserved votive offerings, as well as the architecture and installations within the religious buildings themselves. Within the *naos* of the temple of Zeus Theos (room 1 on the Figure 5.5 above), the installations of cult furniture were relatively well preserved including a number of altars, one of which had channels for liquid libations and bases for further altars or equipment.[82] In the floor of the *naos* of the temple of Aphlad, a bowl was set into the floor of the doorway, perhaps for ritual cleansing; a basin in the centre of the court of the temple of Atargatis may have made reference to the sacred lake at the great Syrian goddess' temple at Hierapolis.[83] Sockets in the floor of the *naos* in Azzanathkona, to either side and in front of the altar, may have held the cult standards, although no trace of the standards themselves were found in the room.[84] Often, to the sides of the *naos* or *pronaos* were subsidiary rooms. As noted above, these were labelled 'sacristies' by the excavators. Some were used as storerooms for temple equipment (e.g. thirteen storage jars were found in room 10 of Azzanathkona).[85] Others had preserved evidence for locking mechanisms and were equipped with niches for storage, and jewellery was found within them (e.g. room 4 of the temple of Zeus Theos on Figure 5.5), while others had benches, perhaps for use by priests, as in the temple of Adonis (room 9 on Figure 5.6).[86]

Another of the main architectural features of Arsacid and Roman sanctuaries at Dura also has a problem with its terminology: that is the type of rooms found around the perimeter of the courtyard that are generally known as 'chapels'. The term 'chapel' is used here to refer to this architectural form (even though it is slightly misleading in its Christian undertone) because it allows consistency about a particular generic form: a room immediately surrounding a courtyard in a Durene religious building which sometimes had benches. Such rooms seem to have been given a range of names in antiquity, judging from inscriptions found in sanctuaries and sometimes found even in the chapel rooms themselves. Again, there is no certain match in either case between the ancient terminology and archaeological remains, but Greek words for spaces dedicated within sanctuaries at Dura which appear in inscriptions found in the 'chapels' include *andron*, *naos*, *oikos*, and *oikodomē*, connoting perhaps a range of ancient names for and uses of these spaces.[87]

The raised perimeter benches in many of the 'chapels' were low platforms like those of the principal rooms of the houses. These were likely used to support couches and reflect the use of the room for ritual dining. Specifically what such rooms were used for probably varied, and ritual dining was only one aspect of the activities attested in this type of room by equipment, objects, inscriptions, and graffiti found within them. For example, food and drink were not only consumed but also probably prepared in some of these rooms: mortars suggesting food preparation were found in room 8D of the temple of Azzanathkona, in which an inscription was also found recording the dedication of an *oikos* in the precinct of 'Artemis, the goddess called Azzanathkona'.[88] On the south side of the temple of Zeus Theos, room 13, another 'chapel', had a fire-blackened floor and wall surrounding a hearth, perhaps also indicative of food preparation.[89] Some 'chapels' even contained a cult image, as in the temple of Aphlad, or had a niche for such a relief.[90]

Inscriptions testify that many of these 'chapels' were dedicated by groups of men, by families, or by priests. 'Chapel J' in the temple of Artemis was dedicated by men who had all taken the Roman name Aurelios and called themselves priests of Artemis and *bouletai* (civic officials).[91] Another room of this form dedicated by priests in the temple of Artemis was called an *oikodomē* in an inscription.[92] In the temple of Atargatis, an inscription (later re-used) testifies to a meeting place dedicated by an association of men.[93] In the temple of Aphlad, a group of men (who are explicitly an association, a *hetaireia*) dedicated the *andron* noted above. The room of the temple of Aphlad in which the *andron* inscription was found (room 1 on Figure 5.7) is a 'chapel' type and had benches around the perimeter, and also contained the cult relief depicting the god himself.[94] An *andron* is a 'men's room' and suggests the gendered divisions of space within sanctuaries, as do the inscriptions recording women in several of the rooms called *salle à gradins*, discussed below. Other rooms in temples are not easily identified in the archaeology but are known from inscriptions, including a wine cellar referred to in dedication in Adonis.[95] As with the words *naos* and *oikos*, it is overall very difficult to map terms for built parts of temples and other architecture directly to terminology found in ancient texts.[96]

Another frequent part of Durene religious buildings was a room with step-like benches, known by the modern French term *salle à gradins* (Figure 5.10). This type of room was found in the temples of Artemis, Atargatis, Azzanathkona, and that of the Gaddé. Generally, the inscribed seats in the temples of Artemis, Atargatis, and Azzanathkona have names of women belonging to prominent Durene families. The earliest such room seems to have been the *salle à gradins* in the temple of Artemis, which was later dismantled; the Roman-era *odeon* in the temple may or may not have replaced some of its functions, but the inscriptions in it relate to men, rather than women.[97] The *salle à gradins* and adjoining room in Azzanathkona were presumed to be a secondary sanctuary unit by the excavators (in addition to more central sanctuary unit 2-5D), and it contained a cult relief of Azzanathkona.[98] The inscriptions on the steps are first and second century CE in date.[99] Most names were those of women, some of whom were of the same families attested on the steps of the temple of Artemis. The *salle à gradins* in the temple of Atargatis was also its *pronaos*, and on its steps were texts that indicate their dedication in 61 CE.[100] The steps in the temple of the Gaddé are an exception, in being within a sanctuary whose main deity was probably not female, and the steps were not inscribed. The use of such rooms with steps further complicates our understanding of Durene religious architecture: the courtyard plan with the

Figure 5.10 Photograph of the *salle à gradins* in the temple of Azzanathkona, showing the cult relief *in situ* with altars beneath it. One of the workers is posed as scale, on the inscribed steps. YUAG e56.

naos at one end and surrounded by chapels follows Babylonian tradition in a general way, but such 'theatral' spaces like the rooms with steps have parallels in Syria, not Mesopotamia.[101] It is not known precisely how these rooms functioned, but they were apparently a place for rituals, perhaps including banqueting, and those of Artemis, Azzanathkona, and Atargatis were probably spaces which were specialized for use by women.

Durene deities were usually represented in paintings or sculpted cult reliefs. As noted above, paintings seem to have been regular in the *naoi* but are not well preserved. Cult reliefs, however, were not found in the *naos* and thus apparently functioned in a different way to the cult statues of Classical temples which would be expected to be found in this location, in the central room of the sanctuary.[102] For example, the only surviving cult relief from of Aphlad was found in a 'chapel' (as seen above, this is probably known in antiquity as an *andron*); that of Azzanathkona was found in the *salle à gradins*.[103] The relief of Azzanathkona (Figures 5.10 and 5.11) demonstrates that the carved relief was perhaps itself an object of worship, as an altar was found directly beneath it; a small altar and other installations were similarly found beneath the cult relief of Aphlad.[104] In the cases of both Aphlad and Azzanathkona, the relief was placed somewhere it was used by a defined group of people (an association of men in the case of Aphlad, a group of women in Azzanathkona).[105] Both gods are also connected to a particular place.

Figure 5.11 Photograph of the relief of Azzanathkona taken when it was accessioned to the Museum in Damascus in the 1930s. In the relief, the goddess Azzanathkona is shown on the left, seated between two lions. She is being crowned by the man standing on the right; above them a man leads a bull over a rocky landscape, probably leading him to sacrifice. YUAG Dam-26.

Together, this may indicate that despite the conventional names of the temples, the reliefs should not be used to indicate the main deity of the entire religious structure within which they were found. Indeed, in the case of the temple of Aphlad, the number of monumental altars that fill its courtyard suggests that Aphlad, the god of Anath, was not the only deity worshipped therein or that different groups worshipped him separately.[106]

Contrasting with the typical courtyard plans common to the Durene sanctuaries of the Arsacid era was the Mithraeum (Figure 5.12). While it is unusual amongst Mithraea in being above ground and not subterranean, its other features are common to such structures throughout the Mediterranean, including a vestibule with two columns, a *cella* with benches, and a *naos* with central cult relief depicting the *tauroctony*, Mithras' slaying of a bull. The features that the Mithraeum shares with its counterparts throughout the Roman empire show that the cult at Dura was connected to this broader practice, evidently via military networks.[107] Many of the Roman military men worshipping in the Mithraeum were members of the twentieth Palmyrene cohort, and its third-century renovation was carried out by Antonius Valentinus, *centurio princeps* of vexillations of the fourth Scythian and sixteenth Flavia Firma legions.[108] Nonetheless the style of the painting as well as the graffiti found within it are also connected to practices in other sanctuaries of Dura.[109]

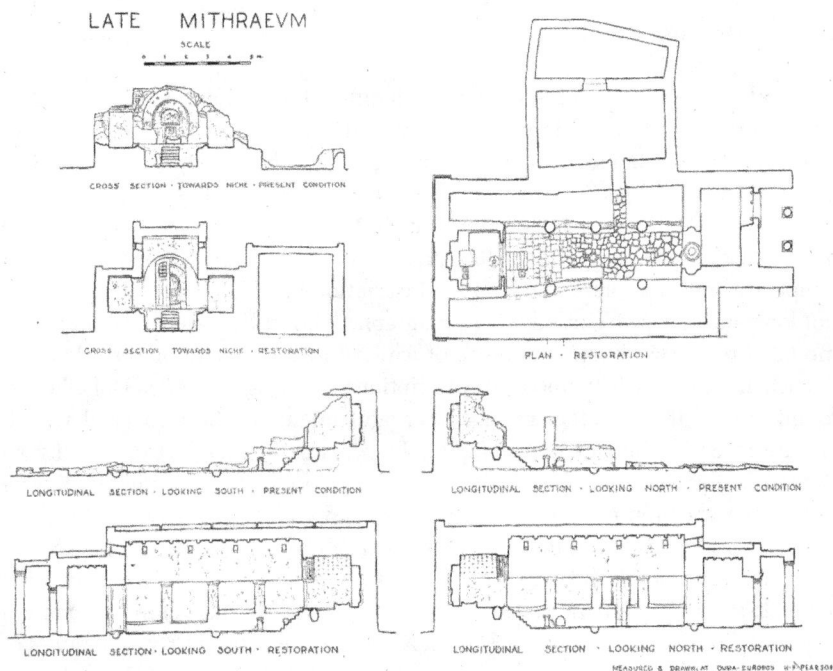

Figure 5.12 Plan and reconstruction of the late Mithraeum by Henry Pearson. YUAG i407.

The Mithraeum was not the only religious building which, in the Roman era at Dura, took on a different form from the Mesopotamian courtyard plans which characterized those of Arsacid Dura. There were also those which were modified from houses (although they shared other features with the earlier temples, including their use of painted interiors for the most important rooms). These were the synagogue and the Christian building. Evolution from private houses in the case of each of these religious buildings probably relates to their origins at the site, which may have been introduced via private practice of the cult within particular families. The privacy and relative inconspicuousness of the use of housing perhaps also served the nature of the religions practiced inside.[110]

The remains of the Christian building in block M8 were poorly preserved. The building itself was a fairly typical Durene house, with some adaptations. Were it not for the subjects of the fragmentary paintings found in one of the rooms, with scenes from the Torah and gospels, little other evidence from Dura would point to the existence of a Christian community.[111] The painted room had a font against its western wall (unique at Dura), suggestive of baptism and hence the initiation of new members into the Christian community at Dura.[112] Like the Christian building, the synagogue inherited its architectural form from its earlier incarnation as a private house, and while both were modified from this form, it is notable that they were not modified in such a way to replicate local sanctuary architecture, which had a range of rooms or 'chapels' around the perimeter, probably to accommodate the range of groups which worshipped there. This may indicate that these religious communities were, at least in terms of religious practice, more communal than others.

Another type of religious building which differed from those typical of Arsacid Dura were the small Roman-era temples with four columns in the centre of nearly square buildings: the temple of the Archers in block A1 and the so-called Dolicheneum in block X7. The temple of the archers was identified by a Latin inscription found within it, recording a dedication by Roman soldiers, including of the fourth Scythian legion and Roman archers of the second Ulpian legion. The temple was not well preserved, and the inscription itself reportedly disintegrated not long after it was recorded and photographed, but it had been decorated with moulded plasterwork and paintings, of which fragments were preserved.[113] The 'Dolicheneum' took its name from inscriptions referring to Jupiter Dolicihenus, found *outside* the building, in the street, and might not be associated with it (Figure 5.13).[114] The worship of Jupiter Dolichenus in this part of the city by Roman soldiers is nonetheless well attested.[115] Within the temple, other gods were mentioned: the mountain god Turmasgade on a door jamb; and *Kyria* ('the lady') on an inscribed relief. It is not clear that either of these were the central deities of the temple. The temple did perhaps have two main deities, as the sanctuary unit has a double structure. Generally, dedicants in and around this part of the Roman-era city were Roman military.[116] The A1 and X7 temples are still courtyard temples of a type, but they differ consistently from earlier religious buildings at Dura, sharing with each other their general shape, the use of four columns in the courtyard, and south-facing sanctuary units (rather than east facing as the others at Dura); they

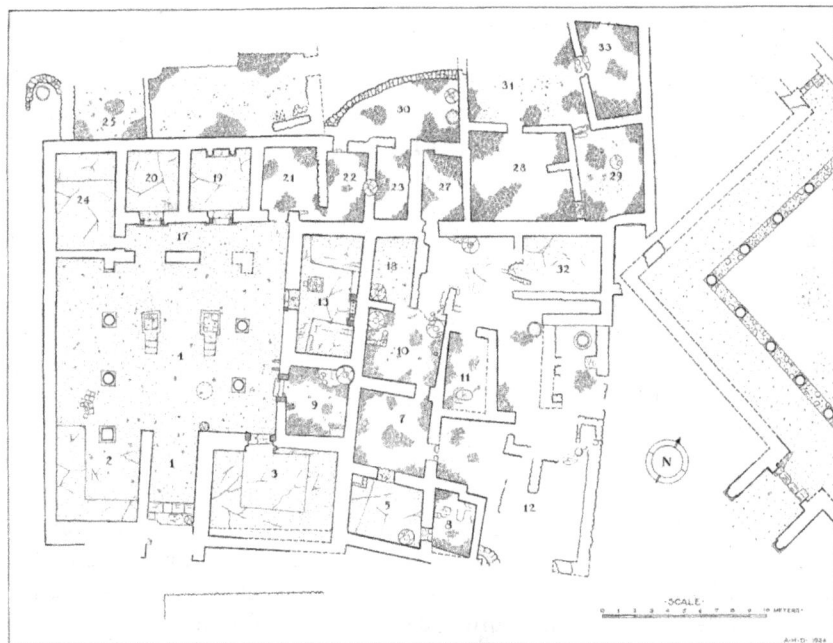

Figure 5.13 Plan made by A. H. Detweiler in 1936 of the 'Dolicheneum' temple (left, entered via room '1'), with buildings probably used as military accommodation in the centre (right of the temple), and the corner of the Roman palace at right. YUAG i400a.

are also both within the part of the city taken over by the Roman military. A small building with a similar plan near Palmyrene gate was suggested to be a Tychaeum following a similar plan, although the evidence for this identification is otherwise thin.[117]

The diversity of cults found at Dura: Mesopotamian, Syrian, Classical, and hybrids of those, was typical of the Arsacid period elsewhere too and reflective of diverse communities with complex heritages.[118] In large part, this seems to have continued under Roman rule, at least until the embankments constructed against the western city walls to try to defend the city against the Sasanians drastically altered the urban landscape. The new temple plans within the part of the city taken over by the Roman military base are one indication of differential religious practice between the civil and military communities (others are myriad, not least the military religious calendar attested by the *Feriale*), but this is not to say the Roman military base excluded existing cult practice, either. Indeed, in the temple of Azzanathkona, there appears to be continuity of religious practice even when the temple found itself well inside the part of the city that had become a Roman military base, and part of the temple building had been taken over for use by the Roman military (i.e. the archive in 13W).[119] In the case of Azzanathkona, perhaps the use in the cult of standards made the use of the continued religious use of the building palatable. Similarly, as has already been noted in Chapter 2, the paintings of Julius Terentius and his men of the twentieth Palmyrene cohort joined an existing painted programme of sacrificial images in the temple of Bel. Even if civilian worship did not continue in the temple when it was swallowed up by the installation of the garrison, religious practice continued within it.

One of the central questions surrounding the religious structures of Dura was who paid for them and who had access to them. As noted already in relation to the 'chapels', certain groups of men bound by origin, occupation, and other affiliations are recorded as having paid for particular parts of the buildings. One of the issues that has arisen from the presence of monotheistic religions at Dura is the extent to which religious communities were competitive with each other. The art of Dura, one of the forms of evidence that is used to testify to such competition, will be discussed in more detail in the next chapter, but it is instructive to note that regardless of the actual subject of the paintings, the technique and style of the paintings found in Dura's religious buildings including those of the monotheistic cults, as with their building materials, and even their graffiti, are in a shared vernacular throughout the site. Materially and architecturally, the sanctuaries share much in common. The 'chapels' in the sanctuaries nonetheless indicate that some of the groups using the buildings did so communally with each other and separately from other groups. An implication of this, as will be further discussed with relation to the paintings in the next chapter, is that religious buildings were not for the sole use of particular families. Further, it sets apart the Mithraeum, Christian building, and synagogue, which had a different architectural form to accommodate their different needs, not only with a different type of religious practice but a particular relationship to other groups within that religious community, and a different relationship to those who were not members.

Within religious buildings, inscriptions record patronage by elite Durenes, and parts of buildings may have been used by members of particular families. Particular buildings had very strong connections with certain families, for instance the temple of Zeus Megistos.[120] This close relationship was, for one thing, spatial: the entrance to the temple was immediately across the road from the main entrance to the House of Lysias, just a few metres away. A member of (probably) the same family is known on an inscription outside the temple which records the dedication of parts of the building in 169/70 CE: 'Seleucos, *strategos kai epistates* of the city, built the arch (*phalis*), the *stoa*, and the *plintheion* (perhaps in this context meaning door trim) for Zeus Megistos on behalf of the safety of himself and that of his children in accordance with a vow.'[121] A *dipinto* inside the temple also records a Lysias (other names not known to be related to the families holding the titles of *strategos* or *epistates* are also recorded in the building).[122] A sculpted relief of the hero Heracles found in room 19, the entrance to a *pronaos-naos* unit, had the Greek remembrance inscription *mnesthe Lysanias* ('may Lysanias be remembered').[123] Within the *naos* of that unit, fragments of the statue of a draped figure were found; this evidence together is perhaps an indication that there was a close relationship between particular families and particular religious buildings, and that some parts of buildings – for example this *naos* in the temple of Zeus

Megistos, one of at least two in the building, may have been for their exclusive use.[124] Elsewhere on the site, in the synagogue, painted inscriptions on ceiling tiles – perhaps not even clearly visible to those using the assembly hall – recorded founders and donors.[125]

Religion at Dura was sometimes therefore deeply entangled with particular elite families and related not only through their patronage of the structures but also in their self-presentation as rulers and with the endorsement of their lineages, some of which were displayed on the walls of the most sacred part of the building, as in the temples of Zeus Theos, Bel, and Zeus Megistos. At Dura, there was no major civic temple, such as the great temple of Bel at Palmyra, but the temple of Artemis had civic features, particularly in the Roman era. The earliest inscription from that building is one recording Seleukos son of Lysias, who is *strategos* and *genearch*.[126] Centuries later, a dedication to Lucius Verus is made by Aurelios Heliodoros, an *epistates* of the city.[127] The relationship between the temple of Artemis and the rule of the city was not simply a formulaic one in inscriptions but one in which the temple served as a locale for administrative practice, and the *odeon* of the temple was used as the *boule* or council of Dura in the Roman era.[128] An inscription honouring the empress Julia Domna was also found on a statue base there, showing that the dedications to the imperial house were not only the purview of the military.[129]

The temple of Bel also had civic aspects.[130] One of the earliest inscriptions from the temple is of 50/51 CE, to Zeus Soter from Seleucos, son of Lysias, a *strategos kai epistates* of the city.[131] Such inscriptions show that religious buildings were an appropriate place for the elites of the city to demonstrate their administrative (and by extension social) power. The *polis* (city) also dedicated an altar to Zeus Megistos in the city tower that formed part of the building after the earthquake which shook the region in 160 CE.[132] Later, in chapel K of the building, a painting shows the eunuch Otes and Iabsumos, the son of Abdaathetos, who are both *bouletes* of Dura, making a sacrifice to five deities, probably the Palmyrene gods Bel, Iarhibol, Aglibol, Allat, and Arsu.[133] This painting is probably of the third century and, as in the temple of Azzanathkona, indicates the continued use by the civic population of a religious structure even when it was within the military garrison.[134] While the building underwent many adaptations, its continued existence as a focus of religious practice shows that religious places retained their significance from the Arsacid into the Roman period, and that some such buildings were used by both military and civilians in the third century.[135]

Families were thus important in Durene religion, and lineage an important part of religious inscriptions and paintings; some families clearly played a role as patrons of particular religious buildings. As already seen, religious groups were also in some cases based on origin. As noted in the previous chapter, the temple known as the 'necropolis temple' was actually a temple for the Palmyrene gods Iarhibol and Bel.[136] Its placement outside the city walls might relate to provision for Palmyrene traders, and a cistern adjacent to the temple could have provided a watering place for animals.[137] The temple in block H1 which became that of the Gaddé was similarly used by Palmyrenes, based on the evidence of extant inscriptions.[138]

Similarities in the plan between Gaddé and the necropolis, in the placement of the sanctuary unit (with long *pronaos* and the *naos* projecting from the exterior of the courtyard), may have something to do with the Palmyrene community that used them, although they are not paralleled in temples at Palmyra (but rather, at Hatra).[139]

At Dura, religious buildings were a focal point for community identities: communities of foreigners as in the temple of Iarhibol and Bel in the necropolis, or those worshipping Aphlad in the *andron* of the building known as the temple of Aphlad, groups of elite women who came together in the temples of Artemis and Atargatis, the community of Jews in the synagogue and Christians with their baptistery, the Palmyrenes and eventually wider Roman military members of the Mithraeum, and many others. It is notable that while these communities were overtly marked out in those religious contexts, they are not, with the exception of the Palmyrenes, clearly evident elsewhere at the site. There is no indication, from current evidence, that these communities clustered within the city in other ways, for instance in particular neighbourhoods or enclaves.

So, some religious communities were bound by socioeconomic class, itself based around perceived descent, such as the secondary *naos* of Zeus Megistos, in which texts note a connection to the family of Lysias and the architecture indicates a more 'private' part of the building. Groupings within religious communities also could be gendered, both in the associations of men who erected 'chapels' in a number of sanctuaries or the women whose names appeared in the *salle à gradins* in the temples of Artemis, Atargatis, and Azzanathkona. Others were based on origins, such as the *andron* to Aphlad within that sanctuary for people from Anath or the temple to Iarhibol and Bel in the necropolis, the temple of the Gaddé, and that in M5, for Palmyrenes. The Roman military integrated into some local religious spaces (e.g. within the temple of Bel, and perhaps the Christian building) but other structures were purpose built for them (such as the temples in X7 and A1). The space of religious buildings was thus used to articulate and reinforce communities and their boundaries. Of the monotheistic religions, we can presume exclusivity, but this need not have extended to other elements of those community's lives. Other religious structures had an explicitly cosmopolitan character, including Zeus Kyrios/Baalshamin.[140]

Many other religious aspects of life and evidence for religious practice were not associated with particular buildings. Graffiti of remembrance, including many of the *mnesthe* formula ('may so-and-so be remembered'), were found on surfaces of fortifications and in houses, as well as in religious buildings.[141] Streets would have been used for processions, and fortification towers formed part of religious buildings. Burnt offerings on altars and towers would create smells and smoke which would be perceptible far beyond the bounds of sanctuaries.

Fortifications and Public Buildings

The dressed gypsum blocks which comprise much of Dura's fortifications were made of local stone quarried from the wadis which bounded the site to the north and south, and which ran across the site itself: this included most of the city walls, the towers, and the citadel. This ashlar masonry characterizes the constructions at Dura which survive from the Hellenistic period, but these are dated by technique rather than inscriptions or absolute dates.[142] In addition to the fortifications, this masonry was used in the construction of early buildings in the centre of the city in the eight-block area designated the 'agora' by the excavators, and the 'palaces' on the citadel and redoubt (the 'Strategeion').

The earliest Hellenistic settlement of the site seems to have been focused in and around the citadel. It is now thought that the road system was not laid out at the time of the colony's foundation, but much later, probably around 150 BCE, based on the stratigraphy of the main street.[143] Indeed, the director of the Franco-Syrian expedition argues on the basis of this stratigraphic evidence that the fortification walls of the city and the layout of the street grid were contemporary, at around this time in the mid-second century BCE.[144] The precise dating of the city's fortifications remains problematic: they seem to have been at least begun in the Seleucid period, but perhaps were still under construction when the Arsacids took control of the site.[145]

The city's walls built of ashlar blocks were constructed using the relatively uniform stones in alternating courses of headers and stretchers.[146] The walls were over 10 metres high and about 3 metres in thickness; the long western stretch was about 856 metres long and the complete circuit would have measured about 3,025 metres.[147] Punctuated with a series of towers, the walls apparently enclosed the entire settled area of the city, as no houses were found outside the city walls. Along the eastern side, the walls have mostly disappeared into the deep river valley below, but on the west side, they are so well preserved that the original wall walk along the summit of the wall is intact.[148] Sections of the western wall were constructed in mudbrick (north of tower 22), perhaps, it is thought, indicative of the original wall which was gradually completed in stone, except in this section (Figure 5.14).[149] The modern road which cuts into the site between towers 25 and 26 exposed the stone masonry foundations of this mudbrick curtain wall, with the foundations believed to be part of that laid out in the Seleucid era.[150] The lack of an external ditch outside the city walls has been explained by the geology of the steppe outside the city, as the upper layer of extremely hard limestone made this difficult to accomplish.[151]

The western wall had a primary gate (that which became known as the Palmyrene gate) which has been dated to the mid-second century BCE, contemporary with the other fortification walls and layout of the town plan.[152] A secondary gate to the south of the primary gate was walled up before the construction of a rampart by the Romans; a Roman sap beneath this section of the city wall perhaps indicates that it had been a weak point in the defences.[153] Access to the city could also be made by a gate on the south side, which opened into the *wadi*, as did a postern gate on the north side near tower 2.[154] A river gate, the *porta aquaria* of the military papyri, was inferred to be southeast of block B2, but no certain trace of it remains, the area having been heavily eroded into the valley below.[155] Near this gate would have been the water-lifting machine to provision the nearby bath in C3.

Figure 5.14 Western city wall, view from north end in 1936–1937, with mudbrick portion visible behind the excavated area in the foreground. The excavated area is block J7, including the Mithraeum. YUAG k88a.

The towers were irregularly spaced along the city wall and took a number of different forms, some projecting only on the exterior of the city, others both internally and externally, and different shapes, including one pentagonal tower (tower 10). The placement of towers seems to have been influenced by a number of factors; on the north and south of the city, they are situated where the topography has given the city an irregular, rather than straight, side, so that each place the wall changed direction is protected, and allowing visibility outwards not to be compromised. Other towers (e.g. towers 14 and 16) align with city grid; potentially, sight lines into the town were also important. A number of towers were also within sanctuaries (towers 1, 3, 15, and 16), the sanctuaries perhaps being sited so as to exploit the access to these. The towers allowed the sanctuaries access to high points and put those parts of the fortification under divine protection.[156]

A mile outside the city, a triumphal arch built by the third Cyrenaean Legion of the Roman army remains partially standing, and fragments of its Latin inscription were preserved, recording its dedication to the Emperor Trajan (Figure 5.15).[157] Three massive enclosures defined by earthworks, visible on aerial photography northwest of the city along the edge of the plateau, are likely to be the remains of Roman campaign camps.[158] Their existence perhaps explains the position of the

WEST ELEVATION RESTORED

A.H. DETWEILER 1937

Figure 5.15 Drawing of the Arch of Trajan outside Dura's city walls, as reconstructed by A. H. Detweiler in 1937. The detailed and shaded stones on the elevation drawing and the black on the plan drawing beneath it indicate the elements which survived; the rest is restored. YUAG.

arch of Trajan, that is, marking the site of victory of the Romans on a battlefield with the Parthians outside the city, which is not known from historical sources.[159]

Under the Romans, the largest change to the fortifications was the massive anti-siege embankment (that which incidentally preserved so many paintings and objects along the western edge of the city), built in several phases, which protected the existing wall circuit. The long western wall where the city was not also protected by steep cliffs was particularly the focus of this work, and two phases of mudbrick and earth embankments destroyed and covered much of what had lain along the interior western edge of the city. The Romans apparently also repaired mudbrick sections of the western city wall and reinforced the main gate with a huge external mudbrick wall.[160]

As noted in Chapter 2, Dura fell to the Sasanians under Shapur I in about 256 CE. The remains of the Sasanian assault on the city include the massive siege ramp near the southwest corner of the city (between towers 14 and 15) and associated saps and countermines.[161] A Sasanian mine and Roman countermine around tower 19 were also excavated, preserving the remains of both Sasanian and Roman soldiers, and of the use of chemicals in combat.[162] The siege camp of the Sasanians on the plain outside the city is not preserved, as winds across the steppe have tended to obliterate standing mudbrick architecture, but its outline has been identified on aerial photographs enclosing a massive area three times as big as the city itself.[163]

The large dressed ashlar blocks which characterized the fortifications of Dura were also used within the city. The Hellenistic period of the so-called *agora*, occupying eight blocks in the centre of the site, is not very well known, although large ashlar masonry of its buildings was re-used in the later buildings, preserving something of its form and outlining monumental public structures in the centre of the city. Traces of earlier inhabitation were also excavated between the later houses which eventually filled this part of the city, including terracotta tubs for bathing and terracotta roof tiles and antefixes.[164] Among the buildings which had been presumed to be Hellenistic in origin but for which most evidence is actually Arsacid is the 'Chreophylakeion' in block G3, the public record office (See p.76). This seems to have remained in use into the Roman period. The building consisted of a courtyard, entered directly from the street, behind which were several rooms, including one which preserved a series of niches for storing records, and graffiti of a Chi-Rho monogram, interpreted as the symbol of the *chreophylakes*, the officials in charge.[165]

Aside from the archives building, the temples, which have several potentially civic functions, and the citadel and redoubt palaces, which probably had administrative functions, no other buildings with a clear public function were excavated at Dura. This is not, of course, to say there were not public spaces; in addition to the potentially unexcavated areas of the city which may yet reveal public structures, streets and other gathering places were available, including small *stoa*-like structures formed by colonnaded frontages of buildings in front of shops, baths, and other buildings.[166] The presence of many houses in the *agora* part of the city during the Roman era is usually described as the private takeover of previously public areas. To some extent, this seems to be true, but it should be noted that among those houses are workshops, inns, bars, and shops, so this part of the city retained a commercial character and was not entirely turned over to domestic occupation.[167]

The shops were mostly single rooms entered directly from the street. Some were internally connected to houses, with a door at the rear of the shop into the adjoining houses, but others consisted of the single room alone.[168] A number of buildings which have the same plans as houses were used as eating and drinking establishments, distinguishable by features such as Bacchic-themed plaster decorations, multiple ovens, additional storage for wine, and multiple dining rooms.[169] Shops were not limited to the *agora* area but were also found along the main street and elsewhere, throughout the city.[170] Workshops were also found in other parts of the city, and kilns were found throughout the city, particularly in block B2, which had such a density it was named by archaeologists the 'block of the potters'.[171] In addition to ceramic vessels, there is also evidence for the production of terracotta objects and glass, and moulds for production of a number of different types of objects were found in houses in the *agora*.

A large market space in block G6, surrounded by columns on two sides and shops on three, seems to be a market space built in the Roman era (the excavators called it a 'Roman market', and while it was certainly in use in the third century, the evidence for its date of construction is not explicit).[172] While the grand colonnaded streets of other Roman-era cities in Syria are in part a result of different local materials and architectural forms, they are also evidence of an investment in public space which is less evident at Dura.[173] There is nonetheless some evidence for the increasing monumentalization of public spaces in the Roman era, for instance in the addition of colonnades as mentioned above, and while Dura may not have evidence for this level of *euergetism* ('doing good deeds', e.g. donations of public monuments by wealthy individuals), there is nonetheless some evidence for this sort of patronage, both in the dedications of parts of religious buildings as described above, and in other examples. For instance, near the remains of an arch on the main road of the city (between the corners of blocks C7 and B8), a fragmentary Greek inscription records something (perhaps the arch) being dedicated by Antigonos son of Marion and an *archiereus* (chief priest), to the magistrate and *euergete* Claudius Sollemnius Pacatianus.[174]

Roman Military Buildings

There is no well-dated archaeological horizon at Dura for the traditional start of the Roman period there in 165; the date, instead, comes from the historical context of Dura (See p.29). Some structures within the city might even be dated as early as the brief Trajanic occupation of the site *c.* 116/117; the central architectural features of Roman-era Dura, however, were probably built starting in the late second and early third century. This included new buildings and buildings of types new to Dura – housing for military accommodation, buildings related to military administration and to officers, an amphitheatre, and the Roman-era temples in blocks X7 and A1 amongst these (Figure 5.16).[175] These buildings would incorporate materials not used previously at Dura, including extensive use of fired (rather than sun-baked) bricks and the use of stone mosaic flooring, but while the forms of buildings were different, they were mostly constructed in the same rubble, plaster, and mudbrick materials as the rest of Dura's structures. Other Roman military buildings took over and adapted existing structures.

The Roman military presence at Dura is testified intensively in the archaeology starting in the late second and early third century. For instance, the headquarters building, or *principia*, in block E7 (mistakenly called the *Praetorium* in the original reports) was built in 211–212 CE.[176] This building was typical of *principia* found elsewhere, with a cross-hall, an *aedes* (chapel for standards) with sockets in the floor to support the standards, a forecourt and forehall, and two tribunals. The date of the building comes from the Latin inscription which was found in the building's central doorway, dedicating the building to the emperor Caracalla.[177]

It is perhaps around the same time that the north side of the city was transformed into a Roman military garrison; a mudbrick curtain wall partially closed it off from the rest of the city, starting against the western city wall and cutting through several blocks, including a house in K5 which has been partially excavated.[178] The Roman military was not, however, shut off from the rest of the city; nor were the civic population completely stopped from entering the base. For example, as noted

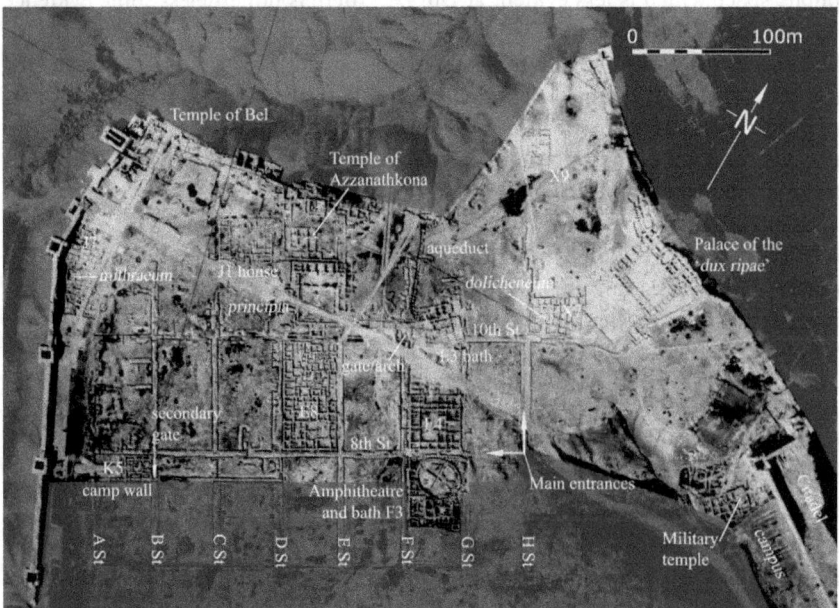

Figure 5.16 Aerial photograph of north end of the site, annotated with building names including the main features of the Roman garrison. Image courtesy Simon James.

already, it appears that access was provided to the temple of Azzanathkona even after part of the building was taken over for use by the twentieth Palmyrene cohort.[179] The *principia* seems to have been further west in block E7 than the original block had been so as to preserve access to an earlier shrine in the southwest corner of the block; both this shrine and the temple of Azzanathkona had impressive axial approaches from the east.[180] The temple of Bel also seems to have continued to allowed civilian access. Admission to the military base was controlled, however, and the perimeter wall which cuts through K5 worked with other measures, such as a gate in B street, and an arched gate which spanned F street.[181]

From the documents, we know a considerable population of legionaries and auxiliaries were present at Dura in the third century, and the buildings in which they were accommodated are another of the building types that appear. Adjacent to the *principia* was, in block J1, a large courtyard house that is likely to have been that of the commander, known in the publications as the 'House of the Prefect'. While there is no evidence other than its form and position to testify to its inhabitants, its partial *peristyle* courtyard is unlike most Durene housing, its plan being more like a Mediterranean town house and appropriate for a Roman military officer or visiting official, and it shares features with officers' housing in other excavated military bases.[182] Block E4 contained a large courtyard house, which had already existed in area when the Roman military took over, which was adapted for military use, perhaps initially as a commander's house, with paintings and a heated room; eventually these features went out of use, and the house was equipped with extensive cooking installations and other features, such as storage of a large number of huge ceramic vessels, which may indicate its use in supporting a larger number of military personnel.[183]

Block E8, which had been made up of typical Durene houses before the military occupation, was modified for use as barracks. This involved dividing up spaces such as courtyards into smaller units, the narrowing of doorways, use of partition walls, additional cooking installations and hearths, decorations (including 'classicizing' paintings), and provision for animals.[184] Evidence of military occupation also came from the objects excavated within the block, including a number of coin hoards, some perhaps representing military pay, as well as a range of military equipment, and clusters of objects which may represent the presence of soldiers' kitbags. Other houses similarly adapted for military use include those found in blocks K5, J7, and X7, although these were less well preserved (in the case of J7 and X7) or poorly recorded (in the case of K5). Nonetheless they can be seen to share many of the same features with (e.g.) E8. Elsewhere on the site, not within the garrison area on the north side, houses were occupied by Roman soldiers but not architecturally modified. For instance, in block C7 the presence of the soldiers is best attested by graffiti that they made, including one in Latin and a pictorial graffito depicting gladiators.[185] The differential modification of houses throughout the city seems to have been chronological, and in some areas (e.g. C7), it is likely the Roman military occupied the houses in the final years of the city, after the civilian population had left. In the agora, houses can be seen to have been occupied by Roman military personnel from the objects found within them, although architectural changes to the houses themselves are relatively ephemeral.[186]

In addition to the basic needs met by accommodation, the provision of administration in the *principia*, and by buildings such as granaries which have not been excavated but which are attested in documentary sources at the site were buildings for the leisure of the soldiers.[187] These included bath buildings and an amphitheatre. Dura's amphitheatre is the easternmost example of a purpose-built Roman amphitheatre that has been excavated.[188] It had an arena measuring thirty-two by twenty-six metres and was a relatively small example of its type; the excavators estimated it could have held about one thousand spectators.[189] The mudbrick superstructure was not well preserved or excavated, but its identification is secure from the building's Latin dedicatory inscription, which also gives its construction date as 216 CE and records its builders as the *vexillarii* of the fourth Scythian and third Cyrenaean legions.[190]

The amphitheatre had been built on remains of an earlier Roman bath in F3, but additional baths were built both inside the military base, in block E3, and outside it, in blocks M7 and C3.[191] Like the amphitheatre, bathhouses were apparently new to Dura in the Roman era; the F3 bath, which was originally thought to have been built in the Arsacid era, has been re-dated as Roman (although, possibly, as early as the Trajanic occupation).[192] The bath buildings share a number of features, including some not otherwise used at Dura such as the extensive use of fired bricks, mosaics, apsidal rooms, concrete vaults, as well as *tubuli* (hollow ceramic tubes for channelling heated air) and other specialized fittings for water and heating like hypocausts (raised floors beneath which heated air could circulate). Each of the baths had water reservoirs for supply, drainage to the street, furnaces for heating, and a series of rectangular rooms and rooms with apses equipped with provisions for bathing, including pools. The rooms were paved with mosaic, fired brick, or hydraulic cement. The fittings including the *tubuli* and *pilae* (the pillars on which raised hypocaust floors stood, made of stacks of round or square fired bricks) were of standardized sizes in all the baths.[193]

While the C3 bath might have fallen within the garrison area together with the region in front of the citadel, the M7 bath adjacent to the main city gate was outside it. It is arguable, then, whether the baths were for exclusively military use. While they were apparently of military construction, it is likely that they were used both by the military and parts of the civilian population.[194] The surviving remains of Dura's water management system all seem to relate to the baths, which each had water reservoirs. The supply seems to have been via pipes in the streets (remains were found in the main street, and in streets A and D, and along the north side of the E3 baths), and while the entire length of these was not excavated and the precise relationships between them is unclear, a series of rubble piers which run from the E3 baths to the north edge of the city probably held an aqueduct, fed by some means (a water screw or other lifting machine) from the river below.[195]

The Roman palace long known as the 'Palace of the *Dux Ripae*' in blocks X3/X5 was the other major Roman structure that has been excavated. This identification is not tenable, however, and the evidence for the office of *dux ripae*, 'commander of the river bank', constructed as it was on a single *dipinto*, is slim (See p.31–32). However, this was nonetheless an important new Roman structure, on an orientation which eschewed the city's established grid. On its eastern-most side, the building was not preserved due to the erosion of the cliff, but most of its plan was preserved, and the palace was based around two large peristyle courtyards. These were the largest courtyards at Dura, and while columns were used extensively in earlier Durene architecture, these true peristyles with columns around all sides of the courtyard are apparently exclusive to Roman buildings, including this palace and the commander's house in J1. Apsidal rooms, too, such as those on the eastern side of this building, occur elsewhere on the site only in Roman-era bath structures. The Roman palace was an elaborate one, particularly by Durene standards, including a furnace and hypocaust, bath structures including a piped water supply, and painted plaster on walls and ceilings.[196] The building likely served both residential and administrative functions for a high-ranking official, something also implied from the character of the objects found in and around the building. Texts from the building also allude to the activities carried out within it, such as those of entertainment: a series of Greek *dipinti* record entertainers, including a tragic actor.[197] Graffiti attest to a range of other activities within the structure, from administrative household accounts in Greek found in what seem to be service rooms to a Latin graffito, found in the room off the south of the first peristyle courtyard, which quotes the opening lines of Vergil's *Aeneid* (See p.76) [198]

The large number of changes to the city, in particular its north side, under Roman rule in the third century are indicative of the sweeping changes to life at Dura which must have occurred at this time. The garrison saw a huge military presence within the city walls: not only members of the Roman military but also a large extended military community which marked a radical change in the urban form and the population of the site.

From this overview of Dura's built environment, a number of things are clear. First, as with the textual evidence, little survives that is securely dated to the Seleucid era, with many of the extant buildings, including most of the temples, being constructed in the Arsacid era. This religious landscape gives a picture of religious diversity, but a diversity which nonetheless uses a local vernacular form and many of the sanctuaries share elements of their architectural form or decoration. These courtyard temples draw on Mesopotamian types, but also have Greek, Syrian, and other influences, which together have formed a hybrid local tradition. Among the shared elements of the temples were 'chapels', in which defined groups within the religious community of that temple came together for religious purposes which seem to have included commensality and sacrifice.

The temples share their method of construction with the houses, which also have in common their main elements of an offset entrance, a courtyard, and a reception room throughout the site, although they varied greatly in size and elaboration. The houses also share a concern for privacy, carefully protecting sight-lines into the house from the street outside, and were shaped by patriarchy and kinship: both by the shape of the household that occupied them and the transmission of property over generations. Over time, houses filled most of the space within the city walls, but the road system, probably of the late second century BCE, was maintained over time, as were some buildings with civic functions, including the archives building in block G3 and the palace on the redoubt.

Major change in the late second and early third century came when a Roman military garrison was built inside the city walls, adapting some structures and building some new ones, completely altering the circulation of the city and presumably displacing a significant proportion of the pre-existing population. The headquarters building inside the garrison and the new Roman palace re-oriented the topography of power within the city. Nonetheless, civic life continued, for some years at least with the *boule* meeting in the temple of Artemis and documents being lodged in the city archive. Within the walls of all these buildings, life at Dura was lived out by its people. The things that enabled their lives – the artefacts recovered at the site, from simple jugs for water to the images of their gods – are the topic of the next chapter.

Chapter 6

THE MATERIAL CULTURE AND ART OF DURA-EUROPOS

The objects which survive from Dura-Europos have been used to tell many stories: for example its paintings were used by Rostovtzeff to invent 'Parthian Art', and its coins by Bellinger to construct a historical narrative for the site. However, the extant material has been deeply shaped by excavation and recording methodologies and by the context of its interpretation. For instance, the most common artefact found in the Near East is pottery, and while much pottery was indeed collected at Dura, even more was discarded: decided in the field to be irrelevant, unimportant, or uninteresting, most of Dura's pottery ended up in the spoil heaps. Similarly, another ubiquitous find is animal bone. At the time of the initial excavations, however, the value of faunal remains to examine such things as dietary practices was not recognized, so it was not collected. The study of Dura's art and objects is then deeply entwined with the history of the excavation, from the moment of excavation to their cataloguing and interpretation.

This chapter will examine the objects of Dura: first, those most ubiquitous finds, the ceramics and the coins. It will then discuss the numerous other categories of evidence which were found in great numbers at Dura, including textiles, jewellery, lamps, metal objects, and glass.[1] The next part of the chapter will examine what has been historically categorized as 'art': the paintings and sculpture of the site, which come almost entirely from religious contexts. There are many other ways the material culture of Dura could be approached, for instance contextually, looking at those objects which occur together in houses, or in military contexts, or in temples. Similarly, it could be argued that studying the 'art' is an artificial or modern category. Approaching the objects of Dura in this way is then not without its caveats, but it does serve to give an overview of artefacts that were excavated: what is extant, why it is so, and how it has been used to explain religion, society, and culture at the site.

As the earlier chapters have shown, little remains from the earliest periods of Dura's existence as a colony, its Seleucid foundation. Just as there are no Greek inscriptions earlier than the Arsacid era, very slight material culture dating to this time has been found. Nonetheless, there has been a strong focus, both in the Yale excavations and those of the Franco-Syrian expedition, on what little Hellenistic ceramic material has been found. This is for a number of reasons, particularly the strong scholarly interest in the Greeks in the East.[2] It is also the case that the recognizability of the imported Greek ceramics in existing corpora was an important factor: broadly speaking, archaeologists trained on Greek pottery and Greek sites were most likely to recognize and be able to categorize Greek materials and more likely to think they were important. Generally, this has been at the expense of ceramics that were produced locally or regionally and gives a somewhat skewed picture of the ceramic record at the site.

The collection and recording of ceramics at Dura suffered from the different priorities of field directors. The earliest director, Pillet, even paid the workmen for particular finds in a way which very much distorts those early records (See p.10). There was also, throughout the excavation, a general disregard for broken pots, which are the sherds that make up the bulk of the ceramic assemblage at any archaeological site. Instead, collection was limited to complete and near-complete pots, or sherds that were noteworthy, usually because they were decorated, inscribed, or a recognizable import.[3] This problem was compounded in the reporting of the ceramics in the publications, which tended to over-emphasize imported vessels.[4] As a result, caution needs to be taken when interpreting the ceramics of the site: most of the ceramic assemblage excavated by the Yale team remains in their backdirt, and those kept and published were a very selective sample.

The Hellenistic ceramics, including imports such as Megarian bowls, Attic and eastern black-glazed wares, and West Slope ware, together give a similar ceramic profile to that found at other Hellenistic sites in Mesopotamia.[5] While imported ceramics would be expected in a newly founded colony, the collection bias was very strongly oriented towards the imported material (which was well known from existing sites and well dated), whereas contemporary locally produced material was unlikely to have been recognized or collected. Work by the Franco-Syrian expedition on the Hellenistic pottery has indeed shown that there were locally produced common and semi-fine wares, and the discovery of wasters (pottery which went wrong when it was being fired in a kiln and was thus not usable) indicate that there was ceramic production at the site itself.[6] The presence of imports and 'imitation' Hellenistic wares indicates a desire on the part of the colony's earliest occupants to replicate ceramics – and perhaps the associated eating and drinking practices – known from elsewhere in the Hellenistic world. The Hellenistic ceramics are also indicative of connections to a wider Hellenistic world, if not necessarily direct ones.

Just as the Hellenistic ceramics are over-emphasized in the published catalogues, common pottery (called 'commonwares') is vastly under-represented. It was not generally collected, with only complete examples kept, even though it was estimated to have formed 95 per cent of the total pottery at the site.[7] The commonware was cream or yellowish in colour, slipped, and was used to make a number of vessel forms, including pottery for storage and serving. The commonware at Dura is usually dated to the third century CE, but it comes from a number of earlier contexts, so its true chronological range is probably from at least the Arsacid era at Dura: here, the lack of recorded stratigraphy (i.e. our ability to date the pottery from the contexts in which it comes or to put it in relative sequence) is a major problem. Kilns excavated, as well as misfired objects, show that there was at least some commonware production at the site.[8]

The green-glazed ceramics, the main fine ware of Dura, have long held the (implicitly ethnic) label 'Parthian green glazed' because a very similar ware had also been found at Arsacid Nippur and at sites like Seleucia on the Tigris (Figure 6.1).[9] It, too, had at least some local production at Dura itself.[10] From the contexts in which it was found (contexts which can be dated because they were sealed beneath structures dated by inscriptions), it was in use at Dura from at least the first century CE, if not earlier, up until the fall of the city. In addition to the commonware and green-glazed ceramics, the other most frequent type of ceramic found at Dura was the brittle ware. This was a thin-walled, brick-red ware used for cooking (cooking pots, 'casseroles', and jugs are all found in this ware). This seems to have been an import from elsewhere in Syria, and unlike the green-glazed ceramics it is typical of eastern Mediterranean ceramics.[11] A small amount of imported Roman ceramics was found in third-century contexts, including African red slip.[12]

Overall, the most frequently used ceramics were locally made commonwares, but cooking pots were sometimes being imported from Syria and fine green-glazed tablewares from Mesopotamia, testifying to links both East and West in the Arsacid and Roman eras. There is no distinctive ceramic associated with the Roman military presence at Dura, and it is likely that they, too, used the locally available pots, although they perhaps used them in different ways. One of the issues with the study of the ceramics is the way that different wares – in this case, the 'Greek and Roman pottery', on the one hand, and the commonware, brittleware, and green glazed on the other, are treated differently and separately.[13] This obscures relative proportions of different types of pottery and the relative importance of the different ceramics at the site over time. Because of the problems with the collection and recording of the ceramics, we do not have a clear picture of the relative proportions of the different types of ceramics at Dura over time, or even within certain buildings. The lack of stratigraphic information and the lack of quantitative evidence make it difficult to give a clear picture of how Dura's ceramic profile changed over time. Generally, though, the green-glazed ware is indicative of deep roots in Hellenistic Mesopotamia; the forms, such as table amphorae, indicate it was used for activities such as reception and commensality. The longevity of its use, throughout most of the history of the site, perhaps shows that 'being Greek' at Dura was in part imagined by way of a Mesopotamian heritage. The brittle ware indicates that there were also strong ties to Syria. The locally produced commonware was overwhelmingly used for most activities in Dura; for cooking and serving and for storage, and it establishes something of the scale of local pottery industry and a degree of local need, self-sufficiency, and range.

Coins were the most frequently recorded object in the field object registers made on site during the Yale expedition. The find-spot of each of these was at the time carefully recorded, with a field number for each coin listed next to a particular context. This information could have been used to provide for example dating information for buildings and associated archaeological deposits. Unfortunately,

Figure 6.1 Green-glazed 'Parthian' table amphorae. These examples were classified as 'vases with three handles' in Dura F. R. 4.1.1: 32-33, nos. II-B-2 and II-B-3. The left vessel, 1935.506, was excavated in the wall street next to block L7, the right, 1935.1285, tower 16. YUAG Yale-1262.

the object numbers which tied each coin to a particular archaeological context became disassociated from the coins themselves at some point after they were moved to Yale, so it is no longer possible to contextualize them. The coins were under the purview of the numismatist Alfred Bellinger; as a numismatist of the mid-twentieth century, he was interested in the coins for their own sake, rather than as archaeological objects.[14] Bellinger noted that 'early and late coins are found in all quarters of the city': his spatial concept of the city was horizontal but not vertical, and he seems not to have realized that examining coins from different depths might have also yielded useful information.[15] Nor were the coins thought of as relating to the places in which they were found, and the published report of the coins recorded the find-spot only for the hoards.[16] While he disregarded the find-spots of coins, Bellinger had a tendency to over-interpret single coin finds: his dates for the foundation of the city, the Arsacid capture of the city, and its fall to the Sasanians all rested on individual coins, pushing the evidence to its extremes, and as a result, many of the central dates for the periodization of the site have since been revised (See chapter 2).[17] Despite these problems, the more than 14,000 coins counted by Bellinger are a useful data set, and they are all from the secure archaeological context at Dura, and not, like so many Roman coins in contemporary collections, of dubious provenance, having been circulated on the antiquities market.[18]

Starting with the Seleucid period, Dura's coins came largely from Western mints, in particular Antioch, but also from Mesopotamian sites, including Seleucia on the Tigris, and these sources continue into the Arsacid period.[19] Arsacid coins themselves, bearing the image of Arsacid king of kings, were relatively rare at Dura. What the coins make clear is a high degree of connectivity (including presumably with regard to trade) Westward, particularly with the coast of the Levant. The coins, even during the time usually considered to be the Parthian era at Dura, are largely drawn from mints such as Antioch.[20] Arsacid-era documents specify debts to be settled in Tyrian silver, indicating that this was a trusted currency (Tyre, off the coast of the Levant, was under Roman control at that time).[21] Bellinger himself noted the continued use of Roman coinage uninterrupted after the Trajanic presence at the site and throughout the second century into the era of Roman control.[22] The numismatic signature of second-century CE Dura indicates strong ties with the Roman world, particularly the Levant, rather than with Parthia itself. It is not a simple story, however, and northern Syria supplied coins to Dura from the first century BCE until its destruction, as did sources in Mesopotamia and Pontus.[23] Regardless of the routes that coins took to eventually reach Dura (e.g. as soldiers' pay, via trade networks, or more directly), it is clear that Dura's regional networks extended in a variety of directions, regardless of whether it was under Arsacid or Roman control at any particular time. Syrian silver and bronze coins of Roman date are not usually found outside the Roman province of Syria and are thought to have been perceived as 'foreign' outside the province (i.e. elsewhere in the Roman world), but they were clearly not foreign to Arsacid Dura.[24] Whether that means the dates for the Arsacid control of Dura should be revised cannot be certainly ascertained from the extant evidence, but it does further complicate the periodization of the site and the overall complexity and indeed highlight the historical haziness of the situation on the Euphrates in the second century.

The coins of Dura come both from stray finds (usually, coins dropped or otherwise casually lost) and from hoards. The term 'hoard' was used at Dura for any group of coins found together; this ranged from a purse dropped in a street to a group of coins sealed in a jar beneath a house floor. Therefore, different hoards represent different activities. Of those which seem to have been deliberately deposited, perhaps due to crisis and the need to cache wealth, the coin hoards fall into roughly two groups: those whose latest coins date to *c.* 253 and those of *c.* 256. As noted in Chapter 2 (See p.35), this is one piece of evidence suggestive of a first Sasanian incursion in the early 250s, followed by the final siege in, probably, 256.[25] Some hoards are thought to have represented collections of soldiers' pay.[26] Others brought together coins from certain mints: for instance a hoard that included a number from Zeugma may be indicative of part of the military community which travelled from there.[27] The hoards of third-century Dura are much more mixed than those at other contemporary Syrian sites, combining both *tetradrachms* and Roman imperial *denarii*.[28]

In addition to coins and ceramics, which are common and found at all Parthian and Roman-era sites, the excavation of Dura also yielded objects which are more rarely preserved. Textiles are exceptional at most archaeological sites, because they require special circumstances (usually, very wet or very dry environments) for their preservation.[29] The rampart built against the city wall provided such dry conditions, and the textiles, while mostly fragmentary, were still so plentiful that the plain examples were left on site and did not become part of museum collections.[30] Because of the special conditions necessary for their preservation, most of the catalogued textiles come from secondary contexts (i.e. dumped within the rampart), rather than from within houses, sanctuaries, or other buildings. Despite the lack of primary contexts for this material, we do know something of Dura's production of textiles: evidence for animal husbandry, textile processing, and textile trading is all found at Dura, from dying installations found in the *agora* and graffiti recording transactions relating to their sale.[31] For many of the textiles found, their fragmentary nature means it is difficult to tell what sort of garment they had been part of, although a number of them were decorated.[32] In addition to locally produced woollen textiles, imports including silk were found. Shoes were also excavated, including those made of leather and of plant fibres. *Caligae*, men's shoes generally associated with the military, were recovered, as were hobnail boots, slippers, sandals, and children's shoes. Like the textiles, these were mostly recovered from the deep secondary contexts in the wall street.[33]

Related evidence is that of painted depictions of clothing, and while it is difficult to make direct connections between what was worn in life and what is shown in idealized depictions in wall paintings, it is clear that dress practices distinguished people of different status, age, and gender. For example, priests are routinely shown with conical white hats; male children, and servants, wear shorter tunics than adults or non-servile men. Women wore head coverings, and elite women are depicted in elaborate jewellery including earrings, with multiple bracelets and necklaces and flat-topped headdresses. The embroidery and jewellery on the headdresses of elite women depicted in paintings (such as Baribonnaea and Bithnanaia on Figures 2.5 and 6.4) probably relates to their marital status, differentiating them from the more plainly dressed unmarried girls.[34] The use of clothing and jewellery as part of how gender was constructed in appearance is also apparent in the objects found in the tombs: *spatulae*, for scooping and applying makeup, and mirrors were found, as were necklaces, bracelets, earrings, bells, rings, and hairpins. These items of adornment were found within the city and associated with women's burials in the necropolis.[35]

Roman soldiers, too, wore distinctive items, including arms and armour, and dress items excavated ranged from humble belt buckles to impressive painted wooden shields.[36] Much of this equipment was very similar to that seen in Europe and elsewhere in the empire, testifying to a degree of standardization in Roman military equipment, reflective of a cohesiveness in the presentation of soldierly identities.[37] The personal appearance of the Roman military at Dura, in both visual evidence such as that of Terentius and his men (see Figure 2.7) and the material culture, testifying to their presence throughout the site (e.g. copper alloy scales of armour, found in military buildings and many other contexts), would have been distinctive from local dress. Other objects, such as copper alloy brooches, may have been used by the Roman military but are not definitively military objects.[38] Some objects are even more ambiguous. For example in block E8, a block converted for use by soldiers, patterning suggests the objects there were part of soldiers' kit bags: these included knives, needles, spoons, tacks, bone pins, and lamps, as well as knucklebones.[39] Only their context indicates these assemblages as military in nature.

Glass objects were excavated at Dura, among which was some very fine but fragmented decorated glassware from the houses, such as imported painted and gilded vessels.[40] Most of the glassware that was collected, however, were the more complete examples from the necropolis and the fill of the wall street.[41] Amongst the Dura material were 'cut glass' tableware, glass bowls, and cups with incised decoration.[42] Glass waste evidence found at Dura indicates some local production, and it has even been suggested that Dura was a regional centre of glass production.[43] Glass objects also included window glass and glass bracelets.[44]

In addition to the ceramic vessels discussed already, other objects were made of clay, including most of the recorded lamps (Figure 6.2).[45] These ceramic lamps would have burned olive oil to provide light. As with the vessels, there was particular attention paid to the early imports by the excavators, to the detriment of more common and local forms.[46] The early (Attic) imports make up a very small proportion of the lamps, with only a handful of examples recorded. These chime with the most recent interpretation of Dura's earliest phases, as one such lamp with a recorded find-spot was from the citadel which seems to have been the focus of the Seleucid settlement. The other Hellenistic lamps also all cluster in this part of the site.[47] By the time of the latest Hellenistic lamp types, they are found all over the site and in the necropolis.[48] Overwhelmingly, the lamps in use at Dura were locally produced; more than half the excavated examples were of a type the excavators believed to be local, and indeed lamp moulds were found on site.[49] These were mostly round lamps with a low profile and nozzle, the earlier examples (probably of the first and second centuries CE) having decoration much like the Hellenistic types; these locally produced mould-made lamps were in use up until the fall of the city.

After the local groups of lamps, the next biggest groups (around fifty of each type were found) were Mesopotamian types and Roman *discus* lamps thought to have been of Syrian manufacture.[50] The provincial manufacture of such typically Roman types has since been recognized as the normal practice.[51] The Roman *discus* lamps are all presumed stylistically to date to the third century and include those whose nozzles are decorated with volutes, sometimes linked to Italian manufacture. The 'picture lamp' types were found throughout the site, decorated with designs including erotic and mythological scenes of the kind that are found throughout the Roman empire. The 'Mesopotamian' lamps, some of which were glazed like the green-glazed ceramic vessels, were wheel-made and had a deep bowl with a broad opening, and no *discus*. These were named for their similarity to examples at Assur, Seleucia, and other Mesopotamian sites, but like the green-glazed vessels, they could have been locally produced at Dura.

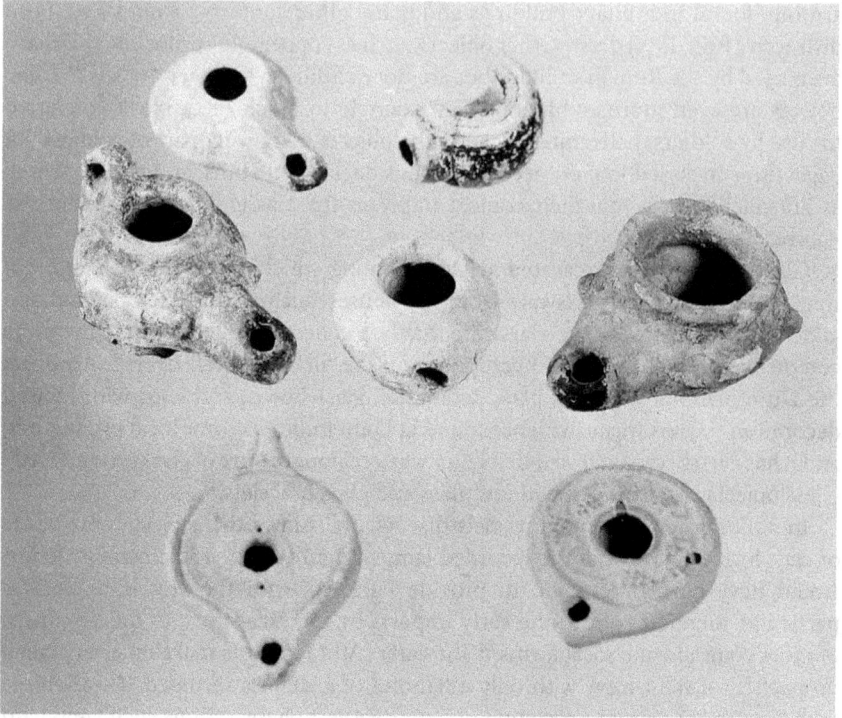

Figure 6.2 Photograph of a selection of different types of ceramic lamps found at Dura. YUAG y261.

Distinctive groups of objects were also found in the necropolis of Dura. While some of the objects, such as ceramics and jewellery, occur within the town walls as well, others occur almost entirely in the context of graves.[52] These included gold leaves arranged as funerary crowns, thin sheets of gold cut with slits which were placed over the eyes and mouths of some of those buried, and miniature vessels (in ceramic, metal, and glass) as well as alabaster vessels.[53]

In addition to these traditional categories of ceramics, coins, and small finds, the texts discussed in Chapter 4 should also be considered material objects: from the inscribed reliefs and altars to the parchments and papyri, these were not just texts but objects. For example the 'double' documents typical of the Arsacid era, parchments with one text open to be read and another copy sealed so that the text could be verified, made the document 'tamper-proof': this implies that these were active texts, meant to be used and consulted.[54] The *feriale*, written on papyrus rather than parchment, also seems to have been an active document and was so well used that it needed repairs in antiquity.[55] Other documents bore sealings, closed with the ring of particular individuals, and a number of cut-stone *intaglios* used to make such sealings, some of them still in their ring settings, were also found at the site.[56]

A range of other types of objects were also excavated at Dura, many of which have still not been thoroughly studied or published. For example many bone objects were found at Dura, but no report was published on these.[57] The bone objects included hairpins and small utensils, small bone vessels, jointed dolls (or figurines), dice, as well as counters. Stone was used for a variety of objects as well. In addition to the sculpture, it was used for objects including grinders and also for portable altars. There were in fact many small altars from Dura, found throughout the site, in houses, streets, gates, and religious buildings, made in stone but also metal and ceramic (including green-glazed examples).[58]

Objects such as the altars not only reveal something about which gods were worshipped and the person who dedicated the altar, in their inscriptions but were also objects which enabled religious practice to occur. As can be seen in the paintings, in which smoke rises from such altars, they were part of a broader religious experience which was also a sensory one, involving the smell of incense and smoke. For religious rituals to occur, both particular places and objects were necessary. Within sanctuaries, in addition to the sculptures and altars, a variety of small objects were recovered, including not only ceramics and coins but knives (perhaps for use in sacrifice), gold leaves (for adorning statues, or votive objects), and terracotta animals (perhaps also votive objects).[59]

The objects of Dura are evidence of the complex web of interconnections within which Dura was placed. While it was not a major trade centre, it nonetheless was a participant in regional and long-distance trade. The small objects of Dura show that it did not look definitively to the East or West but had a complex heritage; there are imports from the Mediterranean and from Mesopotamia, but also much hybrid material which was locally produced. Of course, people and ideas moved to and from Dura as well, as can be seen not only in the massive presence of the Roman army in the third century but in the introduction of apparently new cults, including that of Mithras, Judaism, and Christianity, at the site during the same period. The distinctive locally produced material culture includes much of the sculpture of Dura, as well as the paintings which were found within houses and many of its religious buildings.

The Paintings and Sculpture of Dura

The distinction of 'art' as a category separate from other types of material culture or from architecture is a result of modern disciplinary boundaries. The value afforded to ancient art can be seen even from the first discovery of paintings at Dura, stirring interest as they did, and from this first discovery, the art of Dura was recognized as different or Other. This was accounted for by Breasted in his initial publication of the paintings from the temple of Bel as the 'Oriental Forerunners' (See p.5). Over the course of the excavations, many more paintings – most more fragmentary than those first paintings from the temple of Bel – would be discovered. So too would many sculptures, and together, these were the central evidence for the art of Dura.

This visual culture of Dura has long been taken as one of the site's distinctive features and has made Dura a type site for what has long been known as 'Parthian art', as defined by Rostovtzeff.[60] This art consisted of a number of distinctive stylistic features. Visually, it was characterized by frontality: figures face the viewer directly, not in profile, and look out from the scene rather than at the action within it.[61] This frontal depiction of figures has been generally considered the key trait of 'Parthian' art. Other features of Dura's art, for Rostovtzeff, were its two-dimensionality, detail which was linear rather than modelled, and the composition of scenes in rows, with the heads of figures all at the same level (*isocephaly*). Notable too was the attention paid to the depiction of details such as jewellery and weaponry.

Rostovtzeff was well aware that the visual culture of Dura, and particularly its link to Arsacid control of the site, was a problem; hence he wrote his classic article, 'Dura and the Problem of Parthian Art'.[62] The label 'Parthian' itself was that of Roman authors for the Arsacid empire, and Rostovtzeff did not mean to imply that what he labelled Parthian art at Dura was Iranian in character: rather, it was the art that emerged at Dura under Parthian rule.[63] While a label of 'Parthian' has been applied to material culture (such as the green-glazed pottery, discussed above) and to visual culture, these things are neither definitively associated with the Arsacid regime nor with a particular ethnic group.[64]

Since Rostovtzeff's characterization of 'Parthian' art, the variability of art under the Parthian empire has been further recognized, partly in light of new discoveries. Dura is distinctive from sites such as Old Nisa, which had a different relationship with the Arsacid dynasty, and it is evident that Dura is actually not representative of art under the Arsacids or 'Parthian art' generally but rather one iteration of that.[65] It has now been convincingly shown that 'Parthian art' is a misnomer at Dura.[66] A distinctive visual and material culture associated with Dura is known while the site is under Arsacid control; in that sense, it is chronologically 'Parthian' and a product of the local environment and influence of a range of interactions. Nonetheless, the characterization of 'Parthian' art at Dura has been problematic for several reasons, including that it has had the result of combining a chronologically diverse body of material, from the first to third centuries CE and because of the way that it was used to attribute meaning to the material.

For example in the 1970s Anne Perkins, the then Dura curator at Yale, wrote of Durene art in terms of its deficiencies. Among these were a 'lack of interest in the human body'. Those bodies were 'badly proportioned', and 'perspective, foreshortening, and indication of three-dimensional space are almost totally absent'.[67] While these things are true in one sense, they were applied not only as descriptors but as value judgements. Overall, Perkins' assessment of the art at Dura was that it lacked concern with realism or lacked the ability to produce it.[68] This did not consider Durene art on its own terms but rather in implicit comparison to naturalistic Classical Greek art as a baseline for what can be considered 'good'. This Classical aesthetic underlines her criticism of what she thought was 'little care for visually pleasing relationships'.[69] Perkins noted that fundamental to the art of Dura were 'Costumes, coiffures, attributes, and poses ... drawn from the repertoires of

Greece, Rome, Iran, and Western Asia ... the amalgam of these varied elements ... is the major identifying feature of the style'.[70] Like Perkins' attempt to detangle some of the elements depicted in the art of Dura and their pedigrees, much of the debate concerning Parthian art since Rostovtzeff has centred on the issue of its origins – whether these were Greek, a Hellenistic inheritance, Mesopotamian, or Arab.[71]

Another theme in the study of Durene art, as noted already, concerned frontality. Frontality has been argued to provoke a sense of immediacy between the figures depicted (be they people or deities) and the viewer.[72] In turn, this perceived direct eye contact has been taken to indicate a more personal and spiritual experience of religion in this period and a turn away from the use of cult images, although these interpretations have been questioned.[73] In addition to frontality, Rostovtzeff noted a 'lack of interest in the body' and a 'love of the linear and the spiritual' in Durene art; he saw frontality and spirituality as particularly characteristic.[74]

Durene art has also been characterized as simply bad: poorly executed and lacking in aesthetic virtue. Welles, in his editor's introduction to the first final report on sculpture, wrote of Dura's sculpture that 'little of this is of a high esthetic [sic] or technical quality', and even the author of the sculpture volumes, Susan Downey, herself wrote of Durene sculpture that much of it was 'merely a bad imitation of Greco-Roman types'.[75] 'Bad' means not adhering to Classical tenets of naturalistic depiction (marked by the aforementioned issues of perspective, frontality, and static depictions), and overall in Dura's painting and sculpture, this was 'marked by a lack of concern for the creation of visual reality'.[76] This is a discourse which values a Western over Eastern tradition in art, which has arisen within an Orientalist framework.[77] The survey of Dura's paintings and sculpture that follows attempts to leave aside such judgements and assess what the paintings and sculpture can contribute to our knowledge of Dura when considered in their physical and social contexts (e.g. within religious buildings, or houses), and in chronological perspective.

Paintings

The wall paintings at Dura were found in bath buildings and in some houses, as well as in the Roman palace. By far the largest number of Dura's extant paintings were, however, found in religious buildings, and indeed most of Dura's religious buildings produced at least some fragmentary paintings, typically in the *naos*: paintings were the norm within the innermost parts of Durene sanctuaries (See p.99–102). Only from a few temples, however, did full scenes, or substantial portions of them, survive. The recovery of paintings clustered in the religious buildings along the west side of the site where the deep embankment protected the western walls of a number of structures, including the synagogue, Mithraeum, the temple of Bel, and the Christian building (paintings in houses in blocks M8 and L7 were also preserved because of the same embankment). More fragmentary paintings were found in the temple of Zeus Theos and a number of other religious buildings. Most of the paintings also cluster chronologically, dating to the last decades of the city's existence, in the first half of the third century CE.[78]

In addition to the scholarly problems noted above, the paintings from all of these buildings have had their study hampered by a number of factors. Some paintings were lost almost as soon as they were found, disintegrating when uncovered or when left exposed to weather.[79] Other paintings suffered as a result of early attempts at conservation and removal. As a result, some are now known only from sketches, tracings, or photographs. For these, and indeed even for others which did survive, including the synagogue paintings, there has been a problem of the lack of publication of good quality colour reproductions. Indeed, many of the frequently reproduced images of paintings from Dura are not images of the paintings at all, but painted facsimiles made of them after the excavation. Amongst the most important of these were painted reproductions made by Herbert Gute, including copies he made of the synagogue paintings (Figure 3.9), and while they are useful (particularly in the absence of detailed photographs of the paintings themselves), they present their own problems.[80] Recent conservation work at Yale is making accessible the paintings held there, while the Conon painting, held in Damascus, has recently been conserved and published by Leriche.[81]

In the temple of Bel were found some of the oldest preserved paintings at Dura. The temple as a whole was laden with paintings and graffiti, although its paintings are now usually considered as panels in isolation rather than as part of a painted programme which evolved over centuries.[82] Two of the best preserved scenes depict sacrifices (those of Conon and much later painting of Terentius, as discussed already, Figures 2.5 and 2.7). In addition to those well-known paintings, another from the *pronaos* depicts men named Lysias, Apollophanes, and Zenodotus making sacrifices (Figure 6.3); another sacrificial scene depicts two men, one named Otes, offering incense at an altar to five deities, being assisted by a servant.[83] A mythological scene found in the temple perhaps depicts Dionysus and Ariadne.[84]

Painted scenes were also preserved in the temple of Zeus Theos.[85] In its *naos* were paintings of worshippers, painted in registers on the side walls, including named individuals. The central rear wall was very fragmentary but is thought to have shown a depiction of the god himself, standing on a physical statue base which protruded into the room (Figure 5.9). Of the god, however, only part of his foot survived, together with fragments of four horses and two figures of Nike, and the painting was heavily restored.[86] On the walls to either side of the main painting were apparently three registers, which were also found in a very fragmentary state, but the fragments still attached to the walls indicated that the registers were separated by plaster moulding. The paintings consisted of depictions of life-sized figures, with their names scratched and painted next to their heads; the families included those of Lysias and Bargates. The people depicted were individual men, women, and priests, standing frontally.[87] As with the painting of Conon and his family, the youngest members seem to have been at the bottom of the painting, and older members above in visual hierarchy by age.[88] Among these one of the better

Figure 6.3 Image of a painting from the south wall of the *pronaos* of the temple of Bel, depicting Lysias, Apollophanes and Zenodotus; by the time of the Yale expedition only the feet of the figures and a few other fragments remained: these were removed to Damascus. YUAG Y339.

preserved fragments is one depicting a woman named Baribonnaea, who wears a headdress and a range of detailed jewellery, including a number of necklaces, and whose well-preserved face with staring eyes demonstrates that some paintings at Dura should perhaps be considered true portraiture (Figure 6.4).[89] Painted fragments also showed altars from Zeus Theos, in a further parallel to the Conon painting: these paintings seem also to have depicted members of a particular family performing a sacrifice.[90] The paintings of the temples of Zeus Theos and Bel also show that the rules of isocephalism and frontality are not systematic at Dura: in Zeus Theos, victories are shown in profile, and differently sized figures were found on the rear wall of the *naos* in Bel.[91] But even more than the lack of conformity to the supposed 'rules' of Durene style, these earlier paintings of Dura, probably dating to the Arsacid era, are detailed and skilled in their execution: they look like

Figure 6.4 Photograph of painted fragments of a woman and painted inscription identifying her as Baribonnaea, from the temple of Zeus Theos. YUAG g807a.

actual portraits (of course, what this means is itself complicated, but the paintings are detailed and individual, not schematic and conventional) and were made with skilled brushwork. Faces in particular were carefully rendered, but bodies less so, being used instead as a backdrop for ornamentation, including jewellery which was depicted in detail.[92]

Beyond issues of style in Durene art, the paintings of Baribonnaea and her kin from the temple of Zeus Theos, as with those of Conon and his family from the temple of Bel, indicate importance of the family line in religious practice at Dura.

In both cases, the paintings depict and label individuals of particular families.[93] It is likely that the families funded the religious buildings as well, although in Zeus Theos, the preserved named individuals of the paintings are not the same as the preserved named individuals in inscriptions from that building recording the dedication of parts of the structure.[94] The religious inscriptions, too, showed that the formula of the dedication frequently involves a vow for of the salvation, or safety, of the dedicant and their family.[95] While the paintings and the inscriptions were votive, in as much as they were offerings to the gods to fulfil a vow, they also demonstrate the importance of households and lineages in religious life. Dirven has gone so far as to characterize the cults within the temples of Bel and Zeus Theos as 'family religion'.[96] The diversity within the temples (e.g. the range of individuals depicted in paintings in Bel, and who make dedications of various kinds within it) indicates they were not exclusively for use by particular families, but they may well have used parts of them (e.g. particular chapels; later, perhaps even the secondary *naos* of the temple of Zeus Megistos was restricted for use by the Lysiads). Religious buildings were an appropriate venue to showcase kin ties and patriarchal authority, linking this to the performance of sacrifice to the gods and the building and decoration of the structures themselves.[97]

The later paintings of Dura of the mid-third century CE, from the Christian building, Mithraeum, and synagogue, and the late paintings in the temple of Bel are more linear and flat in style than those of Bel and Zeus Theos. For example, the faces of people are less individual (although still distinct), and less attention is paid to details such a garments and jewellery as well.[98] This can also be seen not only from paintings in religious buildings but also from (perhaps) private contexts, for instance the so-called House of the banquet. From this house just inside the Palmyrene gate, M7-W, were found a number of painted scenes, including one depicting a banquet, whose reclining figures and servants are labelled in both Greek and Palmyrene.[99]

From the Mithraeum came a number of painted scenes, part of an extensive interior programme which included relief sculpture, inscriptions, and graffiti (Figure 6.5).[100] The preserved paintings belong to the final phase of the Mithraeum dated to 240 CE. Surrounding the main relief of Mithras were thirteen scenes depicting Mithras' life and cosmological events.[101] Under the vaulted niche were twelve signs of the zodiac, and a scene of the *tauroctony*, Mithras slaying the bull, on the outer part of the arched niche (this was a third *tauroctony*, as the two sculptured reliefs had the same subject). Paintings on the side walls were of a hunting scene, the significance of which is debated. Some elements of the Mithraeum, including the continued use of an earlier relief (dedicated by Zenobius 170/171 CE), are unusual for Mithraea as they include not only the dedicant but members of his family or military unit. In the context of the painted scenes of lineages from the temples of Bel and Zeus Theos, this relief, while being of the same bull-slaying type found in Mithraea throughout the empire, also has elements with a strong local resonance.[102] Mithraism was an exclusive practice: only members of the cult would have seen the decorations, but they nonetheless did not operate in a vacuum, instead being part of local traditions as well as a broader empire-wide practice of Mithraism.

Figure 6.5 Photograph of Mithraeum shrine *in situ* during excavation, before the paintings were removed and transferred to Yale. The horned altar is visible in the foreground, and at the very top of the image, the three white plaster globules are part of the brace used to keep the structure from collapsing. The relief in the centre of the image shows Mithras slaying the bull, as well as the dedicator and members of his family or military unit. Another *tauroctony* relief is immediately below it, and was retained from an earlier phase of the building. Further paintings above the niche and on the side walls are not visible in this photograph. YUAG G838a.

Less well preserved than the Mithraeum paintings were those of the Christian building.[103] Paintings were found only within the baptistery room of the building (See p.108). Despite the relatively poor preservation, the scenes were sufficiently preserved for a number of biblical scenes to be identified, although the paintings themselves predate a stable form of the text of the New Testament. These include what is perhaps the earliest depiction of Jesus' mother, Mary.[104] Other biblical scenes include David and Goliath, Adam and Eve, and Jesus' healing of the Paralytic and walking on water (Figure 6.6).

The most extensively preserved set of paintings from any building at Dura comes from its synagogue, although only about two-thirds of the main room's paintings were preserved. They are not only exceptional for Dura but are also unique amongst Jewish art (due to the prohibition of the second commandment against graven images), pictorially representing biblical narrative scenes, which run in registers around the main assembly hall of the structure. A previous phase of the synagogue in the earlier third century had painted wall and ceiling decorations

Figure 6.6 Photograph of paintings from North wall of baptistery in Christian building, after they had been removed from the building. The lower scene shows a procession of women approaching a white structure (the figure to the right of the building has been tentatively identified as Mary). Above is part of the scene of Jesus walking on water. YUAG z68.

in a relatively elaborate scheme for a Durene house, but a simple one compared to the scenes that would fill the main room of the synagogue in its later form.[105]

The main room of the synagogue that was preserved beneath the rampart along the city wall had been relatively recently painted, in the mid-240s, when it went out of use as the rampart filled in the building. In its final form before its destruction, a painted niche for the Torah sat in the centre of the main (west) wall, opposite the entrance to the room (Figure 6.7). The niche and the rest of the room was covered in an extensive painted programme. Benches surrounded the perimeter of the room, above which the lower parts of the walls were covered in a painted dado which imitated marble and inlayed stone, and were decorated with painted masks and animals. The dado was surmounted by painted narrative panels, some of which survive on all sides of the room. Each panel contains figural scenes, many of which are biblical in source, including some whose figures are labelled with Greek or Aramaic painted inscriptions, although not every scene is securely identified.[106] Panels include the depiction of the finding of Moses, Exodus, and the crossing of the Red Sea.[107]

The paintings within the synagogue have much in common with those elsewhere in third-century Dura, having a similar style of execution, with

Figure 6.7 Photograph of synagogue paintings as installed in Damascus Museum, showing the Torah shrine on the left. The paintings are the originals, but the architecture in which they were placed was a reconstruction, and the ceiling tiles, just seen at the top of the image, are reproductions. YUAG Dam-382.

people portrayed frontally and relatively schematically, groups of people being *isocephalic*, hierarchical proportions (with more important figures being larger than less important ones), and being relatively static and two-dimensional.[108] The individual people are distinguished not by their faces but by their clothing, which are local types of garments, including 'Greek' draped robes or 'Iranian' tailored (i.e. garments of cut and sewn, rather than draped, cloth) loose trousers and tunics as ways of differentiating people within particular scenes (including biblical figures), with important personages marked out with more elaborate cloaks or other garments.[109] Their poses and gestures are also conventionalized, and they indicate if a figure is (e.g.) singing or at prayer.[110]

The ceiling of the room, constructed with wooden beams and plaster, held painted fired clay tiles, of which 234 were excavated. Their painted decoration included animals, flowers, and astrological symbols like those that were found elsewhere in the city in private houses.[111] The combined use of a range of the motifs and symbols, including the evil eye, was a particular way of emphasizing the sacred space of the synagogue. As with the paintings on the walls, the ceiling tiles used local idioms of architectural decoration (itself drawing on multiple traditions) in a way different than found elsewhere on the site, marking the room as a space for devotion by Jews by including within that normal repertoire some unusual images.[112] The ceiling of the synagogue, like its paintings, used local modes of representation but did this in a way specific to the Jewish community who 'circumscribed their sacred space in particular ways'.[113] Both the ceiling and the paintings on the walls of the synagogue were special and specific to the Jewish community at Dura, but also broadly within the normal local practice: painting on walls of the most sacred part of a religious building, and doing those paintings in panels, was the standard practice in religious buildings at Dura.

Debate continues over the function and meaning of the synagogue paintings as to whether they were meant to be a tool of conversion or whether they held deep symbolism for the Jewish community, and over whether their design relates to copy books or lost manuscript illuminations.[114] In either case, the fact of the paintings' existence has, since their discovery, forced a rethinking of third-century Judaism. There is also much contention over whether some of the scenes of the synagogue paintings, for example that showing the captured Ark at Dagon which includes a depiction of the destruction of cult statues, of the kind other religions in Dura continued to revere, were deliberately denigrating of or competitive with other religions at the site.[115]

From other contexts paintings were also preserved, for instance in bath buildings. From the F3 baths a painting of a flying victory was found on a pillar, and fragments of paintings depicting human faces were also found in the E3 baths, hinting at what had probably once been extensive painted programmes.[116] Such paintings, together with a painting of Aphrodite from house L7-A (the House of the Scribes), and the painted shields generally can be seen to have a more Greco-Roman influence than the other paintings of Dura, and all are associated with the Roman military; they were nonetheless probably locally produced.[117] Also from Dura comes the famed 'shield map'. This is a painted leather parchment which may or may not have once decorated a shield, depicting a map of the coast of the Black Sea (one of the most ancient maps that survives from the ancient world). Rather than a map in the modern sense, it is an illustration of an itinerary of the coastline of the Black Sea.[118]

In addition to the mythological painting from the temple of Bel, mythological paintings were also found in houses of the third century CE, but exclusively in houses converted for use by the Roman military. This includes the aforementioned of Aphrodite in house L7-A and paintings naming the Greek muses in the houses converted into barracks in block E8.[119] Decorative but non-figural wall painting was also found at Dura, including in the palace of the Dux, where geometric and other patterns adorned walls and ceilings.[120] Painting at Dura was not limited to walls: painted wood panels bearing images and inscriptions were also found, even though they were less likely to survive. For example, a wooden panel with a painted victory was found in the Palmyrene gate; its shape shows that it was once part of a larger object.[121]

In a house in block C7 was found a painting of a battle which is unlike other paintings at the site. The painting in house C7-F shows several registers of action;

the fragmentary painting shows figures mounted on horses, with long lances or spears, in an apparent battle scene, and a larger-scale hunting scene adjacent to this.[122] Framing the figural scene is a checkerboard and zigzag pattern which Rostovtzeff thought reproduced the devices of a woven carpet, from which the battle image had been copied.[123] Further, it was thought to have been not contemporary with the use of the house by Durenes, but rather made by a Sasanian captor who stayed in the city after it was captured.[124] It is interesting to note, though, that there is much movement in this painting, including the flying gallop of the horses – unlike the 'static' religious scenes found elsewhere at Dura – and such scenes are found throughout the site in Roman-era buildings, not in paintings but in pictorial graffiti.[125] Pictorial graffiti and *dipinti* are another of Dura's forms of wall decoration but have not been considered alongside the painting (in the same way the terracottas have not been considered sculpture), but they are worth noting.[126] A variety of scenes were scratched into Dura's plaster walls, including a number of images of hunting, religious scenes, and deities, as well as images of animals, buildings, and boats. Despite the 'informal' character of the graffiti, they appear throughout the site in houses and religious buildings alike.[127]

One of the more interesting debates to emerge from the paintings of Dura, and the religious paintings in particular, is the extent to which they can be used as evidence for the nature of the relationships between different communities at the site. Given that this style of painting emerged in Dura under Arsacid domination and continued at Dura under Roman rule, from wherever its influences derived, it was a product of interaction with Arsacid and Roman hegemony. The use of paintings in different religious buildings is complex: the paintings of the Mithraeum, for instance, are part of an exclusive cult which defined itself on the basis of distinction from others and privileged admittance. The form of the building and many of its images, including the central image of Mithras slaying the bull, show that it was part of a much broader religious group, sharing these elements in Mithraea (and presumably Mithraic practice) across the Roman empire. And yet, even in the Mithraeum, a product of Dura's place in a global Roman world, it also had elements which drew on regional cult iconography, such as the way the planets are rendered, which has parallels at Palmyra, and local practices, such as the depiction on one of the reliefs of the dedicant and members of his family or military unit, as was often seen in the religious spaces at Dura.[128] The monotheistic religions of Judaism and Christianity pose an even greater complexity, for while they were, like Mithraism, only for those who had been initiated, they were also, in theory at least, abjuring of any other religious practice. Implicitly and perhaps explicitly, the worship of a single god above all others is also a statement against the Roman empire, which, while flexible in many ways, was not necessarily open to the idea of a power more mighty than itself. After all, in 249 CE, just a few years after the synagogue paintings and those in the Christian building were made, the emperor Decius would issue an edict requiring people to perform sacrifices to the emperor before a magistrate and obtain a certificate which verified this. Whether or not this was enacted on a broad scale, it marked a tension between the state and its gods and other forms of religious practice, especially Christianity which saw severe persecutions at this time.[129]

The content of the synagogue paintings has specifically been taken to indicate a resistance to prevailing norms: an 'anti-pagan' imagery.[130] It is indeed the case that one of the panels of the synagogue paintings depicts the aftermath of the Battle of Eben-Ezer, in which statues to Philistine god Dagon are shown broken into pieces.[131] To a local viewer, such images might indeed be evocative of the desecration of local gods.[132] Even if this was so, however, both the knowledge of such 'pagan' idols, on the one hand, and the hypothetical gentile viewer within the synagogue space, on the other, both imply a Jewish community that was not isolated from its surroundings, just as the style of the paintings, the use of other symbols (like the apotropaic eye), or the nature of religious graffiti within the synagogue all resonate with deeply local practices.[133] This is not to say the practices of the synagogue were not also highly specialized: the prevalence of Aramaic within the building, the presence of a Hebrew prayer, and the fact of the synagogue's existence all show that the community was in some ways set apart from others at Dura. Nonetheless, like Mithraism at Dura, Judaism did not exist in a vacuum and relied for its building, decoration, and even the meaning of its images on local practices.

Sculpture

Like the paintings, much of Dura's sculpture was religious in character, but it was not limited to religious buildings.[134] Sculptures were found within sanctuaries, houses, and other buildings, including fortifications. Wherever it was found, the stone and plaster sculpture was almost entirely religious in subject, being depictions of gods or altars. However, while religious sculpture abounds, the chief representation of deities within temples seems to have been in painting, as already noted. In addition to those paintings, cult reliefs and their accompanying inscriptions are the central evidence for the gods worshipped in the religious buildings of Dura.

Both relief sculptures and those in-the-round were found. Both types of sculptures would have been painted, and some paint survived including red, blue, green, and pink.[135] The reliefs include the cult reliefs depicting a deity and presumed to be the focus of the cult, of which eleven are known.[136] The cult reliefs are typically scenes depicting a static deity to whom an offering is being made by a priest or dedicant. These are usually accompanied by an inscription which names the god, the dedicant, and what is being dedicated (for instance, part of the temple building), often in the formula that indicates the dedication is for the salvation of the house of the dedicant (See p.72–73).[137] Of these types of relief, only a relief to Nemesis, found in the Palmyrene gate, was not found in a building whose purpose was primarily religious (i.e. a sanctuary, although as seen in the previous chapter, the fortifications and indeed this gate had a religious aspect).[138] The cult reliefs were carved in stone and were made to be set into walls. Some were found *in situ*; their scale is small, typically about half a metre in height. Despite their apparently modest size, they are thought to have been 'the chief object of devotion' in the sanctuaries of Zeus Kyrios, Aphlad, Azzanathkona, the Gaddé, and Atargatis at Dura.[139] The relief of Azzanathkona had two altars directly below it: one was stained with evidence of burning incense (the relief itself was covered with soot) and the other had a bowl at its top, for liquid libations.[140] These altars indicate a close relationship between the relief and the act of sacrifice itself. The relief of Zeus Kyrios was set high and prominent in the city wall, a visible signal not only to those within the temple. Others, like those of Azzanathkona and Aphlad, were found not in the *naos* or *pronaos* but in subsidiary rooms ('chapels') of the temples and may have been for the use of particular groups of worshippers within the sanctuary.[141] The cult reliefs were not all found in the same part of the religious building (nor are they all the same period), but the scenes on them and their inscriptions all indicate a votive purpose.

In addition to the cult reliefs, a range of other relief sculptures and three-dimensional sculptures were found. While few three-dimensional sculptures were found in the temples, there were examples, including over-life-size fragments of a statue, from the temple of Zeus Megistos, probably of Baalshamin, with holes in the ears of the statue for the attachment of metal earrings.[142] Statues are also depicted in paintings at Dura, including those of Terentius and Otes in the temple of Bel.[143] A *dipinto* of Iarhibol from the temple of Azzanathkona similarly shows him standing on a statue base.[144] A number of bases which could have supported statues were found in religious buildings.[145] Graffiti also attest to statues in precious metals, and the painting of Zeus Theos stood on a three-dimensional base as if he were a statue (see Figure 5.9).[146] Nonetheless, from the extant evidence, relief sculpture and painting (even paintings *of* sculpture) seem to have been more typical of religious buildings at Dura.[147] Dirven has argued convincingly that the reason deities took this form in Durene sanctuaries was that it reflects the impact of Hellenic and Roman traditions on the ways in which people could interact with representations of the gods: no longer purely the domain of priests and kings alone (as in earlier Mesopotamian and Assyrian practices), at Dura and elsewhere in the Arsacid and Roman eras, the public had greater access to images of the gods, including cult images, and even could dine in their company, within the sanctuary.[148]

A figure which was identified as Heracles was a particularly popular subject for sculpture at Dura: more than forty examples were catalogued. No inscription identifies the nude god, often holding a club and wearing a lion-skin, which in Greek art are the attributes of the hero Heracles (Figure 6.8).[149] However, the same attributes are associated with the Mesopotamian deity Nergal, and the figure could equally be this god, or indeed both, operating contextually or the two having been assimilated.[150] Whoever this nude deity represents, he is present in sanctuaries, public spaces, and houses: more than a quarter of the examples were found within domestic spaces, perhaps indicating that this Heracles figure had a role at Dura as protector of the house or as part of the family cult.[151] He was found also in a range of sanctuaries, but not, apparently, as the main deity in any of the known temples despite his popularity, instead being one of the associated gods, the *synnaoi theoi*. For instance, a number of sculptures of the Heracles figure were found in the temple of Zeus Megistos.[152] Depictions of the Heracles figure were mostly relief sculptures in stone or plaster, but bronze sculpture fragments, in the round, were also recovered.[153] The range of *synnaoi*

Figure 6.8 Photograph taken in 1928–1929 of a stone sculpture of a Heracles-figure with a club and lion, about forty centimetres tall, found in the redoubt palace or in a house nearby. The relief was reportedly left in the house of the governor of Dier ez-Zor. Dura F. R. 3.1.1: no. 28. YUAG b212.

theoi within the religious buildings also shows further that the singular labels to particular gods of each sanctuary can be misleading and that sanctuaries often contained a diversity of gods: for example within both the temple of Adonis and that of Zeus Megistos are found depictions of the camel-riding god Arsu.[154] Both of these buildings have a range of gods within them. In Adonis for example not only the eponymous god and Arsu are known but also a goddess with a mural crown (a Tyche, or Atargatis or Astarte).[155]

While the architectural remains of the large temple of Artemis in block H4 might be taken to indicate that Artemis was Dura's most important goddess, it is not Artemis but a nude female goddess identified as Aphrodite which is found in sculpture throughout the site (Figure 6.9). As with depictions of Heracles, numerous examples of Aphrodite were found, about twenty in all, in both private domestic and religious contexts.[156] The nude female was sometimes accompanied by attributes, like a mirror, or had drapery linking her to Greek depictions of the goddess Aphrodite. Superficially, the ubiquity of Heracles and Aphrodite might seem to indicate Hellenic affiliations. However, the figures identified as Heracles and Aphrodite at Dura share Near Eastern precedents continuing a tradition of the nude hero or goddess. Lacking inscriptions, it is not possible to know what name was attached to these deities at Dura, but it is remarkable that it is precisely these figures, which could read equally as Hellenic or Near Eastern (or a hybrid form of these), which are so ubiquitous at the site. In fact, it is possible that it was precisely their ambiguity, and the fact that they could be read in multiple ways, that made them so popular.

In addition to the relatively common sculptures of the Heracles and Aphrodite figures, a range of other deities are found in sculpture, both within religious buildings and houses. These include depictions of Nike, Allat, Arsu, Hadad, Iarhibol, and Nebo. Many further sculptures are fragments of unidentified deities.[157] Still other fragments of male and female figures are unidentifiable as either human or divine.[158] One of the more enigmatic groups of sculpture found at Dura were plaster blocks with relief busts on them found. Both male and female busts are shown, and while the features are not always clear, Downey identified some as the goddess Athena.[159] These may have been architectural decorations of some sort, meant to have been mounted in walls, but none were recorded _in situ_.[160] Several sculptures of animals were also recorded, including a camel, heads of bulls, and eagles.[161]

Much of the sculpture cannot be securely dated – those with inscriptions are an exception. For this reason, little work has been done on the chronological change in sculpture at Dura. However, recently Dirven has noted that there are distinct traditions within the sculpture at Dura. These are, notably, an earlier phase which has links to Palmyra (including sculpture by Palmyrene artists) and a later one which has a more Roman style of depiction (evident particularly in the relief of Azzanathkona, see Figure 5.11, with the figure crowning the goddess and the shape of the relief itself both having much in common with Roman forms). Finally, Dirven identifies a third group of lesser quality carved in the friable local gypsum.[162]

Bronze survives mostly as figurines and not larger sculptures at Dura, and these were thought to have been imported.[163] It is possible and indeed likely, however, that some large bronze sculptures, if they had existed, would have disappeared or were re-used and melted down in the final years of the city. Suggestions of this have been excavated, such as a life-size bronze foot which was found in the agora in the building known as the Chreophylakeion, as was a silver crown.[164]

Figure 6.9 Image of plaster relief plaque of Aphrodite, from G5-C2, a building identified as Dura's brothel; another example made from the same mould was found in a house in block H2. The nude goddess is shown admiring herself in a mirror held in her hand, standing within an aedicule. Surviving paint showed some features, including her nipples and bracelets, picked out in red. Dura F. R. 3.1.2: no. 21. YUAG 1935.43, Yale-2029.

A graffiti inventory from the temple of Bel also indicates that much metalwork was used at the city that did not survive archaeologically, including golden cult images, jewellery (perhaps for adorning statues), and candelabras in precious metals: items such as these probably became portable wealth when the temples went out of use or were carried off as booty when the city was destroyed.[165] So, while the surviving evidence of religious sculpture emphasizes reliefs, sculpture in the round did occur in religious buildings, both in metal and (as noted above) in stone. Among the small bronze figurines found at Dura, deities included Heracles and Athena alongside other types including musicians and animals.[166]

There was no significant tradition of portrait sculpture in the city: neither funerary, associated with tombs or graves, nor in the public realm, in streets or public buildings.[167] There were, however, a few possible exceptions to this: from the temple of Atargatis came a life-sized female statue, which had stood in the *salle à gradins* where the inscriptions also indicate female members of the cult.[168] In the Roman period, preserved inscriptions may indicate that there had been sculptures of important Roman figures including Lucius Verus and Julia Domna, the Syrian-born wife of the emperor Septimius Severus.[169] From the Roman palace came a male head, but it seems to have been either re-used or unfinished.[170]

Disciplinary traditions have meant that the carved stone and plaster sculptures have been considered separately from the handmade and moulded terracottas, which are considered 'minor' works in terms of art. Dura had a rich assemblage of these.[171] A variety of types of terracottas were found, made by a variety of means including many that were handmade and some fine imported mouldmade examples.[172] Some handmade terracottas may have been toys, particularly the horse-and-rider figures.[173] Others may have had magical significance.[174] The terracottas included some depicting Artemis that may have been produced for use as votive objects, although they were not found in temples (Figure 6.10).[175] Some of the terracotta plaques at Dura are almost identical to examples from Palmyra, perhaps even coming from the same mould and are thus further indication of the strong link between the cities and perhaps even shared elements of religious practice.[176] The medium of terracotta was appropriate for different needs than was sculpture, as shown by the absence of any terracotta Heracles figurines despite their prolific numbers in stone and plaster. A number of terracottas seem to depict cult images, but the modelling is not detailed, and whether they depict divinities or people is not generally clear.[177] There does seem to be a connection, both stylistically and in terms of subject, between figural graffiti found at Dura and the terracottas, both of which frequently depict camels, horses, and 'Parthian' warriors identified by their distinctive dress, with full trousers and tripartite hairstyles.[178]

In addition to the terracottas, also perhaps underappreciated as sculptural production is the extensive use of moulded plaster at Dura, particularly in houses. Decorative plaster was used widely on walls, and decoratively on door frames, but particularly notable are moulded plaster cornices (Figure 6.11). Some included elaborate scenes on Dionysiac themes, others a series of motifs including human heads, fruit, flowers, zodiac symbols, or repeating designs such as a Greek key.[179] The use of plaster for decorative mouldings in the buildings at Dura is characteristic of the site.

Figure 6.10 A selection of terracotta figurines in the Damascus Museum photographed in 1946. Clockwise from top left: a mouldmade medallion of Artemis with a dog or panther (Downey 2003: no. 11), two handmade male rider (?) figures, fragment of a handmade animal figure, and handmade male figure (Downey 2003: no. 70), and a fragment of a mouldmade plaque of a warrior in Parthian dress with a solar disk on the right and lunar crescent on the left (Downey 2003: no. 29). YUAG Dam100.

Figure 6.11 Moulded plaster frieze *in situ* in a house in block C7. Photograph taken in 1931–1932. YUAG e138.

As noted above, while most studies of Durene art have lumped the paintings together as a group, it can now be demonstrated that there is considerable diversity in the style of the paintings and that there are changes in their style over time. The sculpture, too, has not been studied as a chronologically diverse group. As Dirven shows clearly, both in painting and sculpture, broad differences can be seen in both media over time: a more detailed and 'refined' style in earlier, Arsacid, Dura, and a more flat and linear style in the Roman period.[180] With such chronological changes evident, it is clear that not only does the label of 'Parthian art' need to be discarded at Dura but so does the assessment of it as crude or poor. The situation is in fact much more complicated than Durene art simply being a poor imitation of Classical art. Rather, in a range of media, there is evidence of complex cultural interactions. From the Arsacid period when it is first attested, Hellenistic, Mesopotamian, Iranian, and other influences combined to produce something locally meaningful and distinctive.[181]

The Heracles figure which appears so often in stone and plaster sculpture at Dura is an instructive example of the problems and potentials of Durene art: his attributes were connected to that of the Classical hero, and so a Greek name was given to him by excavators. And yet, by the time he appeared at Dura, probably in the first century CE, Hellenistic culture in the Near East had long since become local. 'Greek' visual elements in representation need not have had a 'Greek' meaning. Whether this deity was known as Heracles or as Nergal or whether they had become assimilated, the ubiquity of his image across the site indicates his representation was a local idiom: neither Classical nor Near Eastern, but a third way.[182] Much of the painting and sculpture at Dura similarly negotiates a local place on an almost permanent frontier between empires, drawing on a variety of traditions to create new local meanings.

Overall, there is less evidence in the material culture for a Greek city becoming Orientalized than the prevailing scholarship indicates. In part, this is due to the general absence of Seleucid-era material culture – as with the textual evidence, very little has been preserved and what is extant has been over-emphasized – so there is little baseline on which change can be judged. Whatever Seleucid Dura looked like, by the Arsacid era, when the evidence is plentiful, Hellenism had in effect become part of local and Arsacid visual heritages. The site was distinctive in its diversity of gods and languages, and the material culture and art were ways of negotiating this complex terrain.

The story of Dura's material culture and art has continued long after they were excavated. As noted in earlier chapters (See e.g. p.12), most of the finds were divided between Syria (now in the collection of the National Museum in Damascus) and Yale (now in the holdings of the Yale University Art Gallery and the Beinecke library). As with the division of the finds, the display of the objects itself has a long and often controversial history.[183] Despite myriad problems in their history, including problems in conservation and an international scholarly outcry when the original reconstruction of the baptistery paintings was removed from view in the 1970s, the objects of Dura held by Yale are now more accessible than ever: both in the new permanent gallery which exhibits them (the Mary and James Ottaway Gallery) and in digital form, with the entirety of Yale's collection being available freely online.[184]

Chapter 7

CONCLUSION

Rostovtzeff, in light of his study of Dura's art, characterized the city not as a Greek but as an Oriental one, due to the temples, houses, the religion, and art, 'in spite of occasional Greek names given to Oriental gods'.[1] Decades later, Millar would characterize Dura as Greek on the basis of the preponderance of Greek texts found there, writing that ' ... for all its distinctive regional architecture and art-forms ... Dura always remained a Greek, or in the end a Graeco-Roman city'.[2] These views, each from titans in their fields, show the very different ways that the site of Dura-Europos has been understood, depending on the speciality of the scholar and their world view. These differing views also reveal the necessity of examining a range of categories of evidence: the texts, the architecture, and the material culture all open different windows onto the interpretation of the site. Each of those categories is itself fragmentary, partial, and shaped by the history of their study.

From across these categories of evidence, the picture of ancient Dura-Europos which emerges is one of a site which was cosmopolitan and dynamic: the variety of cults, languages, and diaspora are all indicative of a place which could receive new religions and new ideas. This cosmopolitanism was in some ways a product of its place in a frontier zone and on trade routes. But, while we know of the multiplicity of cults, it is notable that among the many houses excavated across the city, there is no evidence for enclaves, or that people lived separately in a way related to their religious identities. This is not to say Dura was an ancient utopia of multicultural harmony, but it is worth pointing out that on the edge of the Arsacid and Roman empires in the second century, there was a city on the Euphrates in which a diverse population could and did live together and share much in common, despite the presence of people from other places, the presence of many languages, and many religious ideas and gods. Society was structured by gender, kinship, and hierarchy based not only on property and civic titles but also a relationship to the historic past of the site. The major rupture in the way the city was occupied came with the installation of the Roman military garrison within its walls, but many aspects of society continued, adapting to the garrison as best they could.

The fuzziness of the periodization of the site – the lack of firm dates when it passed from Seleucid to Arsacid, and Arsacid to Roman, rule – in some ways masks a larger issue.[3] That is, the reason there is no clear distinction between these periods at Dura is that in some ways, they didn't matter. Thus, Dura was using

Roman currency long before Lucius Verus clashed with Parthia: both the coins and the documents attest to this. In a similar way, the need to ascribe a label to Dura's art, particularly as either Greek or Parthian, has to a certain extent disguised its distinctive local idiom and the ways that it changed over time, from the carefully painted portrait of Baribonnaea wearing her finery in the temple of Zeus Theos to the relief of Azzanathkona, with its Roman framing device and iconography, to the late paintings of the synagogue with their schematic biblical panels.[4]

Dura's art was not beautiful to certain of its beholders: to C. Bradford Welles, for example, it was both ugly and technically bad.[5] Yet, its beauty is perhaps in precisely the way that it appealed to as many ancient beholders as it could, or at least, drew on as many traditions as it might. Thus, in Arsacid Dura, the depiction of the god Aphlad: he stands on two griffons like the god of another place, Jupiter Dolichenus; has a beard like Baal-Shamin, the Semitic lord of the heavens; he wears a headdress like the Mesopotamian god Bel and a Hellenistic *cuirass* typical of the gods of the steppe over his long-sleeved Iranian tunic and trousers.[6] Aphlad is described in the Greek inscription as being of another place – the village of Anath on the Euphrates. A distinctive Durene quality of the relief is the co-presence of such diversity.[7] From within the same room of the temple of Aphlad, another Greek inscription dedicates that room to the same god for the safety not only of the dedicants and their families but of the *strategos*, Seleucos.[8] In this first-century CE inscription, Aphlad, the god of Anath on the Euphrates, protected the general of Dura at the request of his worshippers. His image was still there when, in the mid-third century, it was turned to face the wall of the sanctuary – probably in hopes that one day it might be uncovered – before the building was filled with mudbrick as part of the rampart which tried and failed to secure the city against the Sasanians.

There was a marked change at the site when a Roman military garrison was installed within the city walls, probably in the late second or early third century CE. But, even this was not a complete rupture with the earlier phases of the site, and it seems that local people still had access to some of the religious buildings within the garrison and that civic institutions continued. Some people – like the *strategos* – were able to leverage their existing position to hold on to a measure of power within the city. Some soldiers married, and were divorced from, local women. In the third century, too, the place was more often called Dura in the preserved documents, rather than Europos. It remains unclear why this is the case: whether it indicates the men that held the positions such as that of *strategos* who had also emphasized their link to Dura's colonial past as *Europaioi* were waning or that Dura had remained the local Aramaic name for the site all along, it is not possible to know.

Archaeology conducted in the Middle East by American and European universities was one way that those places jostled for power. Archaeologists were a means by which foreign powers could control knowledge of a place and its past. At Dura, this involved a relationship between the archaeologists and local people which was problematic, involving not only unacknowledged labour but also a projection of those people onto the archaeological remains. Photographs, drawings, and interpretations all elided the ancient and contemporary Middle East.

By the time of the excavations in the 1920s and 1930s, there was already a long history of interventions at the site. Before the city even fell to the Sasanians, an iconoclasm had occurred in the synagogue, gouging out the eyes of some of its figures from the paintings.[9] At some point in antiquity, the tombs of the necropolis were heavily looted. What constitutes authorized and unauthorized interventions at the site has been a product of perspective: Breasted was scathing of the Bedouin who damaged the eyes of the painting of Conon, which had been left unprotected at the site, who are described in the *New York Times* coverage of the discovery of the site as 'prowling' Arabs.[10] The wholesale removal of paintings to museums, done by destroying the buildings and sawing the paintings into panels, was not thought of as destructive.

The place of archaeological sites such as Dura in modern geopolitics continues, with the deliberate destruction of sites by groups such as Islamic State. At sites such as Palmyra, the destruction of monuments has been conducted as spectacle.[11] The political mobilization of antiquities has a long history, and indeed in the Middle East, this is one facet of the colonial legacy.[12] Dura, too, has suffered during the current conflict. The expedition house built by Yale and the site museum built by the Franco-Syrian expedition have both been nearly destroyed, and the site has been looted on a colossal scale, with the circular pits of excavations visible on satellite photographs as covering the site.[13] One of the site guards was reportedly executed. Destruction of sites like Palmyra and Dura is often characterized in the media as a battle between the East and the West, between civilization and barbarians. The situation is of course more complicated.

Unlike Palmyra, Dura has no international visual recognizability and is less useful for spectacular propaganda. The quarrying that is being conducted, that has destroyed so much of the site, is for the recovery of objects: this is worth doing, it is absolutely clear, only because archaeological objects have a monetary value. Whether they are being excavated systematically by agents of ISIS or other groups as a way of raising funds or as a way that people in local communities can make money to feed their families in a dire situation, it is only productive because of the existence of an international market in antiquities.[14] The reason the site is being destroyed is because it is an economic resource, and the objects that are being dug out of the ground can be sold. The destruction of the site is happening for economic reasons and not ideological ones: that economy is based on the value ancient objects have precisely because they are also valued by museums and collectors. The fact of the ongoing looting and site destruction demonstrates the comprehensive failure of decades of international policies on the protection of cultural property and heritage sites.[15] The market for objects continues. There are also difficult questions that foreign archaeologists who have worked in the Middle East must ask ourselves, not only about our presence there but the way that we have engaged (or not) with local peoples, and why it is that those people see (or don't see) the sites they live near or work at as their heritage.[16]

Rostovtzeff claimed that the first inscription found was the little graffito on the Palmyrene gate that thanked the Tyche of Dura, the personified fortune of the site. Dura's Tyche has now abandoned the site, again. Nonetheless, the existence of the vast archive of evidence, the objects and records of the excavation, and the subsequent publications on the site remains accessible. From this, I've tried to look at the way the history of the scholarship has been contingent on particular historical circumstances, and I am aware, as much as one can be, that the implication is this work is itself vulnerable to the same problems. A concern with identity, with connectivity, and diversity and multiculturalism is itself probably predictable in 2016 (as this book was written) when many of those things are under threat, particularly as a foreigner living in Britain as Europe disintegrates. The history of Dura-Europos didn't end in 256, and it won't now: much work remains to be done.

NOTES

Chapter 1

1 On the post-Roman occupation of the site, see Baird 2012a: 320–322.
2 Ousterhout 2011: 93, 116.
3 Sarre and Herzfeld 1911: 386–395; Breasted 1924b: 52–53; Perkins 1973: 1–2. Ammianus Marcellinus, *Rerum Gestarum* 24.1.5; Isidore of Charax, *Mansiones Parthicae* 1.3-4. Other ancient mentions of the site include Zosimos 3.14, and probably Polybius 5.4816 and the Ravenna Geographer, 2.13.
4 Indeed Haynes' image appeared in Punnet Peters' description, which also included a sketch plan Punnett Peters 1897: vol. I. First Campaign, 131–135. On later traveller's maps and other cartography of the site, see de Pontbriand 2012a.
5 Bell's diary and letters are available online: http://www.gerty.ncl.ac.uk/. Accessed 2 February 2016. Bell seems to have seen Dura but not recognized it; there are no tower tombs in the immediate vicinity of Dura, so the place she describes was not the site itself. The tombs she described were perhaps those at Baghouz.
6 Breasted 1924b: 53, 1920: 283.
7 Emberling 2010: 9.
8 As reported by his son, in Breasted 1943: 283.
9 Breasted 1920: 284, 1924b: 57, 1943: 281–299; Emberling and Teeter 2010: 67–70.
10 Emberling and Teeter 2010: 84; details in the June 1920 letters of Breasted, published in Larson 2010: esp. 278–280; Breasted 1943: 313–314; Abt 2011: 247.
11 A 1919 letter from Breasted to Rockefeller quotes Breasted reminiscing about reading his work *Ancient Times* to Rockefeller's children. Emberling and Teeter 2010: 31–32. On Breasted and Rockefeller, see Abt 1996.
12 Bongard-Levin and Litvinenko 2004: 139; Dussaud 1949. Cumont then wrote an afterward to Breasted's initial report on the paintings to the academy: Breasted 1922.
13 That is, on the painting of Julius Terentius and his men making a sacrifice. Breasted was aware of the passage of Isidore of Charax and that the site was also known as Europos (and indeed while he generally calls the site Dura-Salihiyeh, he sometimes calls it Dura-Europos: Breasted 1924b: 37–39).
14 Emberling 2010: 9–10.
15 Breasted 1943: 288.
16 Breasted 1914: v.
17 Scheffler 2003: 254.
18 Wharton 1995: 17–23. The use of the American flag on the convoy is discussed in Emberling and Teeter 2010: 72, and its use at Salahiyeh is shown in the photograph reproduced by Abt 2011: figure 6.11.

19 Wharton 1995: 20.
20 On the 'first-class smash to the jaw' he gave one of his drivers, and the 'oriental palaver' at Meyyadin, as reported by his son, Breasted 1943: 284, 289. On the erasure of the worker in the photograph of the paintings, see plate 8 in Breasted 1924; Emberling and Teeter 2010: 4.58–4.59; Wharton 1995: 36–37.
21 On the name of the temple, see Kaizer 2016.
22 The Conon scene (Breasted's 'Wall of Bithnanaia' would eventually be removed and displayed in the Damascus Museum, and was restored in 2002–2004, as described in Leriche 2012a. The Terentius painting was removed and was sent to Yale University Art Gallery, where it has recently been reinstalled as part of the permanent exhibit, in the Mary and James Ottoway Gallery of Dura-Europos.) On its context, see Heyn 2011.
23 On the organization of archaeology in Syria during the French Mandate, see Gelin 2002, and for an insightful overview of archaeological practice in Syria since the early twentieth century, see Gillot 2010.
24 Finds from this season were reported by Cumont to have stayed in Syria, sent to the museums at Deir ez-Zor or Aleppo. Cumont 1926: 477. Cumont dedicated *Fouilles* to the men of the Army of the Levant who had worked at Dura.
25 Cumont 1926.
26 Cumont 1924.
27 Specifically, Rostovtzeff wrote about a parchment published by Cumont and now known as *P. Dura* 15. Bonnet 1997a: 30–32.
28 On Rostovtzeff's life and in particular on the relevance of Dura to his background in Black Sea archaeology, etc, see Wes 1990: 78.
29 Bongard-Levin and Litvinenko 2004: 142.
30 Rostovtzeff 1926.
31 Ironically, Rostovtzeff's own work at Dura would be rather less speedy in its final publication. Rostovtzeff 1927: 837.
32 Rostovtzeff 1927: 837. Rostovtzeff and others would continue the Pompeii comparison for many years, including repeatedly in publicity. See e.g. the script of a 1937 lecture of Rostovtzeff which outlines the commonalities, including 'excellent preservation … abundance and variety of finds … wall paintings'. Rostovtzeff Manuscript in three parts dated May 1937, marked London University, Michael Ivanovich Rostovtzeff Papers, Manuscripts and Archives, Yale University Library, MS1133.28.173. An extended version of the comparison between Pompeii and Dura can be found in Rostovtzeff 1938: 2–5.
33 Rostovtzeff 1927: 841.
34 On Cumont's life, including his work at Dura, see Bonnet 1997b. His correspondence with Rostovtzeff, including that on Dura (and the 1927 letters relating to this review), has been published in Bongard-Levin et al. 2007: 27.
35 Dura also stood to furnish ancient wall paintings for Rostovtzeff's existing interest in those, including his 1914 book on the topic published in St Petersburg, the argument of which also appeared in Rostovtzeff 1919.
36 In 1927 Breasted and the University of Chicago announced it was to excavate at Dura, and was given consent for the *partage* of finds by the Syrian government, and although this came to nothing, Cumont was prepared to partner with Breasted should Rostovtzeff be unable to secure funds for the project. The details of the 1925–1928 transitional period of Dura's study and the precise machinations of who would excavate at Dura have been published in Bongard-Levin and Litvinenko 2004. The possibility of excavation at Dura seems to have been raised earlier by A. T.

Clay, an Assyriologist at Yale, who had noted Breasted's work and visited Cumont's excavations, but his early death prevented his further involvement. Clay 1924: 193; Hopkins 1979: 24; Bongard-Levin and Litvinenko 2004: 151. A Yale memorandum gives a summary of Clay's plans, in 1925, for Yale to excavate in Iraq to procure tablets for Yale's Babylonian Collection is among Rostovtzeff's papers. 1929 Memorandum, Rostovtzeff, Dura Archive, YUAG. See also Kaizer Forthcoming.

37 A duplicate of this agreement was enclosed with Pillet's contract, with a budget for work, and survives in the Dura archives at Yale. On the historical context of the excavations in the Euphrates valley, see Velud 1988.

38 In the 1940s, when Frank Brown was director of Antiquities in Syria, the papyri were still being studied, and it is clear Syria expected that they would be returned once their study is complete; this return never occurred. See e.g. Brown's March 10 and 20 June 1946 letters to Seymour. Charles Seymour, president of Yale University, Records. Manuscripts and Archives, Yale University Library, RU23.62.537.

39 The funding from the Board was granted for three years in December 1927, to begin in Spring 1928. As noted above, Rockefeller also was the funder of Breasted's expedition and work at Dura, with a personal grant. On the role of Rockefeller and the General Education Board in this period, see Fisher 1983. On the Rockefeller Foundations and the social sciences, including the relationship of Angell to the Social Science Research Council (Angell was advocating for funding for e.g. psychology and law at Yale), see Seim 2013. Angell and Rostovtzeff were both personally involved in the negotiations with the General Education Board, as various letters in the Dura archive attest, e.g. Angell to Rostovtzeff on 18 December 1926. The funding was acknowledged in the published accounts and elsewhere; for example the Bulletin of American Schools of Oriental Research notes the gift from the General Education Board for the work at Dura on the same page of its 1928 Bulletin, in which it announced Rockefeller's two-million-dollar gift to found an archaeology museum in Jerusalem under Albright: 'Two Forthcoming Yale Expeditions in the Orient' 1928. The General Education Board is thanked by Angell in his preface to the first preliminary report on the site, and its contribution to humanistic studies noted. Dura P. R. 1, x. The funding of the board was not meant to be spent outside the United States due to the terms of its charter; a general grant to Yale for humanistic studies circumvented this problem. General Education Board, Appropriations 1.4.636.6674 Yale University Humanities 1925–1929. Rockefeller Archive.

40 General Education Board, Appropriations 1.4.636.6674 Yale University Humanities 1925–1929, including letter of 21 December 1927 on public credit for funding. Rockefeller Archive.

41 Bongard-Levin and Litvinenko 2004; Bongard-Levin et al. 2007. On Cumont's continuing involvement with the Yale-French Academy expedition, see especially Kaizer Forthcoming.

42 'Buried City on the Euphrates' 1928.

43 Rostovtzeff and his wife, Sophie, and Cumont all visited as well, as did Seyrig (of the French School at Athens).

44 Dura P. R. 1: 2; on working under protection of Syrian troops, Hopkins 1979: 32. The Syrian legion used their own tools to undertake the excavation in the first season. On the name of the 'Palmyrene gate' being attributed to Pillet because of the caravan route, see Hopkins 1979: 32–33. Pillet's published report says more simply that it was so named because it faced the direction of Palmyra. Dura P. R. 1: 4. Cumont's description of the gate was brief: Cumont 1926: 12–15.

45   Dura P. R. 1: 2.

46   Hopkins 1979: 119.

47   Pillet's annual reports survive in the Dura Archive, YUAG.

48   E.g. Angell's reply to Rostovtzeff, dated 31 May 1928, which indicates the reason that
     Hopkins and Johnson were appointed as assistants was due to Pillet's 'administrative'
     shortcomings as had been indicated by Rostovtzeff; see also on the issues with Pillet,
     Hopkins' letters to Rostovtzeff on 6 November 1928. Hopkins, while at Dura, wrote in
     a letter to Rostovtzeff dated 5 May 1929, extensively of Pillet's lack of skill at handling
     the workers (including lack of appropriate pay and holidays for Ramadan), and his
     control over both the photographs and the artefacts, which he kept in his personal
     quarters; Hopkins all but directly accuses him of stealing. Dura Archive, YUAG.

49   On the camp inside the citadel, Susan Hopkins made a useful sketch plan in a letter
     to her parents (22 October 1928), which shows the use of one tower as a kitchen, and
     another as a storehouse, the south gate as a garage, and the disposition of the different
     tents. Goldman and Goldman 2011: 95. The workers stayed in tents outside the site,
     adjacent to the river (see e.g. photograph of the black tents in Goldman and Goldman
     2011: 98).

50   Rowell to Bellinger, 28 December 1930. Dura Archive, YUAG. The appointments
     of Rowell and Bellinger to the Dura project were made by Yale's Committee on
     Archaeology, which included Baur and Rostovtzeff among others. James Rowland
     Angell, president of Yale University, Records. Manuscripts and Archives, Yale
     University Library, RU24.92.943, Letter to Angell from B. W. Bacon, Chairman of the
     Committee, on 30 October 1928.

51   Detailed reports of the first four seasons under Pillet were published in the
     Preliminary Reports series: Baur and Rostovtzeff 1929, 1931; Baur, Rostovtzeff, and
     Bellinger 1932, 1933. These are abbreviated as 'Dura P. R.' in the current volume.

52   The clash of personalities with Pillet (including with the Rostovtzeffs, the Hopkins,
     Johnson, and others) is chronicled in the first five chapters of Hopkins 1979. Angell's
     letter, written on 29 April 1931, noted that his services were no longer required
     because 'we are planning, if possible, to go on with work for another year or two
     under somewhat different conditions', and Pillet was to hand over all material to
     Hopkins. Pillet's response from Paris on the 11th of May was not positive, and Angell
     did try to placate him (in a letter of June 8) with excuses of financial problems. Dura
     Archive, YUAG.

53   Pillet's letter from Dura to Angell, dated 26 December 1930. Henry Rowell wrote
     from Dura to Bellinger about the incident a few days later, on December 28th. Rowell
     attributed the deaths not to any person in particular but to the 'papyrus hunt', which
     the team was undertaking in their excavation of the towers. Dura Archive, YUAG.

54   Rostovtzeff, at Dura, to Angell, 16 March 1931. In the same letter, he insists any
     further excavation of the towers, known to be a rich source for papyri, must be done
     without Pillet. Dura Archive, YUAG.

55   Letter to Pillet on 8 January 1931, in which Angell wrote that it was 'impossible to
     make as yet positive statements about our ability to go forward, next year, with the
     Doura excavations'. He received Pillet's letter about the deaths of workmen later in
     January, as he writes to Rostovtzeff in a letter of 22 January 1931. Dura Archive,
     YUAG.

56   It is, however, certainly possible that not all of Pillet's records were returned to Yale,
     given the circumstances of his leaving.

57   Dura P. R. 4, 1.

58 Rostovtzeff 1934.

59 James Rowland Angell, president of Yale University, Records. Manuscripts and Archives, Yale University Library, RU24.92.942. Letter from Angell to Hopkins at Dura. 30 December 1931.

60 Hopkins 1979: 121.

61 On the relationship between the Holy Land and archaeological narratives, see Corbett 2014.

62 Rockefeller Foundation Records RG 1.1 (FA 386) 297.3535, Yale University Archaeology 1929–1931. Rockefeller Archive. Brody notes that 1931–1933 funding came from Yale, but according to Rockefeller records, this internal funding was actually a portion of the Fluid research grant given to Yale by Rockefeller. Brody 2011: 23.

63 Rockefeller Foundation Records RG 1.1 (FA 386) 297.3536, Yale University Archaeology 1932–1938, Interview of Rostovtzeff by David H. Sterns on 25 February 1932. Rockefeller Archive.

64 Hopkins notes du Mesnil's role also as liaison with the French military in Deir ez-Zor. Hopkins 1979: 119.

65 Others present in the sixth season include Van W. Knox of Yale's school of fine arts, as architect, the Louvre's Émile Bacquet to remove the Christian paintings, Maurice le Palud to photograph them, and M. L. Cavro to copy them. From Yale graduate school came Margaret Crosby.

66 Rostovtzeff et al. 1936: 1; Hopkins 1979: 119. The large numbers of works on the excavation teams probably compounded issues of recording in this and other seasons (Simon James, *personal communication*).

67 Susan Hopkins' correspondence from Dura has been published in Goldman and Goldman 2011.

68 D. de Martel signed on behalf of *Le Haut-Commissaire de la Républic Française.* Copy in Dura archive, YUAG. Dated 1 October and signed by Angell on 19 October 1933.

69 Hopkins 1979: 131.

70 Hopkins 1979: 210, 216.

71 Letter from Rostovtzeff, in New Haven, to Angell, 3 January 1933. The letter specifically points out the possibilities for further such finds along the wall street, where houses were preserved beneath the embankment. The support of 'distinguished European scholars' and the Educational Board for the continuation of work is also cited in support of the continuation of work, under Hopkins. Dura Archive, YUAG.

72 The final report on the synagogue was published: Kraeling 1956.

73 Olin 2000: 7, 2001: 127–156.

74 Olin 2000: 9–10.

75 On Gombrich's description of the paintings as 'humble', see Olin 2000: 10; on Goodenough's classification of the community as non-normative, see Wharton 1995: 39.

76 Olin 2000: 14, 18, 2002: 2–3; Weitzmann and Kessler 1990.

77 All of which appeared in the report of the seventh and eighth season, which was published as a single volume: Rostovtzeff, Brown, and Welles 1936. Other works in these seasons included the agora, the necropolis, and the embankment along the desert wall.

78 Baird 2011a: 433.

79 Albright 1935: 147.

80 Rostovtzeff, Brown, and Welles 1936: 2.

81 Hopkins' resignation letter to Angell was dated 1 July 1935: James Rowland Angell, president of Yale University, Records. Manuscripts and Archives, Yale University Library, RU24.92.944.

82 James Rowland Angell, president of Yale University, Records. Manuscripts and Archives, Yale University Library, RU24.92.941: letters from Rockefeller foundation dated 15 February, 19 February, 1 July, and 7 August 1935.

83 The houses, including those in E8 and the House of Lysias, were published in Baird 2014.

84 The plan was included among a number of plans which were provided loose in an enclosure in the rear cover of Rostovtzeff et al. 1944.

85 E.g. on the Pompeii epithet, see the press releases of 25 November and 1 December 1935. On the receipt and display of antiquities at Yale, see e.g. 10 June 1930. James Rowland Angell, president of Yale University, Records. Manuscripts and Archives, Yale University Library, RU24.92.941. Du Mesnil du Buisson, similarly, in the popular French periodical *L'Illustration* entitled an article: 'Doura Europos, La Pompéi de l'orient', Buisson 1936.

86 Hopkins 1932a, b, c, 1933a, b, 1934a, b, 1935.

87 E.g. letter from Wallace Murray, chief, Division of Near Eastern Affairs, in the Department of State, on 9 September 1936, to Angell. Dura Archive, YUAG. Inquiries, in 1936, by the United States, 'regarding the inclusion on the subject of archaeological activities in Syria in the Franco-Syrian treaty negotiations' are recorded in United States Department of State/*Foreign relations of the United States diplomatic papers, 1936. The Near East and Africa (1936), LVII.* Syria and Lebanon, 460–502.

88 This was of course well understood by other nations throughout the nineteenth century. See e.g. Díaz-Andreu 2007.

89 Scott 1988.

90 Correspondence relating to Brown's appointment in Syria, between the president of Yale (Charles Seymour) and the Department of State, in 1946, are preserved in the president's papers. Charles Seymour, president of Yale University, Records. Manuscripts and Archives, Yale University Library, RU23.62.537.

91 Charles Seymour to H. Seyrig, 2 March 1938, Dura Archive, YUAG.

92 Letter from Seyrig, in Beirut, on 28 March 1940 to Charles Seymour. Dura Archive, YUAG.

93 Matheson 1992: 139; Rostovtzeff 1937: 195.

94 The foundation saw its support of Dura ending with the fluid grants to Yale and other universities concluding. Rockefeller Foundation Records RG 1.1 (FA 386) 200.297.3536, Yale University Archaeology 1932–1938.

95 The work of the expedition was published primarily in a series of volumes entitled *Doura-Europos Études*, of which five volumes appeared, followed by *Europos-Doura Varia 1* when Leriche adopted an alternate form of the site name. The houses were published by the author, based on archival work and work in the field with the Franco-Syrian expedition, Baird 2014.

96 I continue to use the name used by the Yale expedition and most modern scholarship, Dura-Europos, or Dura for short, simply to avoid confusion.

97 A useful English summary of the work is given in Leriche, Coqueugniot, and de Pontbriand 2011.

Chapter 2

1   A place called Dura does receive passing mention in a number of ancient sources; see p.157 n.3.
2   Geyer 1988.
3   Stephens 1937; Leriche and Mahmoud 1988: 278.
4   The tablet is field no. K757; Yale Babylonian Collection no. 6518. It dates to *c*. 1900 BCE, the reign of King Hammurabi of Hana. On the relationship of Da-wa-ra to Dura, see Stephens 1937: 187. On the document and the absence of Akkadian at Dura, see Kaizer 2009a: 248–249.
5   Rostovtzeff 1941: vol. 1, 427. Rostovtzeff's main statement on the foundation and early period of the site is Rostovtzeff 1941: vol. 1, 482–489.
6   Isidore of Charax, *Mansiones Parthicae* 1.3-4.
7   Rostovtzeff identified him as a governor of Mesopotamia under Seleucus (a nephew of Seleucus I): Rostovtzeff 1941: vol. 1, 483. On the problem of the possible Nicanors, or Nicator, see Kosmin 2011: 96–97; Edwell 2008: 97–98.
8   On the identities of the figures, see Dirven 1999: 117–119.
9   *P. Dura* 25 and *P. Dura* 32 both include references to Seleucos Nicator as founder of the site. There also seems to have been a cult of the founders, Apollo and Artemis as *archegoi*, as attested in an inscription in a first-century CE inscription in the temple of Artemis: Dura P. R. 3: 63–64, no. D161 (=SEG VII, 352). Further on *P. Dura* 25 (dated to 180 CE and hence belonging to what is generally considered to be Dura's Roman era), and the founders (*progonoi*), see Rostovtzeff 1935a. For Rostovtzeff, the use of the old municipal date (the priest of Seleucus Nikator) was a 'fossilised' survival, not a Roman creation or reintroduction.
10 As Kaizer argues, it seems that rather than being late re-inventions, some 'traditional aspects of worship had been present in the town all along'. Among these include the eponymous Seleucid priesthoods used in dating formulae in Roman-era documents. Kaizer 2015: 99.
11 The translation of the Palmyrene in the image caption is that of Dirven 1999: 230.
12 Kosmin 2011: 97–98.
13 Millar 1993: 446; Kosmin 2011: 99. The other surviving Seleucid document is *P. Dura* 34, a fragmentary contract of 116 BCE recovered from a different tower.
14 On Hellenistic Syria, see especially the papers in *TOPOI* Supple. 4, 2003. Of course, we know relatively little about what a typical settlement would have looked like. Sherwin-White and Kuhrt 1993: 170–180; Millar 1987.
15 Leriche 1997a, 2003, 2004.
16 Bessac 2005a.
17 Downey 1988a: 76–79, 2000: 160. The most recent work in the temple of Zeus Megistos is interpreted as indicating that there was no Hellenistic temple on the site: Downey 2005.
18 Downey 1988a: 89.
19 Baird 2014: 42–43.
20 Downey 1986, 1988b, 1992, 1985a, b. Quote from Downey 1992: 151.
21 Kopsacheili 2011. The dating of the palace itself is circumstantial, based on the size of the foot used in its measurements, as noted by Downey 1986: 27, although its placement does fit into what we now understand.
22 E.g., Downey 2000: 160.

23 On the citadel palace, which partially collapsed into the valley before the excavations began, see Downey 1986, 1988b, 1992. The form of the early town, based around the citadel, has been compared to the site of Jebel Khalid, upstream on the Euphrates, by Kosmin 2011.

24 On the Hellenistic agora the primary work is Brown's report in Dura P. R. 9.1, but see now also Leriche 1996; Coqueugniot 2012a, 2015, 2016. The measurement of fifty-two hectares is based on measurements taken during the author's survey of the site conducted with a total station, a joint project with Simon James which re-surveyed the domestic and military structures in concert with conducting a geophysical survey of the north side of the town. The measurement is slightly short of the ancient size, because it is uncertain exactly how much of the east side of the site has disappeared off the edge of the cliff.

25 The identification of the building as a Chreophylakion is relatively secure, as the monogram of the Chreophylax, the Greek letters chi and rho (in a form later familiar from Christian use), was found repeatedly on compartments used to store documents, although a place called the Chrematisterion is also known (e.g. second-century CE loan document *P. Dura* 20, line 19). Multiple records offices are attested, including from the Arsacid-era documents mentioned above, and later, with the Roman military records. The office of the Chreophylakion is also mentioned in a copy of a succession law, *P. Dura* 12, the surviving record of which is third century CE. The excavated parchment and papyri themselves were all recovered from secondary contexts, and the Chreophylakion is the only securely identified records building at the site. On the inscriptions from the building, including the monogram, see Brown's description in Dura P. R. 9.1: 168–176; the initial description was published in Dura P. R. 5: 81–84, and the building is discussed generally in Dura P. R. 9.1: 28–32, 99–102. For the new investigations of the structure, see Leriche 1996; Coqueugniot 2012a.

26 Hoepfner and Schwandner 1994. Block C7 was the target of re-excavation to attempt to identify early house-plots; see Saliou 2004.

27 Not all archaeologists accept Leriche's re-dating of the site: e.g. Hannestad 2012: 992.

28 Dura F. R. 6: 200–201; Bellinger 1948.

29 Edwell 2008: 102; Gaslain 2012; Edwell 2013.

30 Dura P. R. 1: 6–7; Dura P. R. 3: 17; Dura P. R. 4: 3–4, 56–68.

31 James 2015.

32 Dura P. R. 7/8: 128–129, no. 868.

33 Dura F. R. 6: 203–204.

34 On the civic character of the temple, Downey 1988a: 90. On the inscription, Cumont 1926: 409, no. 52.

35 Downey surmised two major bursts of temple building, from the mid-first century BCE to the mid-first century CE, and then the mid-second century BCE. Downey 1988a: 88–89.

36 On these problems with the naming of temples at Dura and the Gaddé specifically, see Kaizer 2009b: 158–159. Kaizer notes the main deity of the temple was probably Malakbel.

37 Dura P. R. 7/8: 318, no. 916. Kaizer 2009b: 158; Hillers and Cussini 1996: no. 1067.

38 Downey 1988a: 95; Kaizer 2009b: 159.

39 Downey 1988a: 92. A graffito from within the temple gives the compound name Artemis Nanaia, but it is unclear whether the 'Greek' Artemis and 'Babylonian' Nanaia were usually identified within the temple, or if this identification was one made by a particular visitor. Cumont 1926: 411–412, no. 55.

40   Dura F. R. 3.1.1. Downey counts thirty definite depictions of Heracles in sculpture, and eleven more probable examples. At other sites, Heracles is explicitly connected with the Babylonian deity Nergal. On such 'Heracles figures' (as Kaizer notes, when there is no inscription, the figure might as easily be called Nergal), see Kaizer 2000. On the regional significance in the Syrian Djezireh, see Downey 2002.

41   Dura F. R 3.1.2: no. 46 and 202. Hadad also appears on the cult relief in the temple of Atargatis, as her consort.

42   Between Atargaris and Hadad on the relief is a metal standard, which itself is the product of earlier connections to the Near East, emerging from Assyrian worship and transforming over time, including in the light of the Roman use of metal standards: Dirven 2005; Andrade 2013: 1–3.

43   Downey 1988a: 114–115; Dirven 2004: 11–12.

44   Downey 1988a: 125.

45   Kaizer 2009b: 157.

46   Downey 1988a: 89. Further on the paucity of secure evidence from Hellenistic Dura for temples, see Downey 2000: 160.

47   On the mudbrick at Dura, see Gelin 2000a; Leriche 1986, 2000. On the plaster, see Dandrau 1997.

48   On the problem of the 'Parthian' label for what is now referred to as the Arsacid empire for its ruling dynasty, see Hauser 2012: 1001. See also the discussion on the utility of 'Parthian' in Invernizzi 2011: 189.

49   *P. Dura* 18 and 19 for 'Europos in Parapotamia'. For *polis*, see e.g. Dura P. R. 3: 86, no. H.3, a Greek inscription recording the polis' dedication of an altar to Zeus Megistos after an earthquake.

50   *P. Dura* 16, a fragmentary parchment of the late first century CE, is the only mention of the ruler from the parchments of Arsacid period Dura, but the title is also attested on a number of inscriptions of the first century CE: e.g. Dura P. R. 2, 91–93, no. H.4; Cumont 1926, 440–441, nos. 116 and 118. The *strategos kai epistates* was likely a late Seleucid introduction, but there are no direct attestations of the title from that period: Kosmin 2011: 102. It is possible that the *strategos* in charge of Dura may have been *strategos* of the Parthian province of Mesopotamia and Parapotamia within which Dura fell, as interpreted by Sommer 2004: 163. The document Sommer uses, *P. Dura* 20, while found at Dura, does not concern Dura directly but rather the village of Paliga, upstream of Dura (although it is noted that the document was to be lodged at Europos itself).

51   Arnaud 1986.

52   *P. Dura* 18 and 19, in which documents are witnessed by the royal judges and the president and collector of fines.

53   *P. Dura* 20, 21, 22, 24. *P. Dura* 22, dated 133/4 CE, describes the site as 'Europos toward Arabia'. For the herald, see P. R. 7/8: no. 868, the aforementioned inscription concerning the restoration of doors taken by the Romans.

54   *P. Dura* 18 and 19; Millar 1993: 447. On the problems with Parthian periodization at Dura, see Edwell 2013.

55   Andrade 2013: 211.

56   Baird 2014: 249–251.

57   The excavations of the necropolis were published in Dura P. R. 9.2; many tombs had been disturbed in antiquity. Further on the necropolis, see Chapter 5.

58   The painting was published in Breasted 1922, 1924b: 75–88; Cumont 1926: 41–72; Rostovtzeff 1938: 68–74; Perkins 1973: 36–42. The date of the painting is insecure,

and perhaps as early as the first century CE, but in any case, the painting was still *in situ* and remained when the Romans took control of the temple; an inscription of 115 CE from the same temple records a grandson of Konon, Lysias, son of Patroclus (all save Lysias are identified in the painting) as dedicating a chapel on behalf of himself and his grandson. The painting likely predates these two generations, if it was made when Conon was still head of the family, and also attests to the continued relationship between this family and the temple; Cumont 1926: 359–361, no. 5; Dirven 2004: 11–12. The precise identity of the figures in the painting is also less secure than generally admitted, as a painted inscription label on the second figure from the left, one of the priests, gives *his* name as Conon son of Nikostratus, and indeed it is strange that Conon, head of an important family, would be the visually smallest adult of the scene. On the inscriptions, see Breasted 1924b: 101. The painting has been restored relatively recently, and is in the Damascus museum; on the restoration, Leriche 2012a.

59 On the act of sacrifice in Durene paintings, see Elsner 2001: 276. On the context of the painting and its relationship to others in the Temple, see Heyn 2011.

60 The painted inscriptions were not well preserved; Breasted 1924a: 101. The central female figure is generally noted to be Conon's daughter and not his wife, *contra*, following Rostovtzeff, Baird 2014: 216.

61 On the relationship of the jewellery to objects found at the site, see Baird 2016a.

62 E.g. *P. Dura* 24 for a Conon son of Nikostratus, who are *Europaioi*, although the document is fragmentary. On the different documents who note men named Konon, see Andrade 2013: 235–236.

63 E.g. *P. Dura* 26, in which a Roman military veteran buys land on the Khabur; on Dura's control of villages in its territory, see Kaizer 2017.

64 'Caravan cites' appeared in Rostovtzeff's 1928 writings in Russian periodicals after his travels in the region that same year. Bongard-Levin and Litvinenko 2004: 147–149.

65 Olin 2011: 78.

66 Rostovtzeff 1932.

67 Rostovtzeff 1932: 105.

68 Millar 1998a.

69 On Dura's economy, see especially Ruffing 2007.

70 Gawlikowski 1996: 140.

71 Dirven 1999: 34–40.

72 Dirven 1999.

73 Dirven 1999: 191.

74 Dura P. R. 2: 86–87.

75 Downey associates the destruction of the earthquake with an enlargement and alteration of the temple of Zeus Megistos. Downey 1988a: 93.

76 No direct evidence from the site gives us this date, although Cumont recorded a Greek inscription to Lucius Verus made by Aurelios Heliodorus, an *epistates* of the city, in the temple of Artemis, which Cumont believed was a base for a statue of the emperor Cumont 1926: 410, no. 53. For a useful overview of the conflict between Parthia and Rome, see Edwell 2008. The key work on the Roman Near East in English remains Millar 1993.

77 It has been postulated that the site remained nominally under Arsacid control after 165 CE until the late-second-century campaigns of Severus, in the interim being under indirect Roman rule: Luther 2004.

78 Kaizer 2017:67.

79 Downey 1988a: 95–96; Frye et al. 1955: 139–142, no. 6.

80 Downey 1988a: 90, 108,120.

81   Dura P. R. 7/8: 83–84, nos. 845–846; *PAT* no. 1085; Dirven 1999: 260–269.

82   Dura P. R. 7/8: 84, 95–100, nos. 846, 850–852.

83   Dirven and McCarty 2014: 130.

84   Leriche 1997b; Dirven 1999: 273–281; Allag 2004; Rousselle 2005. Kaizer, however, is
     sceptical as to whether the building in which the relief was found should be classified
     as a temple: Kaizer 2017.

85   Kaizer 2015: esp. 99. While there is no direct evidence for the priesthoods under the
     Arsacids, as Kaizer argues (and *contra* the argument that such Hellenic features were
     a Roman re-invention), it is likely that some aspects of Hellenistic worship continued
     throughout the life of the town. Selecus Nicator is of course also present on the Gaddé
     relief of 159 CE. On the Roman 'reassertion' of Hellenic origins, see Spawforth 2006:
     10–11.

86   Millar 1993: 121–122, 467.

87   Leriche and El'Ajji 1999. Reference to members of a *boule* in the temple of Artemis
     was also attested in inscriptions, e.g. Dura P. R. 4, 170–171, no. 343.

88   Dura P. R. 3: 51ff, no. d149; Downey 1988a: 90–91.

89   Ruffing 2000; Baird 2016b: 22–26.

90   Ruffing 2007.

91   Bertolino 1997; Leriche and Bertolino 1997.

92   The date is based on a range of evidence, including the dating of the mudbrick
     construction on the walls of Roman structures. Gelin 2000a: 308–311.

93   Dirven 1999: 191.

94   Dura P. R. 7/8, 85: no. 847.

95   The wall appears on site plans but was otherwise unremarked in the initial
     publications; new investigations provide corrections to the plan and other details:
     James 2007: 37–38. On the Dura military base and its relationship to Roman military
     bases more broadly, see Haynes 2013: 145–163.

96   See discussion in James 2018.

97   The so-called 'Praetorium' in the preliminary reports. Dura P. R. 5: 201–234. The
     dedicatory inscription of the *principia* gives a date of 211–212: inscription no. 556.

98   Dura P. R. 6: 72–77; on the inscription, 77–80, no. 630.

99   Baird 2014: 115–126.

100 Baird 2007a.

101 The publication of the Palace was made in Dura P. R. 9.3. See also Downey 1991, 1993a.

102 Dura P. R. 9.3: 30–31, no. 945.

103 Particularly based on the interpretations of Rostovtzeff, Dura P. R. 9.3, 94–96, and
     Gilliam 1941.

104 On the problem with the title of the *dux ripae*, see especially Edwell 2008: 128–135.

105 Edwell 2008: 135.

106 Dura P. R. 9.3: 97–134.

107 Dura P. R. 9.3: 107–110. The same Antoninus Valentius is recorded in the 'Middle'
     Mithraeum: P. R. 7/8: 85, no. 847. Both the Dolichenus altar and Mithraeum
     inscription are in Latin.

108 Another small military temple has recently been discovered by Leriche and his
     team at the base of the citadel, but it has not yet been fully published. Leriche,
     Coqueugniot, and de Pontbriand 2011: 14.

109 Dura P. R. 5: 131–327.

110 James 2018.

111 Dura P. R. 7/8: 63, 76–80.

112 The final report on the synagogue appeared in 1956 as Dura F. R. 8.1. Its Aramaic
and Iranian inscriptions have now appeared in the third volume of *Inscriptiones
Judaicae Orientis*. The scholarship on the synagogue is extensive, but key recent
works in English include Wharton 1994, 1995: 38–51; Hachlili 1998: 96–197; Noy
2007; Fine 2005: 172–183; Stern 2010; Fine 2011; Rajak 2011; Stern 2012. Earlier
debates hinged around the place of the Dura synagogue paintings as a precursor
to Christian art, and the way they perhaps testify to an unpreserved tradition
manuscript illumination. Further on the synagogue, see chapter 5.

113 IJudO iii Syr84 (=Dura F. R. 8.1, no. 1a). It is unclear whether the date marks the
start or the end of the restoration: Noy 2007: 66.

114 Hachlili 1998: 425.

115 Hachlili 1998: 103.

116 Stern 2010.

117 The final report on the Christian building by Kraeling was published posthumously
in 1967, as Dura F. R. 8.2.

118 On the adaptation of the room, see Dura F. R. 8.2: 23–28.

119 The main preserved scene from the baptistery has generally been thought to be the
holy women at the tomb of Christ (following Kraeling, Dura F. R. 8.2: 190–197),
although there have been questions particularly on this scene from an early date:
e.g., Pijoan 1937. For a recent re-interpretation of the paintings, identifying the
Virgin Mary among their subjects, see Peppard 2016. For other recent re-readings,
see also Klaver 2012.

120 On the context of the Terentius painting among others in the Temple, see Heyn
2011. The painting is Yale no. 1931.386. Julius Terentius is known from elsewhere on
the site, both in documents of the 20th Palmyrene cohort and indeed his tombstone,
which was found in a house in the agora sector of the city: Welles 1941.

121 The date of the painting is based on a number of external factors, including the
funerary inscription found inside the city which gives Terentius' death as occurring
in 239 CE (Dura P. R. 9.1: 176–185, no. 393); the priest Themes, named in the
painting, also appears in a morning report: *P. Dura* 89, also of 239 CE.

122 On the clothing of the soldiers at Dura including this painting, see Dura F. R. 7: 39,
57–66.

123 The figures have also been identified as Roman emperors; for a useful summary of
the debate, see Kaizer 2006: 2. On the figures as Palmyrene gods and the relationship
to the imperial cult, see Dirven 2007.

124 On the diversity of paintings, see Heyn 2011: 223. On the Gad compared to the
Tyche, see Kaizer 2009a: 247.

125 Dura F. R. 7: 30–31; Leriche 1993.

126 This evidence is problematic, however. See Baird 2012a: 313–314.

127 Baird 2012b.

128 Coqueugniot 2012b.

129 Dura P. R. 5: 103–104; Downey 2007: 103.

130 Dura F. R. 6: 181. The date relies on the end of the coin series at Dura – it is worth
noting that civic mints in Syria cease production around the same time, in 256–257;
see Butcher 2012.

131 James 2011.

132 M5: Leriche 1997b: 94; Coqueugniot 2012c: 64. Aphlad (catapult balls stored in
room 3), Dura P. R. 5, 101.

133 Baird 2012a: 314.

134 James 2007: 41.

135 Baird 2012a: 319.

136 Dura F. R. 4.3: 80.

137 Dura F. R. 6: 10; Saliou and Dandrau 1997: 95.

138 On the periodization, see especially Kaizer 2017; Edwell 2013.

139 Ammianus Marcellinus. *Rerum Gestarum* 24.1.5. See also Zosimus 3.14. On the later occupations of the site, including the hermit who apparently lived in the citadel, see Baird 2012a: 321–322.

Chapter 3

1 Yale does not hold the records of Cumont (which reside at the Belgian academy at Rome), although it does hold much correspondence between Cumont and Rostovtzeff. Other records from the excavations are held in personal collections or have been lost. The archives of the Franco-Syrian expedition are in Paris.

2 This is the fifth provision of the *accord* signed in April 1933 by Angell. James Rowland Angell, president of Yale University, Records. Manuscripts and Archives, Yale University Library, RU24.92.941. There is no such provision in the first accord signed by Angel in 1927, which specified only the mechanics of the division of objects and the treatment of special objects (parchments and tablets are given as examples) which were allowed to leave Syria for study, but were to be returned. The first *accord* is preserved with Pillet's contract in the Dura archive.

3 Memorandum of Agreement between Yale University and M. Maurice Pillet, January 1928. Dura Archive, YUAG.

4 E.g. Pillet's 1928 report, part 3, 10–12. Dura Archive, YUAG.

5 E.g. Pillet's 1928 report, part 3, 13–16. Dura Archive, YUAG. The numbers on Pillet's list and captions match those written in Pillet's own hand in the photograph albums he compiled, which were also deposited in the Dura archive.

6 On du Mesnil's objects, Ann Perkins in an unpublished list of Dura material, YUAG archive. On the Louvre objects, for instance, the ceiling tiles and plaster cornices from D5, excavated by Pillet, are among other Durene objects and paintings now on display in the Louvre. Personal collections include those of, for instance, Susan Hopkins, whose correspondence relating to Dura has recently been published: Goldman and Goldman 2011.

7 Some plain textiles were also left at Dura: Dura F. R. 4.2, vii, as were many of the stamped pottery sherds (in the case of these sherds drawings were made and returned to Yale, and it is noted on those drawings that the objects were left at Dura). Still other finds were purchased or traded; Rowell's letters record him trading lamps from Dura for 'better' ones for the Yale collections, while in the Levant, and Rostovtzeff thought nothing of purchasing objects in Baghdad. Rostovtzeff 1935b: 187.

8 See, e.g., James' careful disentangling of du Mesnil's drawings in James 2011: especially figures 14 and 15. Pearson's studies were largely visual, e.g. his 'study of the houses' and his annotated key to the Mithraeum building, both held in the archive, although he did publish a short book on the Synagogue: Pearson 1939.

9 Downey 1993b, 1995, 1997, 2005, 2012.

10 Hopkins 1979: 50–52.

11 Goldman and Goldman 2011: 1–3.

12　Hopkins' retrospective account of Susan's involvement gives slightly different dates; the ones here are based on the earlier archival records (the catalogue she was apparently tasked with under Pillet was not preserved). Hopkins 1979: 37. On being 'the cataloguer', see letter on 26 December 1933, Goldman and Goldman 2011: 206. On her dissatisfaction with the job, her letter of 29 October 1928, see Goldman and Goldman 2011: 100.

13　The author used Susan Hopkins' records as the basis for a database of the artefacts of Dura-Europos, which was the data for (and is an appendix in) Baird 2006. Hopkins reported in his later work that Susan Hopkins compiled a catalogue from the second season, but this documentation is not preserved in the archive (Clark Hopkins notes a system of ink and tags, which might have been superseded by later recording systems when the objects returned to Yale). Hopkins 1979: 53.

14　Clark Hopkins did acknowledge her work in his later account of the excavations: Hopkins 1979: 120.

15　Of the little acknowledgement Susan Hopkins received in publications was her contribution of a study of the steps of the temple of Azzanathkona in Dura P. R. 5.

16　Tracks of one of the Decauville railways used by the Yale expedition were excavated in the 1990s by the Franco-Syrian expedition in the secondary gate: Abdul Massih 1997: 49.

17　This is the average: actual pay was slightly more for men and less for the boys.

18　Hopkins disapproved on the grounds that there was a reduced workforce as a result as some workers did not return after this payment; Hopkins letter to Rostovtzeff, 6 November 1928. Dura Archive, YUAG.

19　Pillet, Report on 1928 (first) season, 9–10. Dura Archive, YUAG. Pillet complains that they often broke objects at the time of discovery, as they were too 'brutal', but that he had improved their performance.

20　Dura P. R. 6, 2: Hopkins' introduction also notes his wife was responsible for the catalogue of finds.

21　That is, a woman who was not there because she was the wife of one of the men working there. Hopkins 1979: 120.

22　Rostovtzeff to Clark Hopkins, 13 February 1932. Dura Archive, YUAG.

23　Wallace Murray (later the head of the division of Near Eastern Affairs with whom Yale would correspond concerning State Department interventions in the securing of permits in Syria) wrote letters in 1932 to consular officers and diplomatic missions throughout the region asking for her protection, including Athens, Istanbul, Baghdad, Beirut, and Izmir. She was introduced as 'a daughter of an old friend of the Secretary'. The letter from Murray to the American chargé d'affaires in Baghdad noted that she would be at 'Dura-Europas [sic], which is described as being on the west bank of the Euphrates River due east of Palmyra. This place does not appear upon any of the maps available in the Department and we are not sure whether it is in Syria or Iraq'.

24　NARA 890d.927.032.

25　On Crosby's involvement with the OSS, Allen 2011, who also discusses many other archaeologists and classicists in this organization. On her work in the Agora, see Rotroff and Lamberton 2006: 52–54. Women at contemporary excavations such as Olynthos had their work plagiarized wholesale: see the case of Mary Ross Ellingson at Olynthos, for example: Kaiser 2014.

26　Hopkins slightly misquoted Bell, who wrote '... the heart *from* sorrow ... '. Bell 1907: 186.

27　Hopkins 1928–1929 Daybook. Dura Archive, YUAG.

28 The 'scientific' notebook is of course a different type of contrivance, and it might be argued these Dura daybooks are more useful than their later counterparts; on reflexive methods, see Hodder 1997. Interestingly, when typescripts of the daybooks were made decades later to assist scholars in the archive, these excluded all but the 'archaeological' information, rewriting them as contemporary documents.

29 Hopkins 1979: 36, 50–53; see also Susan Hopkins' letters in Goldman and Goldman 2011: 56–60.

30 Hopkins 1928–1929 Daybook. Dura Archive, YUAG. The reason for the small number of finds might be that Pillet, while director, had been paying *baksheesh* to workers for finds and then keeping them in his own quarters. Letter from Hopkins (in Athens) to Rostovtzeff, 5 May 1929. Dura Archive, YUAG. Hopkins suggests a solution would be for the Yale representative to make a catalogue that had to be submitted to the university on a monthly basis.

31 E.g. Frank Brown's notebook on the start of excavation in E4, on 31 October 1932. Brown 1932–1933 Daybook. Dura Archive, YUAG. Wall chasing was regular practice in the nineteenth century, but by the 1930s, more advanced methods were being employed, including e.g. the box-grid by the Wheelers at Verulamium and stratigraphic excavations by Danish teams in Hama, Syria: Ploug 1985. A number of earlier excavations at Classical sites had also been employing stratigraphic techniques: Trigger 2006: 290–291. There was occasional attention to stratigraphy and relative relationships within architecture (Brown's work in the agora is notable for this), particularly in later seasons at Dura, but it was not generally utilized in interpretations.

32 21 February 1932. Dura Archive, YUAG.

33 15 November 1930. Dura Archive, YUAG.

34 31 December 1932. Dura Archive, YUAG.

35 Goldman and Goldman 2011.

36 Goldman and Goldman 2011: 211–212. On possible archaeological traces of the expedition's camp, see e.g. the drain visible in citadel photograph FXI10 (as noticed by Simon James, *personal communication*).

37 Goldman and Goldman 2011: 162, 181; Hopkins 1979: 61. Such accusations could, of course, have serious consequences for Johnson's career and Yale's continued permission to excavate the site, despite the fact they seem to have been baseless.

38 Johnson 1932. The care taken and system used are also evident in the photographs, which show the chalk system of numbering the texts used to make his drawings and transcriptions (see e.g. photograph b27).

39 Johnson 1929: 741.

40 Johnson 1929: 741.

41 Johnson 1929: 741.

42 E.g. in a letter from Angell regarding Pillet's contract. 10 January 1928. James Rowland Angell, president of Yale University, Records. Manuscripts and Archives, Yale University Library, RU24.93.943.

43 Dura's use in Detweiler's manual includes the discussion of drawings of extant remains against restored superstructures: Detweiler 1948: 51. Collections of Detweiler's materials are now held at Cornell, the American School at Rome, and the American Schools of Oriental Research, where he was president from 1955 to 1966. His meticulous preparatory drawings made for the site plan of Dura are preserved in the Dura archive at Yale.

44 Detweiler's 1948 manual makes clear that by that time, at least, he was more than aware of the issues of multi-period archaeological surveying. From Frank Brown's 1935 daybook, it is evident that Pearson also helped in the drawing of Detweiler's site plan.

45 Similarly, in Detweiler's later manual, an illustration of methodology includes an architect wearing trousers and shirtsleeves drawing a plan, while workers in Arab dress hold measuring tapes. Detweiler 1948: 28.

46 This quote comes from a typescript by Detweiler reflecting on archaeological work generally, not Dura alone. Detweiler papers, collection no. 15-2-1363, Division of Rare and Manuscript Records, Cornell University Library, Box 20. The same document contrasts the public romanticism surrounding archaeology with the 'everyday matter' of life on an expedition.

47 Detweiler 1948: 50.

48 In the archive, the photographs were taken out of the letters to be filed separately, so while many letters refer to accompanying photographs, it is not generally possible to say precisely what photograph was sent with which letter.

49 Shapin 1989.

50 Baird 2011a.

51 In the second season, Dairaines, the secretary, is said to have been in charge of photography; in the fourth season, Walter, and in the fifth, both Naudy and Walter. In the sixth season, Maurice le Palud was there as photographer (initially, to photograph the paintings specifically). In the seventh, Toll was listed as responsible for photographs.

52 These negative lists were given an alphanumeric sequence, in which a letter which corresponded to the season in which the photograph was taken preceded the numbering, in sequence. These were compiled from the field lists made for the different types of photographs taken (e.g. the film negatives were recorded in Kodak negative albums which supplied sleeves for the negatives and had space to hand-write the subject); glass negatives were written on directly.

53 Baird 2011a: 428, forthcoming.

54 Bohrer has written recently that archaeological photography has always tried to resist being construed as art. For instance, the continued use of black and white for archaeological photography is the 'chosen medium of archaeological science' and seriousness. Bohrer 2011: 140. I agree, but think the case of Classical archaeology is even more complicated in the relationship between 'art' and 'science' as it was a notionally scientific discipline whose main aims included the recovery of art. On black-and-white photography as theoretical stance, Flusser 2000: 42.

55 Baird 2007b.

56 Berg 2008: 2.

57 Of course, there was also a practical issue at play: the workers were used as scale because they were there. But there is also a matter of status. For instance, when Sir Aurel Stein, famed British explorer, visited the site in early 1929, it was Jotham Johnson and Clark Hopkins who posed against the buildings, presumably as they showed their respected guest around the site. The photograph of Stein himself at Dura was taken by Pillet, and he posed not with archaeology, but in front of his tent. Aurel Stein's photographs of Dura, and some related correspondence, are now held at the British Library, having been presented by the Royal Geographical Society. British Library Photo 392/33 (95–118) Album V; Photo 392/33(119–142) Album VI; Photo 392/42.

58 Helbig 2016; Poidebard 1934. Poidebard also took aerial photographs of Dura, in December 1932: Dura P. R. 5: xvi.

59 Interestingly, the portraits of Sir Aurel Stein by Pillet at Dura pose him not in front of the archaeology, but in front of his tent pitched inside the citadel, implicitly foregrounding his status as adventurer and visitor to the site. British Library Photos OIOC 392/42(1) and 392/42(2).

60 As mentioned in letter from Hopkins to Rostovtzeff, 3 February 1933, he was meant to come at the end of the season to take final photographs of everything.

61 A point made well by Wharton 1995. Bohrer has recently made the point that the paintings of Pompeii were photographed so as to minimize their fragmentary nature. Bohrer 2011: 129. The synagogue photographs did have uses, however: In the 1930s, more photographs of the synagogue paintings appeared in the *Illustrated London News* than in the scholarly publications.

62 Wharton 1995: 42.

63 Dura F. R. 8.1, plates 18–25.

64 These series of negatives were given different numbering sequences. The field negatives were designated with a letter (*B* through *K*) for the field season, and then a serial number. Those made at Yale had *X* and *Y* prefixes, and additional object photographs had no letter prefix but began with no. 701 (photographs which were found without a number were added to this series). A series of object photographs, whose sequence was prefaced DAM, was made in Damascus by Toll. The details of the rationale for each sequence are given in Anne Perkins' summary of the archive. Dura Archive, YUAG.

65 Baird and McFadyen 2014.

66 Baird and McFadyen 2014: 16. On translation, see also Lucas 2004: 117.

67 Photographing objects, and indeed plans, was a way of sending information, as documented in one Hopkins' letters to Rostovtzeff. Letter dated 2 June 1932, sent from Athens to New Haven. Dura Archive, YUAG.

68 Baird 2012c: 37–39.

69 On the exclusion of human agency, Bohrer 2011: 81.

70 For contemporary excavations in Syria, see e.g. the object photographs included in Ingholt 1942. In that publication, the captions included mention of stratigraphy, given by level number. The Danish excavations at Hama, conducted at roughly the same time as those at Dura, paid much closer attention to stratigraphy, which can only partially be attributed to the depth and clarity of the strata of Hama's tell – these were later published in Ploug 1985.

71 'Old and New on the Syrian Euphrates', 15. Hopkins Family Papers, Manuscripts and Archives, Yale University Library, MS 290.3.27. The manuscript included a figure list, and photographs taken by Le Palud, of local peoples.

72 Pedersen 2015: 168.

73 Dyson 1998: 199.

74 Bagnall 2007: 285; Winks 1996: 136.

75 Evidence of how the site was used by local people or managed by the directorate of antiquities probably exists, but Syrian archives are inaccessible as the present work was being written in 2016.

76 The details of these donors are given the 1970 Dura report, 12 n31, in the Holburn Grey Papers, Manuscripts and Archives, Yale University Library, RU581.28.392.

77 Welles application, 30 November 1967. Dura Archive, YUAG.

78 Detweiler and Brown wrote to Welles in 1969 saying they would like to help publish the remaining materials, but that it was difficult given how much time had passed, and that they were both heavily committed to other projects. In it, they proposed a volume on architecture and town planning, which they were uniquely qualified to write. These plans, though, would not come to fruition.
Letter from Detweiler and Brown, in Rome, to Welles, at Yale, dated 6 March 1969. Dura Archive, YUAG. Brown was then at the American Academy at Rome, and Detweiler at Cornell University. In his reply of 6 April 1969, Welles describes his position as 'that of custodian of the antiquities, records, and publication funds'. For the quote on the delicate nature of the situation, 1 October 1967. Dura Archive, YUAG.

79 5th and 9th December 1967 letters from Welles to Detweiler. Dura Archive, YUAG.

80 On the career of Welles, see Bagnall 2007.

81 On Perkins' assumption of the Dura editorship, see Dura F. R. 5.1: x. Her book is Perkins 1973. Perkins' book was dedicated to Sophie Rostovtzeff, and she had been close with the Rostovtzeffs: the income from their estate was left to her upon Sophie's death in 1963, until it reverted to the Classics Department upon her death. 1970 Dura report, 4 n8, in the Holburn Grey Papers, Manuscripts and Archives, Yale University Library, RU581.28.392.

82 The report is not dated, but as it refers to gallery accession numbers, presumably dates from after the transfer of the collection to the gallery.

83 Ann Perkins report, 3. Dura Archive, YUAG.

84 As discussed in Baird and McFadyen 2014.

85 Kaplan 1971.

86 Holburn Grey Papers, Manuscripts and Archives, Yale University Library, RU581.28.392.

87 Dura report, 7 n20, in the Holburn Grey Papers, Manuscripts and Archives, Yale University Library, RU581.28.392.

88 Dura report, 12, in the Holburn Grey Papers, Manuscripts and Archives, Yale University Library, RU581.28.392.

89 The dispersal of material was also a problem; for instance, Rostovtzeff's library, including notes and photographs, was bequeathed by his widow Sophie to Welles. Welles had transferred most of it to his Cape Cod house, and it was later sold to the University of Toronto. Dura report, 21–22, in the Holburn Grey Papers, Manuscripts and Archives, Yale University Library, RU581.28.392.

90 Dura report, 23–24, in the Holburn Grey Papers, Manuscripts and Archives, Yale University Library, RU581.28.392.

91 Dura report, 26–27, in the Holburn Grey Papers, Manuscripts and Archives, Yale University Library, RU581.28.392. The report also pointed out that Dura copyright, including the sale of images and publications rights, was shared between the Dura Publications Committee, the Yale Art Gallery, and the Bollingen Foundation; they suggested transferring the Publications committee requests to the gallery for handling, with the proceeds to be divided between them.

92 The volume on painting was initially to have been written by Perkins, and later, the report records it was meant to have been written by Richard Brilliant.

93 Pearson also published his own short guide to the synagogue, under the auspices of the Museum: Pearson 1939.

94 An overview of conservation issues relating to the Dura collection at Yale can be found in Snow 2011.

95 Letter from Alan Shestack, 28 February 1978, in the Holburn Grey Papers, Manuscripts and Archives, Yale University Library, RU581.28.392. The letter also stipulates why the display of the Christian paintings was removed from the gallery, and the precarious state of preservation the paintings were in at the time. This was necessary because of complaints regarding the removal of the 1930s chapel from the galleries and the paintings taken to be conserved for redisplay in a new gallery. Complaints had reached the president of the university.

96 Kiefer and Matheson 1982. Matheson wrote a short synthetic guide to the site and the Yale collection published in the same year, Matheson 1982.

97 Before the opening of the new gallery, Dura material was exhibited in Boston and New York; Chi and Heath 2011; Hoffman and Brody 2011. On the exhibition of Dura at Yale and the different installations, see Brody 2016.

98 James 2004; Downey 2003; Baird 2014; Peppard 2016.

99 Yale University Art Gallery catalogue: http://artgallery.yale.edu/collection/search; the archival photographs are available on ArtStor, which necessitates a subscription. The digitization of the archival photographs, like the new Dura gallery at Yale, was generously funded by James and Mary Ottaway.

100 Quote from Lucas 2001: 44.

Chapter 4

1 The collection included some given by bequest, and many acquired by purchase, some on special shopping trips to Egypt. Once at Yale, the papyri were put into the care of the Department of Classics in the room used as an office by Rostovtzeff and his former student Charles Bradford Welles: Emmel 1989: 48–49. The parchments and papyri are now held by the Beinecke library at Yale.

2 Dura F. R. 5.1.

3 In addition to those published in Cumont 1926 and in the preliminary and final reports, a number of Durene inscriptions were published in Frye et al. 1955. The inscriptions from the Synagogue are included in *Inscriptiones Judaicae Orientis 3,* Noy and Bloedhorn 2004: vol. 3: Syria and Cyprus. Some of the Greek inscriptions are included in *Supplementum Epigraphicum Graecum 7.* The Parthian and Middle Persian inscriptions were published in Frye 1968; Safaitic inscriptions in Macdonald 2005; Hatrene in Bertolino 1997; Leriche and Bertolino 1997; Bertolino 2004; on the Semitic inscriptions of the fortifications, see Bertolino 2005; the Palmyrenean inscriptions appear in *Palmyrene Aramaic Texts,* Hillers and Cussini 1996 and are brought together in their Durene context in Dirven 1999. For an overview of Durene graffiti, Baird 2011b. The pictorial graffiti were published in Goldman 1999; Langner 2001. On graffiti from the Mithraeum, houses, and synagogue respectively, see Francis 1975a; Baird 2016b; Stern 2012.

4 In addition to their publication in Dura F. R. 5.1, many Roman military documents from Dura also appeared in Fink 1971, the documents Fink included are often abbreviated as *RMR* (Roman military records) following Fink's own, separate numbering scheme. When excavated, it was the most extensive military archive known, but since that time, the records at Vindolanda have been excavated.

5 Frye et al. 1955: 169–200; Harmatta 1958; Buisson 1959.

6 Bagnall alludes to the fact that our corpus of *ostraca* at Dura is probably under-representing their frequency at the site: the excavators were not paying attention to individual pot sherds, and they were not usually sifting the earth to recover them systematically. Bagnall 2011: 125.

7 *P. Dura* 15 and 34 are relatively securely dated. The former includes a man named Aristonax, son of Ariston, who was a *Europaios*.

8 *P. Dura* 1.

9 Dura P. R. 6: 411–412; Cumont 1926: 409, no. 52.

10 Ameling 2006; Hammond 1999.

11 Sommer 2006: 430; Arnaud 1986.

12 Parchment *P. Dura* 16B; dedications e.g. Dura P. R. 2: 91–93, no. H.4, a *strategos kai epistates* in 51/2 CE named Seleucos son of Lysias son of Seleucos, in a dedication to Zeus Soter found in the sanctuary known as the temple of Bel.

13 *P. Dura* 18 and 19.

14 Sommer 2004: 163. Sommer bases his argument on *P. Dura* 20, in which Phraates is among his titles *strategos* of Mesopotamia and Parapotamia; whether this position was the highest contemporary administrative office is unclear. On the title of *basileus* (king) being used for Arsacid rulers of important provinces, see Hauser 2012: 1005.

15 On the character of this document, see Millar 1998b: 477.

16 On inheritance, see the third-century copy of the law of succession, *P. Dura* 12.

17 Cumont 1926: 450–452, no. 134; Johnson 1932: 23; Frye et al. 1955: 141. N.B. this inscription was not excavated by Cumont but recovered nearby. On the Arsacid title (*ton proton kai protimomenon kai ton somatophylakon*) of those who sit before the king (earlier this had been a Seleucid title, sometimes translated as the Orientalizing 'noble shaikhs'), see Bellinger and Welles 1935: 126 n21; 142 n88; Yarshater 1983: 709. An Arsacid-era inscription (120/121 CE) from the Temple of Zeus Theos, a man named Seleucos, who is a *Europaioi* and is *ton proton*, which may be related also to the Arsacid court: Dura P. R. 7/8: 214–215, no. 888.

18 On the hereditary title (although covering texts only up until the time of Dura P. R. 3), see Johnson 1932: 17–34. To which can be added the *strategoi* listed in Frye et al. 1955: 140–142; Leriche and El'Ajji 1999: 1345–1346.

19 Baird 2014: 247, 294–295. Among the evidence are especially the inscriptions from the *salle à gradins* of the temples of Artemis, Azzanathkona, and Atargatis, where women's names are recorded, together with those of their husband, being 'of the same father'. The marriage of nieces and uncles and other close-kin marriages are also attested, and while they were not the norm, nor were they extraordinary. It is unclear why they are recorded in such religious contexts, although they do tie into broader concerns with lineage and legitimacy.

20 On the phenomenon of brother-sister marriage in Roman Egypt, see Huebner 2007; Remijsen and Clarysse 2008; Rowlandson and Takahashi 2009.

21 Dirven for example argues that the temples of Bel and Zeus Theos were reserved for the worship of particular families. Dirven 2004: 11–12. Downey agrees that two families were 'primarily responsible for the cult' in Zeus Theos, but notes both Greek and Semitic names appear in painted inscriptions, and that it is possible others worshipped there, Downey 2007: 108.

22 Cumont 1926: 436, nos. 109–110.

23 Dura P. R. 7/8: 215–217, nos. 890–899.

24   From the street separating these two buildings (street 5), a fragmentary stone
      inscription of 169/70 CE records one Seleucos, *strategos kai epistates* of the *polis*, and
      the dedication of a *stoa* and *plinth* to Zeus Megistos. Frye et al. 1955: 139–140, no. 6.
25   P. Dura 17C is among a registry roll of copies dated to 180 CE. I owe these
      preliminary interpretations of Dura's social history to discussions with Claire Taylor.
26   Slaves as personal property in *P. Dura* 17B, 18, 25, 28, and 31. An agricultural slave
      is mentioned in *P. Dura* 23. On slaves related to the Roman military, see e.g. the
      inscription P. R. 9.3: no. 970. On slaves at Dura generally, see Baird 2014: 241–244.
27   *P. Dura* 17B; *P. Dura* 19. The documents use the Greek phrase (translated as 'alias') '*ho
      epikaloumenos*': 'the one surnamed'.
28   On this document, see Saliou 1992; Baird 2014: 50–59.
29   Andrade 2013: 215.
30   Dura P. R. 7/8: 128–134 on 'The Shrine of Epinicus and Alexander', nos. 267–869. The
      deity/deities to whom the shrine is dedicated is not recorded. See also Rostovtzeff
      1935c.
31   Dura P. R. 7/8: 129–130, no. 868. Translation adapted from that in the publication.
32   Dura P. R. 5: 151–152, no. 468.
33   Pollard 2007: 96. As noted by Pollard, Welles himself suggested this in Dura P.
      R. 7/8: 130–131. There is no straightforward pattern, however, of Semitic names
      in religious contexts and Greek ones in public contexts: e.g. the combination of
      Greco-Macedonian and Semitic names amongst the women and their families
      recorded on the steps of the *salle à gradins* of the temple of Azzanathkona.
34   Pollard 2007: 97–98.
35   Zeus Kyrios/Baalshamin, Dura P. R. 7/8: 307–309, no. 915, 31 CE. Artemis
      Azzanathkona, 161 CE, Dura P. R. 5: 142–145, no. 454. Earlier, in the first century,
      the goddess Azzanathkona is known from an inscription, erected by 'Rhechimnaios
      son of Boumaios on behalf of the safety of himself and his children, to Azzanathkona'
      Dura P. R. 5: 177–178, no. 504. Further on the Temple, see Downey 1988a: 110–112.
36   Room W9.
37   See Dura P. R. 5: 180–200, nos. 510–555; Arnaud 1997 esp. 131–132 on the problems
      of using the evidence of names at Dura.
38   Dura P. R. 5: 106–114, no. 416. The relief is now in the National Museum in
      Damascus. The date comes from another inscription which gives the date of the
      founding of the sanctuary, Dura P. R. 5: 113–114, no. 418.
39   Kaizer 2013: 80.
40   On Roman Ana/Anath, see Kennedy 1986.
41   The translation of the Greek as either 'well-being' or 'salvation' are those adopted by
      Dijkstra and Moralee, respectively.
42   On the Greco-Roman formulaic language, see Kaizer 2009a: 240–241; on the language
      requesting personal salvation and its prevalence at Dura (and its rootedness in the
      Near East), see Moralee 2004: 2–3, 56, 79–83. Moralee counted eighteen examples
      of these type of dedication at Dura and noted the compatibility of the notion of
      salvation with Christian and Jewish traditions. At Palmyra, similar inscriptions with
      the formula *for the life of* (the Aramaic equivalent of the Greek *soteria* that occurs
      at Dura) have been shown to be a public representation of social life: at Dura, this
      happened in sanctuaries. At Dura, all the Greek inscriptions using the formula relate
      to the dedication of parts of temples or cult reliefs; Dijkstra compares to the use
      of similar formulae in Nabataean and Hatrene practice. Dijkstra 1995: 3, 81–170,
      259–281 esp. 274.

43 Dura P. R. 5: 113–116, no. 418.

44 Downey 2007: 104; Stern 2012: 183.

45 The description of the place Anath being on the Euphrates in the inscription may, however, indicate that the expected audience was unlikely to be familiar with its location, and thus the worshippers or even the dedicant himself were not from Anath at all: see Kaizer Forthcoming.

46 On peoples from Palmyra, Anath, and Hatra at Dura, see Dirven 2011. On Palmyrenes at Dura, see Dirven 1999; On the Palmyrene religious community, see Downey 2007: 96–102. On Anathenes, see Downey 2007: 103–104.

47 Dura P. R. 7/8: 318–320, no. 916.

48 Dirven 2011: 208; Baird 2014: 258–259.

49 Dura P. R. 7/8: 307–309, no. 915. *PAT* no. 1089. The relief is at YUAG, 1935.45.

50 Translation from the Palmyrene, from Dirven 1999: 213.

51 Dirven 2011: 205.

52 Dirven 1999: 220.

53 The translation of the Palmyrene in the image caption is that of Dirven 1999: 230. On the probability that the sanctuary's primary deity was Malakbel, see Kaizer 2009b: 158–159. Fragments of a relief of Malakbel were found, as described well in Dirven 1999: 248–253.

54 Kaizer 2017: 87–88.

55 Bertolino 1997.

56 Kaizer 2009a: 246.

57 *P. Dura* 25.

58 On the continuation into later Dura of Seleucid cults, see Kaizer 2015: 99.

59 Dura P. R. 5: 218–220, no. 556. The building was dated based on this inscription, which records Septimius Severus as deified (and hence deceased, which happened in early 211) and another dedication of the building to Caracalla's brother Geta (who had been killed in 212). The inscriptions of the building are discussed in P. R. 5: 218–234.

60 Dura P. R. 6: 77–80, no. 629.

61 Graffiti which probably allude to Vergil were found in E4 and the Roman palace. Baird 2011b: 59.

62 Moralee 2004: 82. Moralee doesn't list the examples for the emperor, presumably because these are in Latin, but there are number of *pro salute* inscriptions from military contexts for the salvation of the emperor. E.g. Dura P. R. 5: 226–228, no. 561.

63 James 2018.

64 On the Hebrew parchment, Fine 2005: 173–183.

65 Grenet 1988; Noy and Bloedhorn 2004: 177–209.

66 On the synagogue as a space with Greek and Aramaic bilingualism, see Noy and Bloedhorn 2004: 133. On the importance of Aramaic there, see Noy 2007: 64, and Fine 2011: 304.

67 Fine 2011: 314.

68 *P. Dura* 10. There is debate over whether the text is actually that of Tatian, but in any case it is a gospel harmony and related to Christianity at Dura: Joosten 2003; Crawford 2016. On the fragment as evidence for Tatian's doctrine and its sexual asceticism, see Dirven 2004: 16–17. The Christian community was drawn on locally converted gentile population (not synagogue members), including the Roman army, based on names in graffiti which are also attested among soldiers: Dura F. R. 8.2: 90; Dirven 2008: 49.

69 On the Syriac spelling, Millar 1993: 471.

70 Baird 2011b: 60–61. These appeared in the temple of Azzanathkona during the period the temple was within the Roman military garrison.

71 On the contextual use of different languages at Dura to express and emphasize particular religious aspects in the inscriptions, see Kaizer 2009a: 244.

72 See also Milik 1968 on *P. Dura* 151, possibly a Jewish marriage contract.

73 Syriac is also found on an inscription from the temple of Atargatis, and on inscribed objects. On Syriac at Dura: Millar 1993: 468. Syriac texts on a silver vase from block D5 and a painted ceramic fragment: Dura P. R. 4: 178–181; Drijvers 1972: 50–51. A Syriac inscription on a carved Stele: Dura P.R. 3: 68–71; Drijvers 1972: 49–50, no. 63. The Syriac stele, translated as 'May Khalisa, son of Sennaq, of Qarha, a disciple of Rama be Remembered before the god' uses a formula of remembrance similar to that found in Greek graffiti throughout the site. Baird 2016b, 2011b: 56, 2014: 65. The Syriac at Dura is generally connected to the Christian community. Kaizer 2009a: 237.

74 Bagnall 2011: 104.

75 This is the text of the upper part of the document; the lower section gives an even more complicated lineage: 'Nabusamaus, son of Conon and grandson of Abissaeus, and Acozzis, daughter of Seleucus and granddaughter of Abissaeus'; Acozzis' son signs on her behalf, and he is 'Barnaeus, son of Lysias'.

76 Sommer 2007: 91.

77 Dura P. R. 2: 148–149.

78 The inscription was on a statue base that had been plastered over later in the third century; it seems to have been a statue erected to the Septimius Aurelius Lysias by the *boule* of Europos; the room with steps in the temple of Artemis probably served as the meeting place for the *boule*. Leriche and El'Ajji 1999: 1320–1321.

79 On the onomastic impact of the constitution, see Salway 1994: 133–136. Leriche would put the inscription earlier, between 198 and 212 CE, based on the formula of the inscription of a (probable) statue dedicated to Julia Domna found nearby, given by the *boule* of the *Aurleianoi Antoninianoi Europaoi*: Leriche 1999: 726.

80 Dura P. R. 4: 84–145, nos. 181–275. Baird 2016b.

81 Ruffing 2000.

82 Wine was for the Durene market and for that of a village called Banabela. Dura P. R. 4: 122–123, no. 245.

83 Ruffing 2007.

84 Ruffing 2007: 407.

85 E. g. *P. Dura* 17A, a copy of a loan document relating to vines in the village of Tetyrus. On the Roman military presence on the Khabur, see Gnoli 2007.

86 For a useful overview of Roman military documents, see Phang 2007.

87 On the term 'morning report', see Fink 1971: 179.

88 Fink, Hoey, and Snyder 1940; Nock 1952; Gilliam 1954; Fishwick 1988; Haynes 1993; Reeves 2005; Haynes 2013: 199–206.

89 Beard, North, and Price 1998: 324.

90 Haynes 2013: 203–204.

91 Zeus Betylos: Dura P. R. 4: 68–71, no. 168. Nemesis: Dura F. R. 3.1.2: no. 9, 29–31, 191–192; YUAG 1938.5312.

92 Phang 2007: 290.

93 On the rosters, see also Dura F. R. 5.1: 303ff.; Gilliam 1965; Fink 1971: 9ff.

94 Fink 1971: 18.

95 Salway 1994: 134–135.

96 Baird 2011b: 58–60.
97 On Latin as a language of power (including as a means of displaying power), see Adams 2003.
98 On this transaction, see Sommer 2007: 90.
99 Welles 1951. There is a useful critique in Pollard 2007.
100 Welles 1951: 251, 264. Hopkins also explicitly categorizes the different groups at Dura as racial ones in his pieces for the *Illustrated London News, e.g.* Hopkins 1932a: 239.
101 Welles 1951: 262.
102 Welles 1951: 255.
103 Welles 1951: 255, 264. N.B. the *P. Dura* numbers in Welles are not the final sequence as later published; the documents in question are *P. Dura* 17C and *P. Dura* 23.
104 Welles 1951: 274. Welles' later work on Hellenism in the East repeated this characterization, with a flood of newcomers displacing the population of Greco-Macedonian elite: Welles 1959: 25.
105 Rostovtzeff 1938: 15.
106 Rostovtzeff 1938: 21–22.
107 Rostovtzeff 1938: 30.
108 Rostovtzeff 1938: 31.
109 'Orientalization' typescript by Frank Brown. In the Michael Ivanovitch Rostovtzeff Papers, Manuscripts and Archives, Yale University Library, MS1133.2.18.
110 E. g., Dura P. R. 5: 222.
111 'Orientalization' typescript by Frank Brown, 1. In the Michael Ivanovitch Rostovtzeff Papers, Manuscripts and Archives, Yale University Library, MS1133.2.18.
112 'Orientalization' typescript by Frank Brown, 9. In the Michael Ivanovitch Rostovtzeff Papers, Manuscripts and Archives, Yale University Library, MS1133.2.18.
113 'Orientalization' typescript by Frank Brown, 10. In the Michael Ivanovitch Rostovtzeff Papers, Manuscripts and Archives, Yale University Library, MS1133.2.18. Brown thought what he saw as the failure of Hellenism at Dura was the result of a lack of thoroughly Hellenized original settlers and lack of early civic institutions (he contrasted the situation at Antioch, which he believed had both of these things). On the Bazaar and other anachronistic nomenclature, see Baird 2007b: 35–37. Brown indeed uses 'the West' interchangeably with Hellenic, and 'the Orient', the 'Near East', and 'Middle East' interchangeably: 'Orientalization' typescript by Frank Brown, 8. In the Michael Ivanovitch Rostovtzeff Papers, Manuscripts and Archives, Yale University Library, MS1133.2.18.
114 'Dura-Europos on the Euphrates' typescript by Rostovtzeff, 2–3. In the Michael Ivanovitch Rostovtzeff Papers, Manuscripts and Archives, Yale University Library, MS1133.2.18.
115 'Dura-Europos on the Euphrates' typescript by Rostovtzeff, 3. Emphasis added. In the Michael Ivanovitch Rostovtzeff Papers, Manuscripts and Archives, Yale University Library, MS1133.2.18.
116 On Rostovtzeff's life, Wes 1990. On the racism and Orientalism of Rostovtzeff's work in context, see Shaw 1992: 226.
117 'Orientalization' typescript by Frank Brown, 4. In the Michael Ivanovitch Rostovtzeff Papers, Manuscripts and Archives, Yale University Library, MS1133.2.18.
118 Johnson 1932: 30.
119 Johnson 1932: 31.

120 There are a number of fragmentary contracts that are likely Hellenistic: *P. Dura* 34–37.

Chapter 5

1 There was of course much variation in the precise nature of the socles, the mudbrick, the mortar, and the plaster (*djuss*) used. See especially Dandrau 1997; Gelin 2000a, b; Abdul Massih 2005.
2 Crowfoot 1945: 113.
3 Downey 2000: 160.
4 Wharton 1995: 17–18.
5 Baird 2012c.
6 Baird 2014: 40–49.
7 On the profiles of the stone-and-plaster mouldings at Dura, see Shoe 1943.
8 Houses built on a slope, like those terraced beneath the Redoubt it block C3, are preserved over multiple levels, and a number, including E4 and L7-A, had parts of upper storeys partially preserved when they collapsed within the lower part of the building.
9 Baird 2014: 70–83.
10 Baird 2014: 100–102.
11 Baird 2014: 68, 164–165.
12 Baird 2014: 64–67.
13 Other decorations found in houses (in L7 and D5) included painted tiles, like those of the synagogue, but none of these were found *in situ*.
14 Hauser 2012: 1017.
15 Baird 2016b.
16 Saliou 1992; Baird 2014: 50–59.
17 Previous estimations of population at Dura were based on an average family of two parents, two children, and two slaves: Will 1988. After the Roman garrison is installed, it is likely the population density in the rest of the city became even higher, at least for a time, as people were displaced from the northern side of the site.
18 On endogamy at Dura, see especially Johnson 1932. On brother-sister marriage in Roman Egypt, where it is also textually attested and its economic and social functions, Huebner 2007; Remijsen and Clarysse 2008; Rowlandson and Takahashi 2009.
19 de Pontbriand 2012b.
20 Baird 2014: 248–252.
21 Dura P. R. 1: 24–29; P. R. 2: 12–15, 53–57; Downey 1986, 1985a, 1988b, 1992; Kopsacheili 2011.
22 It is not entirely certain, however, that the redoubt palace replaced the function of the citadel palace, as neither has a secure chronology.
23 Dura P. R. 1: 23–24; Dura P. R. 4: 21–27; Mouton 1992; Leriche et al. 1997; Bessac 2005b.
24 The study of Dura's tombs in de Jong 2017, based on earlier publications, appeared too late to be considered here.
25 Dura P. R. 9.2: 1. Some tombs were also excavated by the French military working under Cumont; see Cumont 1926: 273–277.
26 Buchet 2012.

27 Dura P. R. 9.2: 2.

28 Dura P. R. 9.2: 21.

29 The dating of the dump material is problematic and may relate to dumps from the bath buildings (large amounts of ash were noted), which were Roman in date, or to clearance of debris after the 160 CE earthquake. Dura P. R. 9.2: 3–4. The chamber tombs appear to have gone out of use before the mound began to accumulate, as single inhumations were placed in the entranceways of some, re-using their entranceways, Dura P. R. 9.2: 5.

30 Dura P. R. 9.2: 3.

31 The original publications make partial use of Greek and Latin terminology for the tombs; Toll calls the tombs catacombs (rather than *hypogea* as most chamber tombs in the region would be designated), and each niche is a *loculus*. The publication thus has numbers for each tomb in Arabic numerals, followed by the designation of the *loculi* in Roman numerals.

32 Dura P. R. 9.2: 7.

33 Dura P. R. 9.2: 9.

34 Dura P. R. 9.2: 9.

35 Dura P. R. 9.2: 8. The date of 36 CE in Tomb 47; Dura P. R. 9.2: 26–27 on the 'graffiti' in tomb 4.

36 Dura P. R. 9.2: 8–9.

37 Dura P. R. 9.2: 4–5.

38 Dura P. R. 9.2: 5.

39 Dura P. R. 9.2: 140–150. The tower tombs were demarcated on plans and notes by letters, rather than numbers. The superstructures of the restored tower tombs relied heavily on analogy with the standing tombs at Baghuz, further down the Euphrates, which were also investigated by Toll.

40 Tomb D; Dura P. R. 9.2: 5.

41 Dura P. R. 9.2: 99–100.

42 Dura P. R. 9.2: 95–96. Clay coffins (*sarcophagi*) were found in tombs 3 and 4, and fragmentary remains of others were found in individual internments cut into the mound beneath with the chamber tombs were excavated. Other fragments were found in re-used tombs, but no more precise details were preserved.

43 This was found in tomb 2; Dura P. R. 9.2, 97–98; fragments of the cover of a similar example were noted by Cumont 1926: 277.

44 Dura P. R. 9.2: 19.

45 Some funerary inscriptions were found within the city. That of Julius Terentius (also known from the painting in the temple of Bel) was found, perhaps not yet completed, in a house in the agora: Dura P. R. 9.1: 176–185, no. 393. A sepulchral stele with a Latin inscription (for one Aurelius Celer) was found re-used in the paving of a room in the temple of Artemis: Dura F. R. 3.1.2: no. 81.

46 Dura P. R. 9.3: 21.

47 Dura P. R. 9.3: 21.

48 Dura P. R. 9.3: 22.

49 On the abandonment of the city and burials in E8 and the Dolicheneum, see Baird 2012a: 314. James (2018) believes the burials noted in the Dolicheneum were misattributed by Toll (Dura P. R. 9.2: 6) from another building; this is possible, but in any case, photographs show these burials cut into a plaster floor of a building somewhere in Dura (YUAG i724b).

50 On the tombs in the citadel, see Dura P. R. 9.2: 6–7. On post-abandonment burials in blocks C10 and C11, see Saliou and Dandrau 1997: 95; Buchet 2012: 196–200.

51 On the burials in D1, see Dura P. R. 9.2: 6; Baird 2014: 182, 295–296. The two *sarcophagi* burials, beneath tower 10 and the city walls between towers 4 and 5, are noted in Dura P. R. 9.2: 7, 96.

52 There has been no comprehensive study of the religious buildings of Dura-Europos. The best overview of their architecture can be found in Downey 1988a: 76–130. The temples with Palmyrene associations have been expertly brought together in the appendix of Dirven 1999. On the religious life of Dura, particularly from the point of view of the epigraphy, see Kaizer 2009a, b. A study which brings together the architecture, inscriptions, art, and objects of the Durene religious buildings remains to be done for all but the synagogue and Christian building, which were fairly comprehensively published in the final reports by Kraeling.

53 Nineteen religious buildings include the sixteen structures named as 'temples' by the original excavators and the Christian building, synagogue and Mithraeum, as well as a temple in block X9 which they excavated but did not publish, and two new sanctuaries identified by the MFSDE, one in block M5 and one against the exterior southern end of the citadel. It does not include a small square building with four columns near the Palmyrene gate, which was suggested by the original excavators to be a Tychaeum. Given the similarity of the plan to the Roman-era religious buildings in blocks X7 and A1, it is likely that it was a religious structure of some type, but little further detail was recorded.

54 Downey 1988a: 76–79, 2000: 160.

55 Downey 2005.

56 Downey 1988a: 88–89. The second 'burst' probably followed the earthquake which struck the site in 160 CE, and indeed some inscriptions record building in the year immediately following, in 161 CE, e.g. the dedication to Artemis Azzanathkona, P. R. 5: 142–145, no. 453.

57 Freyberger has used the term 'sacral buildings' for the religious structures of Dura, Freyberger 2002.

58 On the multiple deities in the temple of Zeus Megistos, including Baalshamin, Heracles, two unidentified nimbate gods, and Arsu, see Downey 2008: 417–428. On Malakbel in the temple of the Gaddé, see Kaizer 2009b: 158–159. For the fragments identified as the possible Malakbel relief, see Dura F. R. 3.1.2: no. 6.

59 On temples with towers, staircases, and elevated sections at Dura as a continuation of a Babylonian tradition of temple building, see Downey 1976.

60 The *salle à gradins* in the earlier phase of the temple of Artemis was removed, its stones re-used as paving, but the final form of the building did include the *odeon* with similarly stepped benches, but a U-shape instead. Downey 1988a: 89–92.

61 On the unusual form of the sanctuary, see Downey 1998: 203.

62 The lintel was from the street K entrance and not the larger entrance from street L: Dura P. R. 7/8: 181, 212–213, no. 886, dated to 114 CE.

63 Room Q of the 'temple of Bel'; the entrance to the temple of the Gaddé is recorded in Dura P. R. 7/8: 234–235, 256, and figure 67.

64 The temples of Artemis, Zeus Megistos, Aphlad, and the necropolis temple all included large built altars which were excavated; in Aphlad a number of altars were excavated *in situ*, and many portable altars (in stone, ceramic, and copper alloy) were also found throughout the religious structures of Dura, and elsewhere in streets, fortifications, and houses.

65 On the altars in the courtyard of the temple of Adonis, see Dura P. R. 7/8: 149–150; a similar altar, with a depression without burning so perhaps for libations, was found outside room 1 in the temple of Aphlad (the room in which the cult relief was found). Dura P. R. 5: 103.

66 Dura P. R. 5: 98–130.

67 In the synagogue, human bones are part of a foundation deposit: Dura P. R. 8.1: 19; Magness 2010: 146–147, 2012. On the temple of the Gaddé foundation deposit which contained twenty-one 'amulets', see Dura P. R. 7/8: 241; in the temple of Artemis, a ceramic vessel beneath a paved floor contained ash, animal bones, and bronze objects, Dura P. R. 6: 399; that in the temple of Adonis is uncertain, Dura P. R. 7/8: 137. For a foundation deposit house E4, see Dura P. R. 6: 7.

68 Dura P. R. 7/8: 128–134, nos. 867–868.

69 *Naos* referring to rebuilding of a temple: P. R. 7/8: 129–130, no. 868. Downey uses the term 'sanctuary unit' for the *naos* and *pronaos*.

70 Indeed, while *naos* is sometimes translated by the excavators as 'temple', so is *hieron*, the word used in the description of the building of the foundations of a sanctuary ('hieron') for Aphlad; this was found on the inscription of the cult relief, which itself was found in a room with benches labelled as an *andron* because of another inscription found within it (Dura P. R. 5, no. 416). In some buildings, there is more than one room which has been identified as a *naos* (e.g. Azzanathkona, Aphlad, and Adonis), although in each of these cases, the second *naos* is arguable.

71 See, e.g. the temples of Zeus Megistos, Aphlad, Adonis, and Artemis.

72 This can be seen in the temples of Zeus Theos, Adonis, Artemis, and Azzanathkona. Downey 1988a: 126.

73 Naos paintings in Azzanathkona P. R. 5: 138; Aphlad, P.R. 5: 102–103; Adonis, P. R. 7/8: 158–163; Bel, Breasted 1924a; Cumont 1926: 41ff; Heyn 2011; Kaizer 2016. The temple of Atargaris, too, may have had a depiction of Atargatis and Hadad, Dura P. R. 3, 10; Downey 1998: 209. Fragmentary paintings were also found in the sanctuary in M5, Allag 2004.

74 Dura P. R. 7/8: 196–210; the restoration of the paintings by Brown (figure 50 in Dura P. R. 7/8) takes many liberties with the extant evidence: see Downey 2016. On the intention for the god to appear as a statue, see Downey 2008: 414.

75 There are also paintings of sacrifice in the temple of Zeus Theos: Dura P. R. 7/8: 196–208. On arrangement of the paintings in the temple of Bel and their spatial relationships to each other, see Heyn 2011.

76 The other items held by the priest may be a fillet for the animal and something used to stun it. Cumont 1926: 44–49, 66–70.

77 Dura F. R. 3.1.2: 186. Downey suggests the altar in Azzanathkona was large enough to accommodate the sacrifice of a bull, at 1.44 × 0.9 meters, Downey 1988a: 101.

78 On the ram on the relief of Zeus Kyrios, see Dura F. R. 3.1.2: 33, 208; on the animal remains, see Dura P. R. 7/8: 289. Bulls are also sacrificial victims in the synagogue paintings.

79 E.g. on altar 18 in the courtyard to the temple of Aphlad, Dura P. R. 5: 101.

80 E.g. for leafy branches, those held by people in the paintings of Conon and Terentius, figures 2.8 and 2.11. On incense, wine, and fruit offerings, see the fragments from the temple of Zeus Theos: Dura P. R. 7/8: 196–210; Downey 1988a: 129. Graffiti also attest to (e.g.) bread and barley being offered to the gods, P. R. 7/8: 276–277, nos. 904, 905.

81 I.e. the priests on the paintings from the temple of Bel, and the inscriptions referring to priests in the temple of Artemis, Cumont 196: no. 50; P. R. 3: 55, no. D.152.

82 Dura P. R. 7/8: 187–190.

83 Dura P. R. 5: 103; Downey 1988a: 104.

84 Dura P. R. 5: 138–139.

85 The excavators interpreted this room as a *naos* with a storeroom. Dura P. R. 5: 170–171.

86 Further on the installations in Zeus Theos, see Dura P. R. 7/8: 156–187; Downey 1988a: 114.

87 An *oikos* was erected by Alexander the son of Epinicus but it is not clear what this is, other than something erected to a god according to a vow: Dura P. R. 7/8: 130, no. 869. An inscription recording the *oikos* was built by Barnabous, son of Zebidkonos, son of Rhaeibelos, was found in room 8D in the temple of Azzanathkona. Dura P. R. 5, 142–145, no. 453. On the *andron* in the temple of Aphlad, see Dura P. R. 5: 113–116, no. 418; on the *oikodomē* in the temple of Artemis, see Dura P. R. 3: 55–56, no. D.152. The excavator Frank Brown was aware of the diversity of names for the 'chapels' as they appeared in the inscriptions: P. R. 7/8: 156, n20.

88 The *oikos* was built in 161 CE room 8D. Dura P. R. 5: 142–145, no. 453; Downey 1988a: 100.

89 Dura P. R. 7/8: 192. Downey interprets a 'jar stand' in a chapel of Adonis as evidence for storage in such rooms: Downey 1988a: 120; P. R. 7/8: 141. However, these plaster 'coolers' are not well understood, and most have evidence for polishing on the inside, indicative of their use as mortars. *Amphorae* sunk into the floor of chapels may indicate that some did have storage provision, however, as in another chapel in the temple of Adonis, Dura P. R. 7/8: 157.

90 Downey 1988a: 127. E.g. 'chapel' 13 in the 'Dolicheneum' contained the Kyria ('Lady') relief (Dura F. R. 3.1.2: no. 37, 189–190); 6D in Azzanathkona and K in Bel each had niches probably meant for statues, Dura P. R. 5: 139; rooms 4 and 7 in the temple of the Gaddé contained benches and cult images, respectively, and both contained altars, P. R. 7/8: 245, 248.

91 Cumont 1926: 404–409, no. 50.

92 Found on the north side of the courtyard, the inscription is dated to 33 CE: Dura P. R: 3, 55–56, no. D152. Inscriptions no. D.150 and 157 also record rooms called *oikodomē* in the temple of Artemis: Dura P. R. 3: 52–54, 59.

93 The inscription is dated to 37 CE, and was re-used in later fill in the temple. Frye et al. 1955: 129–131, no. 2; Downey 1988a: 105.

94 The presence of the cult relief in this room led Downey to identify it as one of two *foci* of the temple, the other being the more traditional *naos-pronaos* unit formed by rooms 2A and 2B. Downey 1988a: 112. Without the cult relief, this room would have been identified as a 'chapel'. The *andron* inscription is Dura P. R. 5: 113–116, no. 418; the cult relief 106–114, no. 416. Both were found in room 1 of the temple.

95 Dura P. R. 7/8: 146ff, 171ff, no. 875 in rooms 49 and 50 which were incompletely excavated. 181/2 CE.

96 E.g. the term *exedra* also appears in an inscription referring to a room (or an architectural feature) within a religious building, Cumont 1926: 364, no. 9a. See also discussion in Dura P. R. 7/8, 156 n.20. Downey 1988a: 108.

97 Downey 1988a: 126; Yon 2016: 101–102.

98 Dura P. R. 5: 132; the room behind the *salle à gradins* in Azzanathkona, room 10 (called the *naos* by excavators) contained a number of storage jars, although these were recorded to have contained ash, perhaps relating to sacrificial remains. Dura P. R. 5: 171. Yon 2016: 102–103.

99   On the steps in 9W of Azzanathkona, see Dura P. R. 5: 180–200.
100 On the *salle à gradins* in Atargatis, see Dura P. R. 3: 35–36, 42–50; Yon 2016: 103–104.
101 Downey 1988a: 128. The description of these spaces as 'theatral' and 'Syrian' largely, however, relates to Syrian cults outside Syria, e.g. that at Delos. See also Yon 2016: 104–106. College compares small theatres in religious complexes to those at Seleucia, Colledge 1986: 10.
102 Downey 1998: 210. On the function of statues at Dura, see also Chapter 6 of the present volume and Downey 2008; Dirven 2015.
103 A discussion of the placement of the cult reliefs can be found in Downey 1998. The original publication of the Aphlad cult relief is Dura P. R. 5: 106ff; that of Azzanathkona Dura P. R. 5: 171–176. The cult relief of Atargatis was reported to have been found in the courtyard, but its precise location not well described, Dura P. R. 3: 10; Downey 1998: 208–209.
104 On disposition of Aphlad relief and the other features of the wall in which it was found, see Dura P. R. 5: 103–104; Azzanathkona, Dura P. R. 5: 171.
105 Downey 1998: 208. Almost all the men in the *andron* inscription have 'Semitic' names, and several are related, coming from six different families. Dura P. R. 5: 114. In the temple of Azzanathkona, the goddess is named in inscriptions from a variety of rooms.
106 It should be noted, however, that the discovery of the inscription recording the dedication of the *andron* does not necessarily mean the room in which it was found was the *andron*, and indeed from the same room is the cult relief which records construction of a *hieron* to Aphlad, which may refer to the whole complex, or part of it, or only this particular room. On the Aphlad cult relief inscription, see Dura P. R. 5: 112–114, no. 416. The *andron* inscription is Dura P. R. 5: 113–116, no. 418. Downey suggests the whole complex is meant by *heiron* in Downey 1988a: 112.
107 On the unique features of Dura's Mithraeum, see Dirven and McCarty 2014: 129–132.
108 The Latin inscription of Antonius Valentinus: Dura P. R. 7/8: 85–86, no. 847. On the Mithraic graffiti, see also Francis 1975b.
109 On the graffiti in sanctuaries of Dura, see Stern 2012.
110 On the 'subordinate' nature of the Christian and Jewish buildings at Dura that has been claimed by some, and the typical, relatively interiorized, nature of the other religious buildings at Dura, see Dirven 2004: 4.
111 There is the scrap of gospel harmony preserved at Dura (*P. Dura* 10, see p.77), and the more circumstantial evidence of the presence of Syriac and the ROTAS-SATOR square.
112 Dirven 2008: 43.
113 Dura P. R. 2: 16–17, 57–61, 83–86, no. H1.
114 Three inscriptions noted Jupiter Dolichenus: Dura P. R. 9.3: 107–114, nos. 970, 971, and 972 (the first in Latin, the other two in Greek). One dedication to Jupiter Dolichenus was made by vexillations of the IV Scythica and XVI Flavia firma, as had been the Mithraeum. On the inscription and its relationship to vexillations testified elsewhere at Dura, see Edwell 2008: 140.
115 Dura P. R. 9.3: nos. 971 and 972, both in Greek; James 2018.
116 The structure of the temple in X7 is not independently dated, but it would seem to be Roman, because of its similarities to the A1 temple.

117 The building was also labelled a 'Custom's house'. Dura P. R. 3: 37–39; Downey 1988a: 124.
118 Hauser 2012: 1016.
119 P. R. 5: 152ff. On the continuity of use, see James 2018.
120 Downey 1993b, 1995, 1997, 2004a, b, 2012.
121 Frye et al. 1955: 139–140, no. 6.
122 Frye et al. 1955: 144, no. 11.
123 Dura F. R. 3.1.1: no. 7.
124 Downey 2008: 426.
125 On these, see the discussion in Stern 2010: 487–489.
126 Cumont 1926: 409, no. 52.
127 Cumont 1926: 410, no. 53.
128 Graffito in Odeon, Dura P. R. 3: 31.
129 Dura P. R. 3: 51–52, D.149.
130 On the name of the temple of Bel and the variety of gods within it, see Kaizer 2016.
131 Dura P. R. 2: 91–93, no. H4.
132 Dura P. R. 2: 86–90, no. H4.
133 Cumont 1926: 122–134, plates 40–48; Dirven 1999: 295–302.
134 Downey 2007: 112–113. Downey also notes the presence of further altars testifying to Roman military worship within the temple and nearby.
135 Downey 1988a: 110.
136 Dura P. R. 7/8: 318, no. 916. Kaizer 2009b: 158; Hillers and Cussini 1996: no. 1067.
137 Dirven 1999: 41–66.
138 Dirven 1999, 2011: 204; Downey 2007: 96–102.
139 Downey 1988a: 126, 2007: 100.
140 On the religious communities of Dura, see especially Downey 2007; Kaizer 2009b; Dirven 2011.
141 On remembrance graffiti at Dura, see Baird 2011b, 2016b; Stern 2012.
142 Bessac 1988; Bessac, Abdul Massih, and Valat 1997; Bessac 2005a.
143 Leriche 1997a, b, 2003, 2004.
144 Leriche 2012b.
145 On Dura's place in the Arsacid political system and problems with dating, see Gaslain 2012.
146 For a summary of the Franco-Syrian expedition's discoveries with relation to the fortifications, see Leriche 2012b: 15–20. A summary of the finds related to the fortifications by the Yale expedition was written by von Gerkan, in Dura P. R. 7/8: 4–61.
147 The disappearance of most of the eastern edge of the fortification walls into the Euphrates valley makes precise measurement of the ancient perimeter of the city on the site impossible. The surviving circuit measures *c.* 2150 meters, not including the citadel walls inside the city itself.
148 On the conservation and restoration of Dura's fortification walls (using the example of those of the redoubt/strategeion), see Mouton 1992; Bessac 2005b.
149 Gelin 2005.
150 Dura P. R. 7/8, 48; Leriche 1986.
151 James 2015: 329.
152 Al-Mahmoud and Leriche 1992: 12–16; Gelin, Leriche, and Abdul Massih 1997.
153 Abdul Massih 1997: 50.

154 On Franco-Syrian cleaning of the south gate, Leriche and Al Ajji 2004: 16; Bertolino and Abd el Aziz 2005.

155 The *porta aquaria* is mentioned in *P. Dura* 106. On the river gate placement, see Leriche 1997a: 201–205. For a full discussion of the river gate, see James 2018.

156 Downey 1988a: 112. On the tower 15 relationship to the temple of Aphlad, see Dura P. R. 7/8: 35.

157 Dura P. R. 1: 6–7; Dura P. R. 3: 17; Dura P. R. 4: 3–4, 55–68, no. 167.

158 James 2015: 328–345. It has not been possible, however, to ground-truth these observations due to the current conflict in Syria.

159 James 2015: 342.

160 Leriche 1986: 79–80; Gelin, Leriche, and Abdul Massih 1997.

161 Leriche 1993.

162 The primary initial publications were in Dura P. R. 6: 188–205; Du Mesnil du Buisson 1937, 1933, 1934. The Franco-Syrian expedition's work was also revealing of some aspects of the Sasanian assault on the site, Gelin, Leriche, and Abdul Massih 1997. The siege works have been restudied, drawing on these works together with archival and field evidence, by James 2005, 2011.

163 The Sasanian camp was indicated by dotted line by the French army map of Dura, reproduced e.g. Rostovtzeff 1938, figure 4. On aerial photographs, see Kennedy and Riley 1990: 109–114.

164 Dura P. R. 9.1: 3–27. On the antefix, see Dura P. R. 9.1: 165.

165 On the niches and their markings, see Dura P. R. 9.1: 99–102 ('building A'), 168–176, nos. 936–938. Cleaning and re-study of the building was undertaken by the more recent Franco-Syrian expedition: Coqueugniot 2012a, 2015, 2016: 128–129.

166 E.g. along the main street in front of block B8. On changes at Dura under the Romans but lack of colonnaded streets like other Roman sites in the east, see Downey 2000: 170.

167 On the inns, shops, and food establishments that were classed as houses, see Baird 2014: 186–200.

168 Baird 2007a: 415–423.

169 Baird 2007a: 423–432.

170 About three-quarters of identified shops are in the agora section of the city; the rest are elsewhere. A total of 164 shops were excavated by the Yale expedition, enumerated in Table 1 of Baird 2007a.

171 On block B2, Allara 2002. Kilns have also been found in the excavation of block C11 by the Franco-Syrian expedition. See also F. R. 4.1.3: 2; Baird 2014: 184–186.

172 Brown's description of the market implies the Roman date is due to the orderliness of the structure in contrast to the oriental disorder of the Parthian-era 'bazaar'; I am less convinced it is distinct from Arsacid-era structures in this part of the site, in character or plan. Dura P. R. 9.1: 62–64; Baird 2007b.

173 Butcher 2003: 247.

174 Dura P. R. 4: 72–76, no. 169.

175 A full study of the Roman military base can be found in James 2018, following new fieldwork and archival work, including James 2007.

176 Dura P. R. 5: 201–237.

177 Dura P. R. 5: 218–220, no. 556.

178 On the perimeter of the base, see James 2007: 36ff.

179 James 2018. Leriche et al., however, see discontinuities in the temples within the military base: Leriche, Coqueugniot, and de Pontbriand 2011: 29–30.

180   On this 'pre-principia shrine', James 2018.

181   On the gates, see James 2007.

182   Dura P. R. 5: 235–237; Haynes 2013: 152; Baird 2014: 151–152. House D5-F on the
      south house of the site did, however, have a peristyle courtyard in an earlier phase,
      so the feature was not entirely unknown locally.

183   Dura P. R. 6: 4–49; Baird 2014: 134.

184   Baird 2014: 116–126.

185   Baird 2011c: 240.

186   Baird 2012b.

187   On the Roman military granaries, see *P. Dura* 106 and 108.

188   The original publication of the amphitheatre was in Dura P. R. 6: 68–77. On Dura's
      position as the easternmost example, see Dodge 2009.

189   Dura P. R. 6: 76.

190   Dura P. R. 6: 77–80, no. 630.

191   On the baths of Dura, see Dura P. R. 6: 49–105; Koloski-Ostrow 2011.

192   On the F3 bath, see Dura P. R. 6: 49–83. It is there dated as Parthian; on its Roman
      dating, see Pollard 2004: 132–143. James 2018 suggests the F3 baths are Trajanic in date.

193   Dura P. R. 6: 102–104.

194   On e.g. the use of vaults of fired bricks as military technology, and the introduction
      of vaulting tubes, see Lancaster 2015: 66, 110–111. The mosaic inscription from C3,
      however, was not in Latin, as the other military inscriptions, but in Greek: Dura P. R.
      6: 104–105, no. 631.

195   A second water-lifting device is presumed to have existed near block B2 to supply
      the C3 baths, but only the pipes leading towards the bath were excavated. Dura P. R.
      6: 100–101.

196   Dura P. R. 9.3: 1–96; Edwell 2008: 128–135; Baird 2014: 148–151. The 'Roman
      palace' name follows that of James 2018.

197   Dura P. R. 9.3: 30–40, nos. 945–950. The *tragodos* (member of a tragic chorus or
      performer of tragedy) is partially restored in no. 948.

198   Household account: no. 958; Vergilian graffito, no. 960.

Chapter 6

1   Some classes of Durene objects have been the subjects of final reports: the ceramics,
    lamps, terracottas, bronze objects, glass, textiles, stone and plaster sculpture (and,
    as a separate volume, the Heracles sculptures), coins, and the arms, armour, and
    military equipment.

2   As noted by Sherwin White and Kuhrt, 'It has long been customary to search the
    middle east microscopically for any evidence of something Greek – almost to the
    exclusion of the existing cultures'. Sherwin-White and Kuhrt 1993: 141.

3   There was no explicit collection strategy, and what was being collected changed
    over time and depending on the part of the site and the ware: green-glazed sherds
    were initially kept, because they were seen to be fine ware, but the numbers proved
    too burdensome, and only new types (forms) or those 'sufficient' to give the
    reconstruction were collected. The complete vessels were split between Yale and
    Damascus; the sherds were held in the dig house and apparently later dumped on

site. Dura F. R. 4.1.1: 1. Large storage jars were also left *in situ* or on site, not seen as being worth the effort to transport: Dura F. R. 4.1.3: viii.

4   Baird 2012c.

5   Dura F. R. 4.1.2: 2–6 on the Greek imports; Hannestad 1983: vol. 2.1 and 2.2, 95.

6   Alabe 1990, 2005, 2012. See p.117.

7   Dura F. R. 4.1.3: 1. Just over 400 vessels were catalogued.

8   Dura F. R. 4.1.3: 2, 43; Allara 1992, 1994; Baird 2014: 166.

9   Dura F. R. 4.1.1, Punnett Peters 1897: vol. I. First Campaign; Debevoise 1934; Valtz 1984, 1991, 2002.

10   Dura F. R. 4.1.1: 6.

11   Dura F. R. 4.1.3: 58–59; Bartl, Schneider, and Böhme 1995; Vokaer 2009, 2010: 116–117.

12   Dura F. R. 4.1.2:14–16; Pollard 2004: 124–125.

13   This methodology continues in the Near East; see the critique of the ceramic catalogue of Jebel Khalid in Baird 2015.

14   On the types of information which can be gleaned from coins, such as issues relating to context or identity, see now e.g. Howgego 1995; Howgego, Heuchert, and Burnett 2007; Lockyear 2007, 2012.

15   Dura F. R. 6: ix.

16   Bellinger, in his coin report, noted that contextual information was not important because ' … in no case that I have found is the place of finding of importance for the identification of the coin'. Dura F. R. 6: ix.

17   On the date of 113 BCE, see Dura F. R. 6: 200–201; on the date of the fall of the city from numismatic evidence, see Dura F. R. 6:181; Bellinger 1943: 65–71.

18   The total is that given by Bellinger: Dura F. R. 6: ix.

19   Newell and Bellinger believed that Dura minted its own coins for a time, although this was based on types which were not found elsewhere and their poor quality; Bellinger and Newell 1940; Newell 1941.

20   Edwell 2008: 100–101.

21   E.g. *P. Dura* 20 and 23.

22   Dura F. R. 6: 205.

23   Clark 1978.

24   On the perception of the coins of Roman Syria as 'foreign', see Burnett 2007; Butcher 2012.

25   James 1985; MacDonald 1986; Baird 2012a.

26   Hoards 1 and 10; Dura F. R. 6: 165–166, 175–176.

27   Dura F. R. 6: 177, Hoard 11; Dura P. R. 7/8: 422ff; Dura P. R. 9.1: 259–260. A hoard with Zeugma coins has been linked to the house in the agora which was probably used a brothel. On the 'brothel' of Dura, see Baird 2014: 196–199.

28   Bland 1991: 11.

29   On the textiles at Dura, main examples were published in Dura F. R. 4.2; Cumont 1926: 251–253. N.B. a number of the textiles in the catalogue come from the 'Citadel Necropolis', the burials there probably post-date the occupation of Dura as an urban environment.

30   Most textiles remain at Yale; others were in the collection of the Trocadero museum in Paris (now the *Museum de l'homme*). Dura F. R. 4.2: vii.

31   Baird 2014: 183–184. On the graffiti relating to textiles, see especially those of house B8-H, including discussion in Ruffing 2007: 402–404.

32 The clothing worn is also attested to in the paintings; on dress practices at Dura, see Baird 2016a.

33 Gansser-Burckhardt 1953; Kaplan 1971. On footwear in the Roman army, see van Driel-Murray 1986a, b, 2001.

34 On headdresses and marital status Dura, see Klaver 2016: 380.

35 Baird 2016a.

36 On the arms, armour, and military equipment, see Dura F. R. 7.

37 Dura F. R. 7: 260–262.

38 Baird 2016a: 39–40.

39 Baird 2014: 121–122.

40 Among the exceptional glassware is a fragment with the painted inscription *Thetis*, YUAG 1931.588.a, from house C7-F; Grossman 2002: 18. Quite a few cut-glass items were published from the same house, which may indicate only that particular attention was paid during its excavation. The glass vessels of Dura were published in Dura F. R. 4.5, which catalogued almost 800 items, many of which were not given a find-spot within the site. There is also a problem with dating the material: Hellenistic examples were recorded, and Clairmont divided the rest of the glass into Early and Middle Imperial (Roman) periods. There is in this characterization a false lacuna for Parthian-era Dura, much of which falls into the 'Early' Imperial material in this framework.

41 Dura F. R. 5: 1.

42 Dura F. R. 4.5: 56–86.

43 Grossman 2011: 278. On the context of Dura's early glass, see Jackson-Tal 2004.

44 Grossman 2011: 277.

45 The lamps were catalogued in Dura F. R. 4.3. According to that final report, almost 500 lamps were recorded. N.B. the total numbers of different lamp types given in the introduction to the *Final Report* do not match the number in its catalogue. Baur created his own typology for Dura, eschewing the (still) standard typologies of e.g. Loeschcke 1919.

46 Baird 2012c: 37–38.

47 These are F. R. 4.3 types 1 (Attic) and 2 (Hellenistic); the find-spots of the latter were in the Citadel and adjacent blocks B2 and C3. Type 2, the 'Hellenistic' lamps are a type found throughout the Mediterranean and Mesopotamia; some were given quite early dates (third century BCE) on comparison with Corinth and Antioch.

48 F. R. 4.3: type 3.

49 These are types 4 and 5, 256 total catalogued lamps (the chief difference between these two groups is the lack of handle in group 5). Bailey believes some groups of the local types came from Palmyra: Bailey 1988: vol. 3. Roman provincial lamps, 283. Moulds were found at Dura for these types, made of both clay and of plaster (F. R. 4.3: nos. 36, 37, and 122). Other evidence for local production is more circumstantial, but includes the inscription on a lamp (made pre-firing) of the name of a man attested elsewhere on site. F. R. 4.3: 23.

50 The 'Syrian' Roman lamps were type 6, the Mesopotamian, type 8; 57 and 52 examples, respectively, were catalogued. On the possibility they were 'Syrian' imitations of Roman prototypes, see Dura F. R. 4.3: 45. Bronze lamps of Roman type were also found, F. R. 4.3: nos. 422–454.

51 Harris 1980.

52   N.B., however, the types of jewelry and ceramics that occur in the necropolis are of a different profile from that within the city, e.g. a large proportion of table amphora from the necropolis. On the jewellery, see Baird 2016a.

53   On the gold leaves and gold sheets placed on faces, see Dura P. R. 9.2: 22, 114–116. Similar objects were found in Parthian graves at Assur, Nineveh, and Ur. See e.g. the gold 'spectacles' like those at Dura in Curtis 1976. Gold leaf wreaths are found in funerary contexts throughout the Hellenistic world.

54   Double documents of Arsacid era found at Dura: *P. Dura* 18–22 and 24.

55   Dura F. R. 5.1: 191; *P. Dura* 54.

56   E.g. the double document with five sealings, dated to 87 CE, *P. Dura* 18. On the intaglios, see Guiraud 1992.

57   An archival report was written, however: Russell 1976.

58   These tended to be published only in passing, or if they had an inscription. Glazed altars and *thymiateria* were not included in report on green-glazed pottery: FR 4.1.1: 1. Altars were noted in preliminary reports, sometimes only as the background for their inscriptions, but they have not been systematically catalogued or studied, although Downey notes a few in Dura F. R. 3.1.2: 141–145. Fifty-three altars of known find-spot, made of stone, plaster, or ceramic, were listed in the object registers (which cover only the 5th–10th seasons of work); only some of these were published.

59   E.g. knife blade from the temple of Artemis, G679; a gold leaf from the temple of Atargatis, K236; terracotta animal from Azzanathkona, E1012 (YUAG photo Dam 87, a quadruped, not listed in Downey 2003.).

60   E.g. Colledge 1977, 1986; Mathiesen 1992. Colledge puts 'Parthian' art in quotes, and outlines well some of the difficulties in understanding this hybrid style in Colledge 1986: 12–14.

61   Frontality seems to have emerged in north Syria and Mesopotamia in the first century BCE and continues until the Sasanian period, or about the period of Roman power in Syria itself. Dura F. R. 3.1.2: 287; Drijvers 1990: 69.

62   Rostovtzeff 1935b. On the nature of Parthian Dura, see Baird 2014: 21–23.

63   Rostovtzeff 1938: 90. Indeed, for Rostovtzeff, Parthian art had its roots in Central Asia.

64   Hauser 2012: 1018–1019; Invernizzi 2011: 189–190.

65   Invernizzi 2011: 191. Invernizzi shows that 'Parthian' material at Old Nisa is a continuation of Hellenistic forms.

66   Dirven 2016.

67   Perkins 1973: 35–36.

68   E.g. with respect to the depiction of nude bodies, Perkins 1973: 114. On 'Durene style', see Perkins 1973: 114–126. Her summary of Durene painting and sculpture was that the style was 'characterized by frontal, two-dimensional, static, schematically drawn figures set in the available space with little or no meaningful visual connection'. Perkins 1973: 117.

69   Perkins 1973: 116.

70   Perkins 1973: 117.

71   Greek origins: Will 1959. Greek via the descendants of Greek culture Schlumberger 1960. Mesopotamia, in particular Babylonia (as College and Perkins, above); from Arab tribes of the Syrian and Mesopotamian desert, via the form of baetyls, Pietrzykowski 1985: 58–59.; from traditional Syrian chapels, Drijvers 1990: 75. On the historiography of the debate around Parthian art, see Dirven 2016: 68–73.

72   Avi-Yonah 1961; Pietrzykowski 1985; Hauser 2012: 1018.

73   Dirven 2015: 255.

74 Rostovtzeff 1935b: 238. Rostovtzeff traces frontality to Iranian nomads in southern Russia in the third century BCE. Rostovtzeff 1935b: 239. Ever the modernizer, Rostovtzeff also saw Iranian elements of Durene art as part of a 'nationalization' of Parthian art: Rostovtzeff 1935b: 295. Hopkins saw the people depicted in Durene paintings as 'purely Syrian and the frontality … due to Eastern influence' Hopkins 1936: 3. The architectural background of the paintings, however, was for Hopkins Hellenistic: Hopkins 1936: 5, 1941. For Downey's assessment of frontality in Durene art, see Dura F. R. 3.1.2: 283–287.

75 Welles, Dura F. R. 3.1.1: vii; on the sculpture as bad imitation, this comment notes particularly the sculptures of Hercules and Aphrodite. Dura F. R. 3.1.2: 293. One of these issues – around technical quality – can be explained in part with regard to the available material, the course-grained and friable local stone which did not take fine carving. Even the painted programme of the Mithraeum is derided as 'no great artistic achievement' in Dura P. R. 7/8: 104.

76 Quote from Dura F. R. 3.1.2: 277.

77 Wharton 1995: 20.

78 Dirven 2016: 79.

79 Perkins 1973: 37.

80 The painted reproductions of Gute are not always clearly marked as such, and they have in many publications taken on the status of the original paintings themselves. See, for instance, the use of Gute's paintings (obfuscated with the label 'exhibition photograph') in Peppard 2016.

81 At Yale, see e.g. the work done on the baptistery paintings and the Terentius painting. Terentius, YUAG 1931.386, Hoffman and Brody 2011: plate 37, and on restoration of Dura material at Yale, see Snow 2011; on the Conon scene in the Damascus museum and its restoration, see Leriche 2012a. According to Hopkins, the paintings at Dura were not true fresco (made on wet plaster), but painted in tempera on dry plaster.

82 Heyn 2011: 228. The situation in Bel with a great number of paintings and graffiti is mirrored in all temples of Dura where the building's preservation was sufficient to allow these things to survive. The dating of the painting of Conon is not secure: dates from the first to third century CE; see Dirven 2016: 80 n. 64.

83 The Otes painting was not from the *naos-pronaos* as were the others, but came from room K, a chapel off the courtyard of the temple. Cumont 1926: 72–73. For a photograph of what remained when the Yale expedition documented the paintings published by Cumont, see e.g. YUAG d295.

84 Heyn 2011: 221–223, 2016.

85 So, while the paintings of Dura are characterized as depicting sacrifice, this is true only of the Conon and Terentius scenes from Bel and probably the temple of Zeus Theos. Elsner 2001.

86 The painting was reconstructed by Frank Brown. The paintings from this room were *in situ* only along the very base of the wall; the rest 'exist solely in the form of several thousand small fragments', Dura P. R. 7/8: 196. On the problems of his reconstructions throughout Dura, see Downey 2016.

87 Dura P. R. 7/8: 202; on families and religious buildings at Dura, see also Yon 2016: 112.

88 The family relationship is attested by several of the fragments, one naming Bargates son of Zabinus and another one
 – naus, son of Bargates.

89 Dirven 2016: 81–82.

90 Dura P. R. 7/8: 202–208.
91 Dirven 2016: 80–81.
92 Dirven 2016: 81–82.
93 Dirven 2004: 11–12.
94 Dura P. R. 7/8: Lintel inscription from Zeus Theos (114CE), no. 886; dedication of chapel (120/121 CE) no. 880, both naming a Selecus as the dedicant.
95 See Chapter 4; Moralee 2004.
96 Dirven 2004: 12. Downey also had proposed that the temple of Zeus Theos was used only by a particular family: Downey 1988a: 114–115.
97 On the Bel paintings and patriarchal authority, see Wharton 1995: 62.
98 Dirven 2016: 82–83.
99 Baird 2014: 74–75. Rostovtzeff believed the paintings in M7-W were funerary: Rostovtzeff 1935b: 274. The surviving portion of the painting is at Yale, YUAG 1938.59999.1147; see Brody and Hoffman 2014: plate 178.
100 Dura P. R. 7/8: 62–134. On the graffiti, Francis 1975a.
101 Dura P. R. 7/8: 105–110.
102 Dirven and McCarty 2014: 130–132. For paintings in a Mithraeum elsewhere in Syria, at Hawarte, see Gawlikowski 2007.
103 Dura F. R. 8.2: 40–88.
104 Peppard 2016. On the interpretation of the processional scene of women from the baptistery, see Klaver 2012.
105 Dura F. R. 8.1: 34–38.
106 On the panels and their different readings, see Hachlili 1998: 98–135. In addition to scenes based on biblical chapters include elements from other sources, including folk stories. Hachlili 1998: 194.
107 The panels were given alphanumeric codes based on their position: the first letter denotes which wall (W for west, N for north, etc), the second letter which register (A for the top, B the middle, C the bottom), and a number based on a left-to-right ordering on whichever wall it is on (e.g. WC1 is the leftmost panel on the bottom register of the west wall).
108 Hachlili 1998: 136.
109 Hachlili 1998: 136–142. Further on the dress in the synagogue paintings, see Goldman 1992, 2001.
110 Hachlili 1998: 177.
111 Such tiles were found in houses in blocks L7 and D5; Stern 2010: 489–490.
112 Stern 2010: 496–497.
113 Stern 2010: 502.
114 Goodenough 1964: vol. 9–11; Weitzmann 1971; Gutmann 1992.
115 Elsner 2001; Dirven 2004; Rajak 2011, 2013.
116 Dura P. R. 6: 63–67.
117 Dirven 2016: 83.
118 Cumont 1925; Arnaud 1988, 1989; Hălmagi 2015. Discovered by Cumont, the 'shield map' is now in Paris at the Bibliothèque nationale de France (Ms. *Suppl. Gr.* 13554[2] V; viewable online: http://gallica.bnf.fr/ark:/12148/btv1b105388698).
119 Baird 2014, figures 3.3 and 3.19.
120 Dura P. R. 9.3: 21, 23, 24–25.
121 The painted victory, Dura P. R. 2, 8; YUAG 1929.288; Hoffman and Brody 2011, plate 2. The painted Latin inscription on a wooden *tabella ansata*, Dura P. R. 2: 148–151.
122 Rostovtzeff and Little 1933.

123   Rostovtzeff 1935b: 284.
124   Rostovtzeff 1935b: 286. A Sasanian date is accepted in Dura F. R. 7: 42; Goldman and Little 1980; De Waele 2004. This dating is largely based on the 'Iranian' character of the dress and horse fittings to identify a possible historical Sasanian battle. I am unconvinced (there is no reason a painting depicting Sasanians could not belong to Dura's Roman era), but it is possible and there is a dearth of good comparanda. The house in which it was found was near the centre of the city, adjacent to a triumphal arch, from which there are no definitive Sasanian coins or small finds (unlike, e.g., in the siege mines where distinctive Sasanian material culture was found).
125   Of course, it could then be argued that the battle scenes in graffiti are also Sasanian. On the pictorial graffiti including mounted warriors, see Goldman 1999. See also Dura F. R. 7: 40–43.
126   The pictorial graffiti from Dura were catalogued by Goldman 1999. They appear in the corpus of Langner 2001.
127   On the graffiti of Dura, see Baird 2011b; Stern 2012; Baird 2016b.
128   Dirven and McCarty 2014: 130.
129   Rives 1999.
130   Elsner 2001.
131   Panel WB4. Elsner 2001: 282.
132   Du Mesnil du Buisson 1939: 77.
133   Dirven 2004: 8; Stern 2012.
134   The sculptures were published in two volumes by Susan Downey, one on the Heracles sculptures, and the other on the rest of the stone and plaster sculpture, Dura F. R. 3.1.1 and 3.1.2. In addition to Downey's catalogue, a relief of Bel was found by the Franco-Syrian expedition; see Rouselle 2005.
135   Dura F. R. 3.1.2: 5.
136   Ten were catalogued by Downey in Dura F. R. 3.1.2; a further cult relief to Bel has been discovered by the Franco-Syrian team in block M5, Leriche and Al Mahmoud 1994: 412–415. The reliefs that are not certainly religious in subject might have been so, depicting unidentified male/female figures. The idea of the 'cult relief' is that of Will 1955.
137   On the formula, see Moralee 2004.
138   Dura P. R. 1: 65–68; Dura F. R. 3.1.2: no. 9.
139   Downey 2008: 415.
140   Dura P. R. 5: 171.
141   Downey 1998: 209.
142   Downey 1988a: 95, 2008: 417. Dura F. R. 3.1.2: 67–70, 209–210, nos. 50–51.
143   On statues depicted in religious paintings at Dura, see Downey 2008: 429–433. Otes painting in Cumont 1926: plate 55.
144   Dura P. R. 5: 153–156.
145   Dura F. R. 3.1.2: 149–152.
146   As pointed out by Dirven, the lack of extant three-dimensional cult statues is not necessarily an indication they did not exist: Dirven 2015: 259.
147   'in the end … the dearth of sculpture in the round from the site reinforces the idea that such three-dimensional cult statues, as opposed to paintings or reliefs, were largely foreign to religious practices and worship at Dura-Europos' Downey 2008: 435. Downey had indeed earlier noted that even most three-dimensional sculptures in sanctuaries were found against walls: Dura F. R. 3.1.2: 2.
148   Dirven 2015: 266–267.

149   Inscriptions preserved do indicate the name of dedicants in some instances: Dura F. R. 3.1.1: 38.
150   Seyrig 1944; Christides 1982; Kaizer 2000; Downey 2002.
151   Baird 2014: 177–179.
152   At least four are from the temple of Zeus Megistos; two from the temple of Atargatis was found in the cistern there, perhaps relating to an earlier cult or desanctifcation of the temple. Dura F. R. 3.1.1: 37, 39. On Hercules as *synnaos theos*, see Dura F. R. 3.1.1: 59–61.
153   Dura F. R. 3.1.1: no. 27.
154   Arsu in Adonis, Dura P. R. 7/8: 165–167; Dura F. R. 3.1.2: no. 43. In Zeus Megistos, Dura F. R. 3.1.2: no. 42 and 44.
155   The goddess with mural crown in the temple of Adonis: Dura P. R. 7/8: 163–165; Dura F. R. 3.1.2: no. 33.
156   Dura F. R. 3.1.2: nos. 11–30; on finding places, 168–169. A mould for a small relief of Aphrodite was also found in C5 by the Franco-Syrian expedition: Queyrel 2012.
157   Dura F. R. 3.1.2: 46–90.
158   Dura F. R. 3.1.2: 91–115.
159   Dura F. R. 3.1.2: 116–130; Baird 2014: 77–78.
160   Downey counted thirty-six examples of such blocks, although the precise number is unclear due to duplicate entries in records made by Hopkins. The blocks are much deeper than the normal relief sculpture, perhaps indicating that they functioned in a different way and were not meant to be set into walls.
161   Dura F. R. 3.1.2: 134–140.
162   Dirven 2016: 77–79. Downey discusses the chronology, including the dated sculpture, in Dura F. R. 3.1.2: 227ff. The different qualities of the stone have been used in the past to differentiate imports, etc., but the different attributes would have also been perceptible in antiquity. On the different stones, see Dura F. R. 3.1.2: 4.
163   Dura F. R. 3.1.2: vi, 3.
164   Dura P. R. 5: 83.
165   Cumont 1926: 369–372 nos. 12, 385–387; Downey 1988a: 109; Dirven 2015: 266; Downey 2008: 431.
166   Dura F. R. 3.1.2: 3.
167   Dura F. R. 3.1.2: 1.
168   Female statue from the *salle à gradins* in the temple of Atargatis, Dura F. R. 3.1.2: no. 108 (published in Cumont 1926, 205–206 and plates 73, 79, its current whereabouts are unknown).
169   Julia Domna inscription, given by the *boule*, found in the courtyard of the temple of Artemis, Dura P. R. 3: 51–52, no. D149; YUAG 1930.626. The Greek inscription was presumed to be part of a statue base, but at just over six inches thick could not have supported a statue on its own. On that recording Lucius Verus, see Cumont 1926: 410, no. 53.
170   Dura F. R. 3.1.2: no. 76; YUAG 1938.5350.
171   The terracotta figurines and plaques have been published outside of the final reports series, in Downey 2003.
172   For a particularly unusual and fine example within the Dura terracotta assemblage, e.g. the Hermes figure from the necropolis, see Downey 2003: no. 57. Downey believed most of the mould-made examples to be imported, probably from Syria due to their Near Eastern iconography, and noted the strong relationship between the coroplastic production in Palmyra and Dura. Downey 1996, 2003: 21. A mould

found at Dura, for a plaque depicting a warrior in 'Parthian' dress, indicates there was certainly some local production, Downey 2003: 74–75, no. 31.

173 Downey 2003: 15, 140–141; Baird 2014: 232.

174 E.g. an example which seems to have been deliberately broken and deposited, Baird 2014: 180–181.

175 Downey 2003: 13, 2008: 433.

176 Downey 1996: 253.

177 Downey 2003: 14.

178 Downey 2003: 17–19; Goldman 1990.

179 Baird 2014: 73–74, 283. Cumont 1926: 226–237. The 'Orthonobazus' frieze is now in the Louvre; on the architectural mouldings of Dura more broadly (including carved stone examples), see Shoe 1943. Further examples were excavated by the Franco-Syrian expedition, Allag 2012.

180 Dirven 2016: 84.

181 Hauser 2012: 1019.

182 On the third space and creolization at Dura (drawing on the work of Stuart Hall), see Sommer 2016. For the application of the third way in a different Roman provincial context, see Rothe 2012. For the application of creolization in another Roman provincial context, see Webster 2001.

183 On the history of the Dura collection at Yale, see Brody 2016.

184 The Yale Art Gallery can be searched online at: http://artgallery.yale.edu/collection/search. The photographs of the expedition, including many of the objects and art made in the field, are also available online (links correct in December 2016): http://www.sscommons.org/openlibrary/#3|collections|7730479||Yale20University20 Art20Gallery3A20Dura2DEuropos20Collection|||

Chapter 7

1 Rostovtzeff 1935b: 295.

2 Millar 1993: 469–470. Millar is justifiably followed by many, including Elsner, who writes that 'to judge by the preponderance of epigraphic evidence – the city's basic culture was Greek'. Elsner 2001: 275.

3 On the periodization, see especially Edwell 2008, 2013.

4 On the chronology of Dura's art, see especially Dirven 2016.

5 Dura F. R. 3.1.1: vii.

6 Kaizer 2013: 80–82. Dura F. R. 3.1.2: 193–194, no. 1.

7 I am not suggesting that each of these elements came directly from a particular 'source', only that a multitude of traditions underlie Durene visual language at this time.

8 Dura P. R. 5: 114–116, no. 418.

9 Pierce Kelley 1994.

10 22 June 1922, 'Art of Third Century in Syrian Ruins', *New York Times*, 7.

11 Harmanşah 2015.

12 De Cesari 2015.

13 Casana and Panahipour 2014; Casana 2015.

14 On looting as a human right (in lieu of other economic resources), see Hardy 2015.

15 Brodie 2015.

16 This is not to say that some Western archaeologists have not been doing this in Syria
    already: see e.g. Loosley 2005. The Franco-Syrian expedition under Pierre Leriche
    has also, of course, been a joint one and put considerable resource into engaging with
    Syrian archaeologists, including training, and into stabilizing and curating the site.

BIBLIOGRAPHY

Abdul Massih, J. 1997: 'La porte secondaire à Doura-Europos', P. Leriche and M. Gelin (eds), *Doura-Europos Études* 4, 47–54.

Abdul Massih, J. 2005: 'Etude ethno-archaeologique sur la fabrication du Djousse dans la valee de l'Euphrate: Doura-Europos (Salhiye) et Deir ez-Zor', P. Leriche, M. Gelin, and A. Dandrau (eds), *Doura Europos-Études V, 1993–1997*, 199–211.

Abt, J. 1996: 'Toward a Historian's Laboratory: The Breasted-Rockefeller Museum Projects in Egypt, Palestine, and America', *Journal of the American Research Center in Egypt* 33, 173–194.

Abt, J. 2011: *American Egyptologist: The Life of James Henry Breasted and the Creation of his Oriental Institute*, Chicago.

Adams, J. N. 2003: *Bilingualism and the Latin Language*, Oxford.

Alabe, F. 1990: 'La céramique de Doura-Europos', *Doura Europos-Études* [III], Syria LXIX, 1992, 49–63.

Alabe, F. 2005: 'Céramiques hellénistiques d'Europos à Doura: hasards ou cohérances?', *Doura Europos Études* 5, 163–198.

Alabe, F. 2012: 'Vaisselle d'Europos Hellénistique: la carrière en contrebas de la rue principale et son comblement', P. Leriche, G. Coqueugniot, and S. Du Pontbriand (eds), *Europos-Doura Varia* 1, 161–184.

Albright, W. F. 1935: 'A Summary of Archaeological Research during 1934 in Palestine, Transjordan, and Syria', *American Journal of Archaeology* 39, 137–148.

Allag, C. 2004: 'La sanctuaire de la rue principale (M5) de Doura-Europos: la décoration murale', in *Doura-Europos Etudes V, 1994–1997*, Paris, 99–112.

Allag, C. 2012: 'Graffiti et corniches à Europos-Doura', P. Leriche, S. De Pontbriand, and G. Coqueugniot (eds), *Europos-Doura Varia* 1, 124–141.

Allara, A. 1992: 'L'îlot des potiers et les fours à Doura-Europos. Étude Préliminaire', *Dura-Europos Études 1990*, Syria, Tome LXIX, 101–120.

Allara, A. 1994: 'Osservazioni sulle fornaci per ceramica di Dura-Europos sull' Euphrate', *Rivista Di Archeologia* 18, 129–134.

Allara, A. 2002: *Problemi di Architettura domestica a Dura-Europos sull'Euphrate. L'Isolato Dei Vasai (B2)*, Naples.

Allen, S. H. 2011: *Classical Spies: American Archaeologists with the OSS in World War II Greece*, Ann Arbor.

Al-Mahmoud, A., and Leriche, P. 1992: 'Bilan des campagnes 1998–1990 à Doura-Europos', *Doura-Europos Études 1990*, Syria, Tome LXIX, 3–28.

Ameling, W. 2006: 'Strategos. II Hellenistic States', in H. Cancik and H. Schneider (eds), *Brill's New Pauly*.

Andrade, N. J. 2013: *Syrian Identity in the Greco-Roman World*, Cambridge.

Arnaud, P. 1986: 'Doura Europos, microcosme grec ou rouage de l'administration arsacide? Modes de maîtrise du territoire et intégration des notables locaux dans la pratique administrative des rois arsacides', *Doura Europos Études 1986, Syria, Tome LVIII*, 135–155.

Arnaud, P. 1988: 'Observations sur l'orginal du fragment de carte du pseudo-bouclier de Doura-Europos', *Revue des études anciennes* 90, 151–162.

Arnaud, P. 1989: 'Une deuxième lecture du "bouclier" de Doura-Europos', *Comptes Rendus. Académie des Inscriptions et Belles Lettres* 113, 373–392.

Arnaud, P. 1997: 'Les salles W9 et W10 du temple d'Azzanathkôna à Doura-Europos: développement historique et topographie familiale d'une "sale aux gradins"', *Doura Europos Études IV*, 117–143.

Avi-Yonah, M. 1961: *Oriental Art in Roman Palestine*. Studi semitici 5, Rome.

Bagnall, R. S. 2007: 'Charles Bradford Welles (1901–1969)', in M. Capasso (ed.), *Hermae. Scholars and Scholarship in Papyrology*, Pisa, 283–286.

Bagnall, R. S. 2011: *Everyday Writing in the Graeco-Roman East*, Vol. 69, Berkeley.

Bailey, D. M. 1988: *A Catalogue of the Lamps in the British Museum*, Vol. 3. Roman Provincial Lamps, London.

Baird, J. A. 2006: 'Housing and Households at Dura-Europos: A Study in Identity on Rome's Eastern Frontier', Leicester.

Baird, J. A. 2007a: 'Shopping, Eating and Drinking at Dura-Europos: Reconstructing Contexts', in L. Lavan, E. Swift, and T. Putzeys (eds), *Objects in Context, Objects in Use: Material Spatiality in Late Antiquity*, Leiden, 413–437.

Baird, J. A. 2007b: 'The Bizarre Bazaar: Early Excavations in the Roman East and Problems of Nomenclature', *TRAC '06: Theoretical Roman Archaeology Conference Proceedings*, Oxford, 34–42.

Baird, J. A. 2011a: 'Photographing Dura-Europos, 1928–1937. An Archaeology of the Archive', *American Journal of Archaeology* 115, 427–446.

Baird, J. A. 2011b: 'The Graffiti of Dura-Europos: A Contextual Approach', in J. A. Baird and C. Taylor (eds), *Ancient Graffiti in Context*, New York, 49–68.

Baird, J. A. 2011c: 'The Houses of Dura-Europos: Archaeology, Archive, and Assemblage', in *Dura-Europos: Crossroads of Antiquity*, Chesnut Hill, 235–250.

Baird, J. A. 2012a: 'Dura Deserta: The Death and Afterlife of Dura-Europos', in N. Christie and A. Augenti (eds), *Urbes Extinctae: Archaeologies of Abandoned Classical Towns*, Aldershot, 307–329.

Baird, J. A. 2012b: 'Re-excavating the Houses of Dura-Europos', *Journal of Roman Archaeology* 25, 146–169.

Baird, J. A. 2012c: 'Constructing Dura-Europos, Ancient and Modern', in K. Lafrenz Samuels and D. Totten (eds), *Making Roman Places, Past and Present*, Portsmouth, 34–49.

Baird, J. A. 2014: *The Inner Lives of Ancient Houses: An Archaeology of Dura-Europos*, Oxford.

Baird, J. A. 2015: 'Jebel Khalid: Counting Sherds, or Sherds that Count?', *Journal of Roman Archaeology* 28, 877–881.

Baird, J. A. 2016a: 'Everyday Life in Roman Dura-Europos: The Evidence of Dress Practices', in T. Kaizer (ed.), *Religion, Society and Culture at Dura-Europos*, Cambridge, 30–56.

Baird, J. A. 2016b: 'Private Graffiti? Scratching the walls of Houses at Dura-Europos', in R. Benefiel and P. Keegan (eds), *Inscriptions in Private Places. Brill Studies in Greek and Roman Epigraphy*, Leiden, 13–31.

Baird, J. A. Forthcoming: 'Exposing Archaeology: Time in Archaeological Photographs', in D. Hicks and L. McFadyen (eds), *Archaeological Photography*, London.

Baird, J. A., and McFadyen, L. 2014: 'Towards an Archaeology of Archaeological Archives', *Archaeological Review from Cambridge* 29, 14–32.

Bartl, K., Schneider, G., and Böhme, S. 1995: 'Notes on Brittle Wares in North-eastern Syria', *Levant* 27, 165–177.

Baur, P. V. C., and Rostovtzeff, M. I. (eds) 1929: *The Excavations at Dura-Europos Conducted by Yale University and the French Academy of Inscriptions and Letters. Preliminary Report of First Season of Work, Spring 1928*, New Haven.

Baur, P. V. C., and Rostovtzeff, M. I. (eds) 1931: *The Excavations at Dura-Europos Conducted by Yale University and the French Academy of Inscriptions and Letters. Preliminary Report of Second Season on Work, October 1928-April 1929*, New Haven.

Baur, P. V. C., Rostovtzeff, M. I., and Bellinger, A. R. (eds) 1932: *The Excavations at Dura-Europos Conducted by Yale University and the French Academy of Inscriptions and Letters. Preliminary Report of Third Season of Work, November 1929-March 1930*, New Haven.

Baur, P. V. C., Rostovtzeff, M. I., and Bellinger, A. R. (eds) 1933: *The Excavations at Dura-Europos Conducted by Yale University and the French Academy of Inscriptions and Letters. Preliminary Report of Fourth Season of Work October 1930-March 1931*, New Haven.

Beard, M., North, J., and Price, S. 1998: *Religions of Rome*, Cambridge.

Bell, G. L. 1907: *Syria : The Desert and the Sown*, London.

Bellinger, A. R. 1943: 'The Numismatic Evidence from Dura', *Berytus* 8, 61–71.

Bellinger, A. R. 1948: 'Seleucid Dura. The Evidence of the Coins', *Berytus* 9, 51–67.

Bellinger, A. R., and Newell, E. T. 1940: 'Seleucid Mint at Dura-Europos', *Syria* 21, 77–81.

Bellinger, A. R., and Welles, C. B. 1935: 'A Third Century Contract of Sale from Edessa in Osrhoene', *Yale Classical Studies* 5, 95–154.

Berg, K. A. 2008: 'The Imperialist Lens: Du Camp, Salzmann and Early French Photography', *Early Popular Visual Culture* 6, 1–18.

Bertolino, R. 1997: 'Les inscriptions Hatréennes de Doura-Europos: étude épigraphique', *Doura-Europos Études IV*, Beirut, 199–206.

Bertolino, R. 2004: *Corpus des inscriptions sémitiques de Doura-Europos*. Supplemento n. 94 agli Annali (Sez. Orientale) 64, Naples.

Bertolino, R. 2005: 'Les inscriptions semitiques de Doura-Europos', P. Leriche, M. Gelin, and A. Dandrau (eds), *Doura Europos-Études V, 1993–1997*, 127–130.

Bertolino, R., and Abd El Aziz, G. 2005: 'La porte sud de Doura-Europos', P. Leriche, M. Gelin, and A. Dandrau (eds), *Doura Europos-Études V, 1993–1997*, 91–97.

Bessac, J. C. 1988: 'L'analyse des procédés de construction des remparts de pierre de Doura-Europos. Questions de méthodologie', *Syria* 65, 297–313.

Bessac, J. C. 2005a: 'Carrières et topographie à Doura-Europos', *Doura Europos-Études V, 1993–1997*, 247–258.

Bessac, J. C. 2005b: 'Restitution en pierre du mur nord du socle du Strategion de Doura-Europos et archéologie expérimentale', P. Leriche, M. Gelin, and A. Dandrau (eds), *Doura Europos-Études V, 1993–1997*, 79–89.

Bessac, J. C., Abdul Massih, J., and Valat, Z. 1997: 'De Doura-Europos à Aramel: étude ethno-archéologique dans des carriéres de Syrie', *Doura Europos Études IV*, 159–197.

Bland, R. 1991: 'Six Hoards of Syrian Tetradrachms of the Third Century AD', *The Numismatic Chronicle* 151, 1–33.

Bohrer, F. N. 2011: *Photography and Archaeology*, London.

Bongard-Levin, G., and Litvinenko, Y. 2004: 'Dura-Europos: From Cumont to Rostovtzeff', *Mediterraneo Antico* 7, 135–159.

Bongard-Levin, G., Bonnet, C., Litvinenko, Y., and Marcone, A. 2007: *Mongolus Syrio Salutem Optimam Dat : La Correspondance entre Mikhaïl Rostovtzeff et Franz Cumont*, Paris.

Bonnet, C. 1997a: *La Correspondance Scientifique de Franz Cumont conservée à l'Academia Belgica de Rome*, Rome.

Bonnet, C. 1997b: 'La vie et l'oevre de Franz Cumont: Introduction biographique', in C. Bonnet (ed.), *La Correspondance Scientifique de Franz Cumont Conservée À l'Academia Belgica de Rome*, Brussells, Rome, 1–67.

Breasted, C. 1943: *Pioneer to the Past. The Story of James Henry Breasted Archaeologist*, Chicago.

Breasted, J. H. 1914: *Ancient Times. A History of the Early World*, New York.

Breasted, J. H. 1920: 'The First Expedition of the Oriental Institute of the University of Chicago', *Journal of the American Oriental Society* 40, 282–285.

Breasted, J. H. 1922: 'Peintures d'epoque Romaine dans le désert de Syrie', *Syria* 3, 177–206.

Breasted, J. H. 1924: *Oriental Forerunners of Byzantine Painting. First-Century Wall Paintings from the Fortress of Dura on the Middle Euphrates*. Oriental Institute Publications 1, Chicago.

Brodie, N. 2015: 'Syria and its Regional Neighbours: A Case of Cultural Property Protection Policy Failure?', *International Journal of Cultural Property* 22, 317–335.

Brody, L. 2011: 'Yale University and Dura-Europos: From Excavation to Installation', in L. Brody and G. Hoffman (eds), *Dura-Europos: Crossroads of Antiquity*, Chesnut Hill, 17–32.

Brody, L. 2016: 'Dura-Europos and Yale: Past, Present and Future', in T. Kaizer (ed.), *Religion, Society and Culture at Dura-Europos*, Cambridge, 206–218.

Brody, L., and Hoffman, G. (eds) 2014: *Roman in the Provinces. Art on the Periphery of Empire*, Chesnut Hill.

Buchet, L. 2012: 'Europos-Doura analyse des restes Humains', P. Leriche, G. Coqueugniot, and S. Du Pontbriand (eds), *Europos-Doura Varia* 1, 191–200.

'Buried City on the Euphrates', *The Times* 1928: 13.

Burnett, A. 2007: 'The Roman West and the Roman East', in C. Howgego, V. Heuchert, and A. Burnett (eds), *Coinage and Identity in the Roman Provinces*, Oxford, 171–180.

Butcher, K. 2003: *Roman Syria and the Near East*, London.

Butcher, K. 2012: 'Syria in the Roman Period, 64 BC–AD 260', in W. E. Metcalf (ed.), *The Oxford Handbook of Greek and Roman Coinage*, Oxford; New York.

Casana, J. 2015: 'Satellite Imagery-Based Analysis of Archaeological Looting in Syria', *Near Eastern Archaeology* 78, 142–152.

Casana, J., and Panahipour, M. 2014: 'Satellite-Based Monitoring of Looting and Damage to Archaeological Sites in Syria', *Journal of Eastern Mediterranean Archaeology and Heritage Studies* 2, 128–151.

Chi, J. Y., and Heath, S. 2011: *Edge of Empires. Pagans, Jews, and Christians at Roman Dura-Europos*, New York.

Christides, V. 1982: 'Heracles-Nergal in Hatra', *Berytus* 30, 105–115.

Clark, J. R. 1978: 'Measuring Changes in the Ease of Trade with Archaeological Data: An Analysis of Coins Found at Dura Europos in Syria', *Professional Geographer* 30, 256–263.

Clay, A. T. 1924: 'The So-Called Fertile Crescent and Desert Bay', *Journal of the American Oriental Society* 44, 186–201.

Colledge, M. 1977: *Parthian Art*, London.

Colledge, M. 1986: *The Parthian Period*, Leiden.

Coqueugniot, G. 2012a: 'Le Chreophylakeion et l'agora d'Europos-Doura: Bilan des recherches, 2004–2008', P. Leriche, G. Coqueugniot, and S. Du Pontbriand (eds), *Europos-Doura Varia* 1, 93–110.

Coqueugniot, G. 2012b: 'Des espaces sacrés dans la tourmente: les lieux de culte d'Europos-Doura durant le siège sassanide de la ville (milieu du IIIe s. de n.è.)', P. Leriche, G. Coqueugniot, and S. Du Pontbriand (eds), *Europos-Doura Varia* 1, 215–230.

Coqueugniot, G. 2012c: 'Un sanctuaire au dieu Bêl le long de la rue principale d'Europos-Doura (îlot M5)', P. Leriche, G. Coqueugniot, and S. Du Pontbriand (eds), *Europos-Doura Varia* 1, 47–64.

Coqueugniot, G. 2015: 'The Hellenistic Public Square in Europos in Parapotamia (Dura-Europos, Syria) and Seleucia on the Tigris (Iraq) during Parthian and Roman Times', in S. Chandrasekaran and A. Kouremenos (eds), *Continuity and Destruction in the Greek East*, Oxford, 71–81.

Coqueugniot, G. 2016: 'Ancient Near-Eastern Traditions and Greco-Roman Culture in the Agora of Europos-Doura (Syria)', in R. A. Stucky, O. Kaelin, and H. P. Mathys (eds), *Proceedings of the 9th International Congress on the Archaeology of the Ancient Near East*, Vol. 2, Wiesbaden, 2:119–132.

Corbett, E. D. 2014: *Competitive Archaeology in Jordan: Narrating Identity from the Ottomans to the Hashemites*, Austin.

Crawford, M. R. 2016: 'The Diatessaron, Canonical or Non-canonical? Rereading the Dura Fragment', *New Testament Studies* 62, 253–277.

Crowfoot, J. W. 1945: 'Dura-Europos', *Antiquity* 19, 113–121.

Cumont, F. 1924: 'Une dédicace de Doura-Europos, colonie romaine', *Syria* 5, 346–358.

Cumont, F. 1925: 'Fragment de bouclier portant une liste d'étapes', *Syria* 6, 1–25.

Cumont, F. 1926: *Fouilles de Doura-Europos (1922–1923)*, Paris.

Curtis, J. 1976: 'Parthian Gold from Nineveh', *British Museum Yearbook*, 47–66.

Dandrau, A. 1997: 'Gypse, Plâtre et Djousse', *Doura-Europos Études IV*, Beirut, 155–157.

De Cesari, C. 2015: 'Post-Colonial Ruins: Archaeologies of Political Violence and IS', *Anthropology Today* 31, 22–26.

De Jong, L. 2017: *The Archaeology of Death in Roman Syria. Burial, Commemoration, and Empire*, Cambridge.

De Waele, A. 2004: 'The Figurative Wall Painting of the Sasanian Period from Iran, Iraq, and Syria', *Iranica Antiqua* 39, 339–381.

Debevoise, N. C. 1934: *Parthian Pottery from Seleucia on the Tigris*, Ann Arbor.

Detweiler, A. H. 1948: *Manual of Archaeological Surveying*, New Haven.

Díaz-Andreu, M. 2007. *A World History of Nineteenth-Century Archaeology. Nationalism, Colonialism, and the Past*, Oxford, 255–269.

Dijkstra, K. 1995: *Life and Loyalty. A Study in the Socio-Religious Culture of Syria and Mesopotamia in the Graeco-Roman Period Based on Epigraphic Evidence*, Leiden.

Dirven, L. 1999: *The Palmyrenes of Dura-Europos. A Study of Religious Interaction in Roman Syria*, Leiden.

Dirven, L. 2004: 'Religious Competition and the Decoration of Sanctuaries. The Case of Dura-Europos', *Eastern Christian Art* 1, 1–19.

Dirven, L. 2005: 'ΣΗΜΗΙΟΝ, SMY', Signum. A Note on the Romanization of the Semitic Cultic Standard', *Parthica* 7, 119–136.

Dirven, L. 2007: 'The Julius Terentius Fresco and the Roman Imperial Cult', *Mediterraneo antico* 10, 115–127.

Dirven, L. 2008: 'Paradise Lost, Paradise Regained. The Meaning of Adam and Eve in the Baptistery of Dura-Europos', *Early Christian Art* 5, 43–57.

Dirven, L. 2011: 'Strangers and Sojurners: The Religious Behavior of Palmyrenes and Other Foreigners in Dura-Europos', in G. Hoffman and L. Brody (eds), *Dura-Europos: Crossroads of Antiquity*, Chesnut Hill, 201–220.

Dirven, L. 2015: 'Cult Images in Cities of the Syrian-Mesopotamian Desert during the First Three Centuries CE', in M. Blömer, A. Lichtenberger, and R. Raja (eds), *Religious Identities in the Levant from Alexander to Muhammed: Continuity and Change*, Turnhout.

Dirven, L. 2016: 'The Problem with Parthian Art at Dura', in T. Kaizer (ed.), *Religion, Society and Culture at Dura-Europos*, Cambridge, 68–88.

Dirven, L., and McCarty, M. 2014: 'Local Idioms and Global Meanings: Mithraism and Roman Provincial Art', in L. Brody and G. Hoffman (eds), *Roman in the Provinces. Art on the Periphery of Empire*, Chesnut Hill, 125–142.

Dodge, H. 2009: 'Amphitheatres in the Roman East', in *Roman Amphitheatres and Spectacula: A 21-Century Perspective*, Oxford, 29–45.

Downey, S. B. 1976: '*Temples à escaliers*: The Dura Evidence', *California Studies in Classical Antiquity* 9, 21–39.

Downey, S. B. 1985a: 'The Second Citadel Palace at Dura-Europos and the Early History of the Iwan', *American Journal of Archaeology* 89, 329.

Downey, S. B. 1985b: 'Two Buildings at Dura-Europos and the Early History of the Iwan', *Mesopotamia* 20, 111–129.

Downey, S. B. 1986: 'The Citadel Palace at Dura-Europos', *Doura Europos Études 1986*, *Syria, Tome LVIII*, 27–37.

Downey, S. B. 1988a: *Mesopotamian Religious Architecture. Alexander through the Parthians*, Princeton.

Downey, S. B. 1988b: 'Further Observations on the Citadel Palace of Dura-Europos', *Doura-Europos Études 1988, Syria, Tome LXV*, 343–347.

Downey, S. B. 1991: 'The Palace of the Dux Ripae at Dura-Europos', *Histoire et cultes de l'asie Centrale Préislamique. Sources écrites et documents archéologiques*. Actes du colloque international du CNRS (Paris, 22–28 Novembre 1988), Paris, 17–21.

Downey, S. B. 1992: 'Archival Archaeology, Frank Brown's Notes on the Citadel Palace at Dura Europos', *Dura-Europos Études 1990, Syria, Tome LXIX*, 141–151.

Downey, S. B. 1993a: 'The Palace of the Dux Ripae at Dura-Europos and "Palatial" Architecture in Antiquity', in R. T. Scott and A. R. Scott (eds), *Eius Virtutis Studioso: Classical and Postclassical Studies in Memory of Frank Edward Brown (1908–1988)*, Hanover, 183–198.

Downey, S. B. 1993b: 'New Soundings in the Temple of Zeus Megistos at Dura-Europos', *Mesopotamia* 28, 169–193.

Downey, S. B. 1995: 'Excavations in the Temple of Zeus Megistos at Dura-Europos, 1994', *Mesopotamia* 30, 241–250.

Downey, S. B. 1996: 'Terracotta Plaques as Evidence for Connections between Palmyra and Dura-Europos', *Les Annales Archaeologiques Arabes Syriennes. Special Issue Documenting the Activities of the International Colloquium. Palymra and the Silk Road.* 42, 253–260.

Downey, S. B. 1997: 'Excavations in the Temple of Zeus Megistos at Dura-Europos, 1992', *Doura-Europos Études IV*, Beirut, 107–116.

Downey, S. B. 1998: 'Cult Reliefs at Dura-Europos: Problems of Interpretation and Placement', *Damaszener Mitteilungen* 10, 201–210.

Downey, S. B. 2000: 'The Transformation of Seleucid Dura-Europos', in E. Fentress (ed.), *Romanization and the City: Creation, Transformations, and Failures*, Portsmouth, 155–172.

Downey, S. B. 2002: 'Heracles in the Djezireh: Dura-Europos, Tell Sheikh Hamad and Hatra', *Documents D'archéologie Syrienne I. The Syrian Jezira, Cultural Heritage and Interrelations. Proceedings of the International Conference Held in Deir Ez-Zor April 22nd–25th, 1996*, Damascus, 271–276.

Downey, S. B. 2003: *Terracotta Figurines and Plaques from Dura-Europos*, Ann Arbor.

Downey, S. B. 2004a: 'Sculptures of Divinities from the Temple of Zeus at Dura-Europos', in *Doura-Europos Etudes V, 1994–1997*, Paris, 153–161.

Downey, S. B. 2004b: 'Zeus the Greatest in Syria', *Parthica* 6, 117–128.

Downey, S. B. 2005: 'Excavations in the Temple of Zeus Megistos, 1994–1998', in *Doura-Europos Etudes V, 1994–1997*, Paris, 41–55.

Downey, S. B. 2007: 'Religious Communities at Dura-Europos', *Mediterraneo Antico* 10, 95–114.

Downey, S. B. 2008: 'The Role of Sculpture in Worship at the Temples of Dura-Europos', in Y. Z. Eliav, E. A. Friedland, and S. Herbert (eds), *The Sculptural Enviornment of the Roman Near East. Reflections of Culture, Ideology and Power*, Leuven and Dudley, MA, 413–435.

Downey, S. B. 2012: 'Temple of Zeus Megistos: Brief Report on Excavations, 1992–2002', P. Leriche, G. Coqueugniot, and S. Du Pontbriand (eds), *Europos-Doura Varia* 1, 65–75.

Downey, S. B. 2016: 'The Dangers of Adventurous Reconstruction: Frank Brown at Europos-Doura', in T. Kaizer (ed.), *Religion, Society and Culture at Dura-Europos*, Cambridge, 199–205.

Van Driel-Murray, C. 1986a: 'Leatherwork in the Roman Army. Part One', *Exercitus* 2, 1–6.

Van Driel-Murray, C. 1986b: 'Leatherwork in the Roman Army. Part Two', *Exercitus* 2, 23–27.

Van Driel-Murray, C. 2001: 'Vindolanda and the Dating of Roman Footwear', *Britannia* 32, 185–197.

Drijvers, H. J. W. 1972: *Old-Syriac (Edessean) Inscriptions*, Leiden.

Drijvers, H. J. W. 1990: 'The Syrian Cult Relief', in H. G. Kippenberg (ed.), *Genres in Visual Representations: Proceedings of a Conference Held in 1986 by Invitation of the Werner-Reimers-Stiftung in Bad Homburg (Federal Republic of Germany)*, Leiden, 69–82.

Du Mesnil Du Buisson, R. 1933: 'Sixième campagne de fouilles a Doura-Europos (Syrie)', *Comptes Rendus. Académie des Inscriptions et Belles Lettres*, 193–204.

Du Mesnil Du Buisson, C. 1934: 'Compte rendu de la septième campagne de fouilles a Doura-Europos (Syrie)', *Comptes Rendus. Académie des Inscriptions et Belles Lettres* 78, 176–187.

Du Mesnil Du Buisson, C. 1936: 'Doura Europos, la Pompéi de l'orient', *L'Illustration*, sec. 4854.

Du Mesnil Du Buisson, C. 1937: 'Une guerre de mines', *Revue Du Genie Militaire*, 5–27.

Du Mesnil Du Buisson, R. 1939: *Les peintures de la synagogue de Doura-Europos (245–256 après J. C.)*, Rome.

Du Mesnil Du Buisson, C. 1959: 'Inscriptions sur jarres de Doura-Europos', *Mélanges de L'université Saint Joseph* 36, 3–49.

Dussaud, R. 1949: 'Franz Cumont (1868–1947)', *Syria* 26, 168–172.

Dyson, S. L. 1998: *Ancient Marbles to American Shores. Classical Archaeology in the United States*, Philadelphia.

Edwell, P. M. 2008: *Between Rome and Persia. The Middle Euphrates, Mesopotamia and Palmyra under Roman Control*, London.

Edwell, P. M. 2013: 'The Euphrates as a Boundary between Rome and Parthia in the Late Republic and Early Empire', *Antichthon* 47, 191–206.

Elsner, J. 2001: 'Cultural Resistance and the Visual Image: The Case of Dura-Europos', *Classical Philology* 96, 269–304.

Emberling, G. 2010: 'Introduction', in G. Emberling (ed.), *Pioneers to the Past: American Archaeologists in the Middle East, 1919–1920*, Chicago, 9–14.

Emberling, G., and Teeter, E. 2010: 'The First Expedition of the Oriental Institute, 1919–1920', in G. Emberling (ed.), *Pioneers to the Past: American Archaeologists in the Middle East, 1919–1920*, Chicago, 31–84.

Emmel, S. 1989: 'Antiquity in Fragments: A Hundred Years of Collecting Papyri at Yale', *The Yale University Library Gazette* 64, 38–58.

Fine, S. 2005: *Art and Judaism in the Greco-Roman World: Toward a New Jewish Archaeology*, Cambridge.

Fine, S. 2011: 'Jewish Identity at the Limus. The Earliest Reception of the Dura Europos Synagogue paintings', in E. S. Gruen (ed.), *Cultural Identity in the Ancient Mediterranean*, Los Angeles, 289–306.

Fink, R. O. 1971: *Roman Military Records on Papyrus*, London.

Fink, R. O., Hoey, A. S., and Snyder, W. S. (eds) 1940: *The Feriale Duranum*, New Haven: Yale Classical Studies 7.

Fisher, D. 1983: 'The Role of Philanthropic Foundations in the Reproduction and Production of Hegemony: Rockefeller Foundations and the Social Sciences', *Sociology* 17, 206–233.

Fishwick, D. 1988: 'Dated Inscriptions and the Feriale Duranum', *Syria* 115, 349–361.

Flusser, V. 2000: *Towards a Philosophy of Photography*, London.

Francis, E. D. 1975a: 'Mithraic Graffiti From Dura-Europos', in J. R. Hinnels (ed.), *Mithraic Studies. Proceedings of the First International Congress of Mithraic Studies* Vol. 2, Manchester, 2: 424–445.

Francis, E. D. 1975b: 'Mithraic Graffiti From Dura-Europos', in J. R. Hinnels (ed.), *Mithraic Studies. Proceedings of the First International Congress of Mithraic Studies*, Vol. 2, Manchester, 2: 424–445.

Freyberger, K. S. 2002: 'The Sacral Buildings of Dura-Europos', *Documents d'archéologie Syrienne I. The Syrian Jezira, Cultural Heritage and Interrelations. Proceedings of the International Conference Held in Deir Ez-Zor April 22nd-25th, 1996*, Damascus, 277–281.

Frye, R. N. 1968: *The Parthian and Middle Persian Inscriptions of Dura-Europos*, London.

Frye, R. N., Gilliam, J. F., Ingholt, H., and Welles, C. B. 1955: 'Inscriptions from Dura-Europos', *Yale Classical Studies* 14, 123–213.

Gange, D., and M. Ledger-Lomas. 2013: *Cities of God: The Bible and Archaeology in Nineteenth-Century Britain*, Cambridge.

Gansser-Burckhardt, A. 1953: 'The Leather Findings from Dura-Europos', New Haven.

Gaslain, J. 2012: 'Quelques remarques sur la politique impériale des parthes arsacides et la prise d'Europos-Doura', P. Leriche, S. Du Breil De Pontbriand, and G. Coqueugniot (eds), *Europos-Doura Varia* 1, 124–141.

Gawlikowski, M. 1996: 'Palmyra and Its Caravan Trade', *Les Annales Archaeologiques Arabes Syriennes. Special Issue Documenting the Activities of the International Colloquium. Palymra and the Silk Road* 42, 140–145.

Gawlikowski, M. 2007: 'The Mithraeum at Hawarete and Its Paintings', *Journal of Roman Archaeology* 20, 337–361.

Gelin, M. 2000a: 'Histoire et urbanisme d'une ville a travers son architecture de brique crue: L'exemple de Doura-Eurpos (Syrie orientale hellenistique, Parthe et Romaine)'.

Gelin, M. 2000b: 'De l'euphrate à l'oxus: exemples de l'utilisation de la brique cuite à Doura-Europos et à Termez', in *La Brique Antique et Médiéval*, Rome, 53–69.

Gelin, M. 2002: *L'archéologie en Syrie et au Liban À l'époque du mandat 1919–1946: Histoire et Organisation*, Paris.

Gelin, M. 2005: 'Le rempart en briques crues de Doura-Europos: La muraille Grecque', P. Leriche, M. Gelin, and A. Dandrau (eds), *Doura Europos-Études V, 1993–1997*, 213–236.

Gelin, M., Leriche, P., and Abdul Massih, J. 1997: 'La porte de Palmyre à Doura-Europos', in P. Leriche and M. Gelin (eds), *Doura Europos Études*, Vol. 4, Beirut, 4:21–46.

Geyer, B. 1988: 'Le site de Doura-Europos et son enviornment géographique', *Syria* 65, 285–295.

Gilliam, J. F. 1941: 'The Dux Ripae at Dura', *Transactions and Proceedings of the American Philological Association* 72, 157–175.

Gilliam, J. F. 1954: 'The Roman Military Feriale', *Harvard Theological Review* 47, 183–196.

Gilliam, J. F. 1965: 'Dura Rosters and the "Constitutio Antoniniana"', *Historia: Zeitschrift Für Alte Geschichte* 14, 74–92.

Gillot, L. 2010: 'Towards a Socio-Political History of Archaeology in the Middle East: The Development of Archaeological Practice and Its Impacts on Local Communities in Syria', *Bulletin of the History of Archaeology* 20, 4–16.

Gnoli, T. 2007: 'Some Considerations about the Roman Military Presence along the Euphrates and the Habur', *Mediterraneo Antico* 10, 71–83.

Goldman, B. 1990: 'Foreigners at Dura-Europos: Pictorial Graffiti and History', *Le Muséon* 103, 5–25.

Goldman, B. 1992: 'The Dura Synagogue Costumes and Parthian Art', in *The Dura-Europos Synagogue: A Re-Evaluation (1932–1992)*, Atlanta, 53–77.

Goldman, B. 1999: 'Pictorial Graffiti of Dura-Europos', *Parthica* 1, 19–106.

Goldman, B. 2001: 'Graeco-Roman Dress in Syro-Mesopotamia', in *The World of Roman Costume*, Madison, 163–181.

Goldman, B., and Goldman, N. 2011: *My Dura-Europos. The Letters of Susan M. Hopkins, 1927–1935*, Detroit.

Goldman, B., and Little, A. M. G. 1980: 'The Beginning of Sasanian Painting and Dura-Europos', *Iranica Antiqua* 15, 283–298.

Goodenough, E. R. 1964: *Jewish Symbols in the Greco-Roman Period*, Vol. 9–11, New York.

Grenet, F. 1988: 'Les Sassanides a Doura-Europos (253 ap. J. C.). Réexamen du matériel épigraphique iranien du site', in *Géographie Historique Au Proche-Orient (Syrie, Phénicie, Arabie, Greques, Romaines, Byzantines)*, Paris, 133–158.

Grossman, R. A. 2002: *Ancient Glass. A Guide to the Yale Collection*, New Haven.

Grossman, R. A. 2011: 'Ancient Glass from Dura-Europos in Perspective', in G. Hoffman and L. Brody (eds), *Dura-Europos: Crossroads of Antiquity*, Chesnut Hill, 275–279.

Guiraud, H. 1992: 'Intaglios from Dura-Europos', *Yale University Art Gallery Bulletin*, 49–85.

Gutmann, J. 1992: *The Dura-Europos Synagogue: A Re-Evaluation (1932–1992)*, Atlanta.

Hachlili, R. 1998: *Ancient Jewish Art and Archaeology in the Diaspora*, Leiden.

Hălmagi, D. 2015: 'Notes on the Dura-Europos map', *Revista Cicsa* New Series 1, 41–51.

Hammond, N. G. L. 1999: 'The Roles of the *Epistates* in Macedonian Contexts', *The Annual of the British School at Athens* 94, 369–375.

Hannestad, L. 1983: *Ikaros: The Hellenistic Settlements. The Hellenistic Pottery from Failaka. With a Survey of Hellenistic Pottery in the Near East* Vol. 2.1 and 2.2, Aarhus.

Hannestad, L. 2012: 'The Seleucid Kingdom', in D. T. Potts (ed.), *A Companion to the Archaeology of the Ancient Near East*, Chichester, 984–1000.

Hardy, S. 2015: 'Virtues Impracticable and Extremely Difficult: The Human Rights of Subsistence Diggers' in A. González-Ruibal and G. Moshenska (ed.) *Ethics and the Archaeology of Violence*, New York, 229–239.

Harmanşah, Ö. 2015: 'ISIS, Heritage, and the Spectacles of Destruction in the Global Media', *Near Eastern Archaeology* 78, 170–177.

Harmatta, J. 1958: 'Die Parthischen Ostraka aus Dura-Europos', *Acta Antiqua Academiae Scientiarum Hungaricae* 6, 87–175.

Harris, W. V. 1980: 'Roman Terracotta Lamps: The Organization of an Industry', *Journal of Roman Studies* 70, 126–145.

Hauser, S. R. 2012: 'The Arsacid (Parthian) Empire', in D. T. Potts (ed.), *A Companion to the Archaeology of the Ancient Near East*, Chichester, 1001–1020.

Haynes, I. P. 1993: 'The Romanisation of Religion in the "Auxilia" of the Roman Imperial Army from Augustus to Septimus Severus', *Britannia* 24, 141–157.

Haynes, I. 2013: *Blood of the Provinces. The Roman Auxilia and the Making of Provincial Society from Augustus to the Severans*, Oxford.

Helbig, D. K. 2016. '*La trace de Rome*? Aerial Photography and Archaeology in Mandate Syria and Lebanon', *History of Photography* 40.3, 283–300.

Heyn, M. K. 2011: 'The Terentius Frieze in Context', in L. Brody and G. Hoffman (eds), *Dura-Europos. Crossroads of Antiquity*, Chesnut Hill, 221–233.

Heyn, M. K. 2016: 'Gesture at Dura-Europos. A New Interpretation of the So-Called "Scène Énigmatique"', in T. Kaizer (ed.), *Religion, Society and Culture at Dura-Europos*, Cambridge, 89–98.

Hillers, D. R., and Cussini, E. 1996: *Palmyrene Aramaic Texts*, Baltimore.

Hodder, I. 1997: '"Always Momentary, Fluid and Flexible": Towards a Reflexive Excavation Methodology', *Antiquity* 71, 691–700.

Hoepfner, W., and Schwandner, E. L. 1994: *Haus und Stadt im Klassischen Griechnenland*, Munich.

Hoffman, G., and Brody, L. 2011: *Dura-Europos: Crossroads of Antiquity*, Chesnut Hill.

Hopkins, C. 1932a: 'Dura-Europos Discoveries: The Unexpected in Archaeology', *Illustrated London News*, London.

Hopkins, C. 1932b: 'The Oldest Frescoed Church: New Relics of Early Christian Art', *Illustrated London News*, London.

Hopkins, C. 1932c: 'Papyrus from Roman Army Archives, and Pagan Religious Art Relics: Syrian "Finds"', *Illustrated London News*, London.

Hopkins, C. 1933a: 'Jewish Prototypes of Early Christian Art?', *Illustrated London News*, London.

Hopkins, C. 1933b: 'Third Century Art at Dura-Europos: Sculpture Reliefs, Wall-Paintings and Woven Fabric', *Illustrated London News*, London.

Hopkins, C. 1934a: 'The Tragedy of a Buried City Told by Its Ruins', *Illustrated London News*, London.

Hopkins, C. 1934b: '"The Most Brilliant Record" of the Mysterious Mithraic Cult', *Illustrated London News*, London.

Hopkins, C. 1935: 'Roman Painted Shields and Temple Sculptures from Dura-Europos: The Famous Syrian Site Yields Fresh Tresure', *Illustrated London News*, London.

Hopkins, C. 1936: 'Aspects of Parthian Art in the Light of Discoveries from Dura-Europos',
    Berytus 3, 1–30.
Hopkins, C. 1941: 'The Architectural Background in the Paintings at Dura-Europos',
    American Journal of Archaeology 45, 18–29.
Hopkins, C. 1979: *The Discovery of Dura-Europos*, New Haven.
Howgego, C. 1995: *Ancient History from Coins*, New York.
Howgego, C., Heuchert, V., and Burnett, A. 2007: *Coinage and Identity in the Roman
    Provinces*, Oxford.
Huebner, S. R. 2007: '"Brother-Sister" Marriage in Roman Egypt: A Curiosity of
    Humankind or a Widespread Family Strategy?', *The Journal of Roman Studies* 97,
    21–49.
Ingholt, H. 1942: 'The Danish Excavations at Hama on the Orontes', *American Journal of
    Archaeology* 46, 469–476.
Invernizzi, A. 2011: 'Parthian Art—Arsacid Art', *TOPOI* 17, 189–207.
Jackson-Tal, R. E. 2004: 'The Late Hellenistic Glass Industry in Syro-Palestine: A
    Reappraisal', *Journal of Glass Studies* 46, 11–32.
James, S. 1985: 'Dura-Europos and the Chronology of Syria in the 250s AD', *Chiron* 15,
    111–124.
James, S. 2004: *The Excavations at Dura Europos. Final Report 7, Arms and Armour and
    Other Military Equipment*, London.
James, S. 2005: 'The Deposition of Military Equipment during the Final Siege at Dura-
    Europos, with Particular Regard to the Tower 19 Countermine', *Carnuntum Jahrbuch*,
    189–206.
James, S. 2007: 'New Light on the Roman military base at Dura-Europos: Interim
    Report on a Pilot Season of Fieldwork in 2005', in A. S. Lewin and P. Pellegrini (eds),
    Proceedings of the Later Roman Army in the East Conference, Potenza, 2005, Oxford,
    29–47.
James, S. 2011: 'Stratagems, Combat and "Chemical Warfare" in the Siege-Mines of Dura-
    Europos', *American Journal of Archaeology* 115, 69–101.
James, S. 2015: 'Of Colossal Camps and a New Roman Battlefield: Remote Sensing,
    Archival Archaeology and the "Conflict Landscape" of Dura-Europos, Syria', in D. J.
    Breeze, R. Jones, and I. A. Oltean (eds), *Understanding Roman Frontiers*, Edinburgh,
    328–345.
James, S. 2018: *The Military Base of Dura-Europos*, Oxford.
Johnson, J. 1929: 'A Trade for Halliburton. Archaeology the Adventurous, as Viewed by
    One Whose Present Address Is "Fouilles de Doura-Europos, Salihiyeh Euphrate, Syria"',
    Princeton Alumni Weekly 29, 741–742.
Johnson, J. 1932: 'Dura Studies', Philadelphia.
Joosten, J. 2003: 'The Dura Parchment and the Diatessaron', *Vigilae Christianae* 57,
    159–175.
Kaiser, A. 2014: *Archaeology, Sexism, and Scandal: The Long-Suppressed Story of One
    Woman's Discoveries and the Man Who Stole Credit for Them*, New York.
Kaizer, T. Forthcoming: *Bibliotheca Cumontiana; Scripta Minora VII*.
Kaizer, T. 2000: 'The "Heracles Figure" at Hatra and Palmyra: Problems of Interpretation',
    Iraq 62, 219–232.
Kaizer, T. 2006: 'A Note on the Fresco of Iulius Terentius from Dura-Europos', in *Altertum
    und Mittelmeerraum: Die Antike Welt Diesseits und Jenseits der Levante*. Oriens et
    Occidens, Band 12, Stuttgart, 150–159.

Kaizer, T. 2009a: 'Religion and Language in Dura-Europos', in H. M. Cotton, R. G. Hoyland, J. J. Price, and D. J. Wasserstein (eds), *From Hellenism to Islam. Cultural and Linguistic Change in the Roman Near East*, Cambridge, 235–253.

Kaizer, T. 2009b: 'Patterns of Worship in Dura-Europos. A Case Study of Religious Life in the Classical Levant Outside the Main Cult Centres', in C. Bonnet, V. Pirenne-Delforge, and D. Praet (eds), *Les Religions Orientales dans le monde Grec et Romain: Cent ans après Cumont (1906–2006)*, Brussells, Rome, 153–172.

Kaizer, T. 2013: 'Local Religious Identities in the Roman Near East', in M. R. Salzman (ed.), *The Cambridge History of Religions in the Ancient World*, Vol. 2 From the Hellenistic Age to Late Antiquity, Cambridge, 2 From the Hellenistic Age to Late Antiquity: 54–86.

Kaizer, T. 2015: 'Dura-Europos under Roman Rule', in J. M. Cortés Copete, E. Muñiz Grijalvo, and F. Lozano Gómez (eds), *Ruling the Greek World. Approaches to the Roman Empire in the East*, Stuttgart, 91–102.

Kaizer, T. 2016: 'Revisiting the "Temple of Bêl" at Dura-Europos: A Note on the Fragmentary Fresco from the Naos', in M. K. Heyn and A. I. Steinsapir (eds), *Icon, Cult, and Context: Sacred Spaces and Objects in the Classical World*. UCLA Cotsen Institute of Archaeology Press Monographs 82, Los Angeles, 35–46.

Kaizer, T. 2017: 'Empire, Community and Culture on the Middle Euphrates. Durenes, Palmyrenes, Villagers and Soldiers', *Bulletin of the Institute of Classical Studies* 60.1, 63–95.

Kaplan, B. 1971: 'Report of the Leatherwork from Dura-Europos, Yale Archive', New Haven.

Kennedy, D. L. 1986: 'Ana on the Euphrates in the Roman Period', *Iraq* 48, 103–104.

Kennedy, D., and Riley, D. 1990: *Rome's Desert Frontier from the Air*, London.

Kiefer, K. M., and Matheson, S. B. 1982: *Life in an Eastern Province. The Roman Fortress at Dura-Europos. Checklist of the Exhibition at the Yale University Art Gallery 24 March-5 September 1982*, New Haven.

Klaver, S. 2012: 'The Brides of Christ: "The Women in Procession" in the Baptistery of Dura-Europos', *Eastern Christian Art* 9, 63–78.

Klaver, S. 2016: 'Dress and Identity in the Syrian-Mesopotamian Region: The Case of the Women of Dura-Europos', *ARAM* 28, 1–2, 375–391.

Koloski-Ostrow, A. O. 2011: 'Dura-Europos: Water, Baths, Latrines, and the Goddess Fortuna in a Desert City', in *Dura-Europos: Crossroads of Antiquity*, Chesnut Hill, 251–273.

Kopsacheili, M. 2011: 'Hybridisation of Palatial Architecture: Hellenistic Royal Palaces and Governors' Seats', in A. Kouremenos, S. Chandrasekaran, and R. Rossi (eds), *From Pella to Gandhara Hybridisation and Identity in the Art and Architecture of the Hellenistic East*. BAR International Series 2221, Oxford, 17–45.

Kosmin, P. J. 2011: 'The Foundation and Early Life of Dura-Europos', in G. Hoffman and L. Brody (eds), *Dura-Europos: Crossroads of Antiquity*, Chesnut Hill, 95–109.

Kraeling, C. H. 1956: *The Synagogue*, A. R. Bellinger, F. E. Brown, A. Perkins, and C. B. Welles (eds), New Haven.

Lancaster, L. C. 2015: *Innovative Vaulting in the Architecture of the Roman Empire: 1st to 4th Centuries CE*, Cambridge.

Langner, M. 2001: *Antike Graffitizeichnungen. Motive, Gestaltung und Bedeutung*, Wiesbaden.

Larson, J. A. 2010: *Letters from James Henry Breasted to His Family August 1919 – July 1920 Letters Home during the Oriental Institute's First Expedition to the Middle East*, Chicago.

Leriche, P. 1986: 'Chronologie du rempart de brique crue de Doura-Europos', *Doura-Europos Etudes 1986, Syria 58*, 61–82.

Leriche, P. 1993: 'Techniques de guerre sassanides et romaines à Dura-Europos', in *L'armée Romaine et les barbares du IIIe au VIIe Siècle*, Paris, 83–100.

Leriche, P. 1996: 'Le Chreophylakeion de Doura-Europos et la mise en place du plan hippodamien de la ville', in *Archives et Sceaux du Monde Hellénistique*, Paris, 157–169.

Leriche, P. 1997a: 'Pourquoi et comment Europos a été fondée à Doura?', in *Escalavage, Guerre, Économie en Grèce Ancienne. Hommages À Yvon Garlan*, Rennes, 191–210.

Leriche, P. 1997b: 'Tranchée sur la rue principale et fouille d'un sanctuaire et d'une maison de i'îlot M5 à Doura-Europos', *Doura-Europos Études IV*, Beirut, 81–94.

Leriche, P. 1999: 'Salle à gradins du temple d'Artémis à Doura-Europos', *Topoï 9*, 719–739.

Leriche, P. 2000: 'La brique crue en Mésopotamie et en Asie centrale hellénisées (IVe siècle av. n.è. - IIIe siècle de n.è.)', in P. Boucheron, H. Broise, and Y. Thébert (eds), *La Brique Antique et Médiéval*, Rome, 11–30.

Leriche, P. 2003: 'Europos-Doura Hellénistique', in *TOPOI Supplement 4, La Syrie Hellénistique*, Lyon, 171–191.

Leriche, P. 2004: 'La rue principale et l'urbanisme d'Europos-Doura. Etude Preliminaire', *Parthica 6*, 145–159.

Leriche, P. 2012a: 'Les peintures d'Europos-Doura au Musée National de Damas', P. Leriche, G. Coqueugniot, and S. Du Pontbriand (eds), *Europos-Doura Varia 1*, 143–155.

Leriche, P. 2012b: 'Europos-Doura. Quinze années de travaux de la mission Franco-Syrienne (1986–2001)', P. Leriche, G. Coqueugniot, and S. Du Pontbriand (eds), *Europos-Doura Varia 1*, 11–46.

Leriche, P., and Al Ajji, E. 2004: 'Présentation des travaux de la mission (1994–1997)', in *Doura-Europos Etudes V, 1994–1997*, Paris, 1–40.

Leriche, P., and Al Mahmoud, A. 1994: 'Doura-Europos. Bilan des recherches récentes', *Comptes Rendus. Académie Des Inscriptions et Belles Lettres 138*, 395–420.

Leriche, P., and Bertolino, R. 1997: 'Les inscriptions Hatréennes de Doura-Europos: le contexte archéologique et historique', *Doura-Europos Études IV*, Beirut, 207–214.

Leriche, P., Coqueugniot, G., and De Pontbriand, S. 2011: 'New Research by the French-Syrian Archaeological Expedition to Europos-Dura and New Data on the Polytheistic Sanctuaries in Europos-Dura', in J. Y. Chi and S. Heath (eds), *Edge of Empires: Pagans, Jews, and Christians at Roman Dura-Europos*, New York, 9–33.

Leriche, P., and El'Ajji, E. 1999: 'Une nouvelle inscription dans la salle à gradins du temple d'Artémis à Doura-Europos', *Comptes Rendus. Académie Des Inscriptions et Belles Lettres*, 1312–1346.

Leriche, P., Gelin, M., Gharbi, M., and Yon, J. B. 1997: 'Le palais du Stratège à Doura-Europos', *Doura Europos Études IV*, 55–80.

Leriche, P., and Mahmoud, A. 1988: 'Bilan des Campagnes de 1986 et 1987 de la mission Franco-Syrienne à doura-Europos', *Doura-Europos Études 1988, Syria, Tome LXV*, 261–282.

Lockyear, K. 2007: 'Where Do We Go from Here? Recording and Analysing Roman Coins from Archaeological Excavations', *Britannia 38*, 211–224.

Lockyear, K. 2012: 'Dating Coins, Dating with Coins', *Oxford Journal of Archaeology 31*, 191–211.

212 *Bibliography*

Loeschcke, S. 1919: *Lampen aus Vindonissa*, Zurich.

Loosley, E. 2005: 'Archaeology and Cultural Belonging in Contemporary Syria: The Value of Archaeology to Religious Minorities', *World Archaeology* 37, 589–596.

Lucas, G. 2001: 'Destruction and the Rhetoric of Excavation', *Norwegian Archaeological Review* 34, 35–46.

Lucas, G. 2004: 'Modern Disturbances: On the Ambiguities of Archaeology', *Modernism/ Modernity* 11, 109–120.

Luther, A. 2004: 'Dura-Europos zwischen Palmyra und den Parthern. Der politische status der region am Mittleren Euphrat im 2. Jh. n. Chr. und die Organisation des palmyrenischen Fernhandels', in R. Rollinger and C. Ulf (eds), *Commerce and Monetary Systems in the Ancient World: Means of Transmission and Cultural Interaction*. Oriens et Occidens 6, Stuttgart, 327–351.

MacDonald, D. 1986: 'Dating the Fall of Dura-Europos', *Historia* 35, 45–68.

Macdonald, M. C. A. 2005: 'The Safaitic Inscriptions at Dura Europos', in E. Cussini (ed.), *A Journey to Palmyra. Collected Essays to Remember Delbert R. Hillers*, Leiden, 118–129.

Magness, J. 2010: 'Third Century Jews and Judaism at Beth Shearim and Dura Europus', in D. M. Gwyn and S. Bangert (eds), *Religious Diversity in Late Antiquity*, Leiden, 133–166.

Magness, J. 2012: 'The 'Foundation Deposit' from the Dura-Europos Synagogue Reconsidered', in B. D. Wescoat and R. G. Ousterhout (eds), *Architecture of the Sacred. Space, Ritual, and Experience from Classical Greece to Byzantium*, Cambridge, 231–247.

Matheson, S. B. 1982: *Dura Europos. The Ancient City and the Yale Collection*, New Haven.

Matheson, S. B. 1992: 'The Tenth Season at Dura-Europos 1936–1937', *Syria* 69, 121–140.

Mathiesen, H. E. 1992: *Sculpture in the Parthian Empire : A Study in Chronology*, 2 Vols, Aarhus.

Milik, J. T. 1968: 'Parchemin judéo-araméen de Doura-Europos, an 200 ap. J. C.', *Syria* 45, 97–104.

Millar, F. 1987: 'The Problem of Hellenistic Syria', *Hellenism in the East: The Interaction of Greek and Non-Greek Civilizations from Syria to Central Asia after Alexander*, London, 110–133.

Millar, F. 1993: *The Roman Near East 31 BC–AD 337*, Cambridge, Mass.

Millar, F. 1998a: 'Caravan Cities: The Roman Near East and Long-Distance Trade by Land', in *Modus Operandi. Essays in Honour of Geoffrey Rickman*, London, 119–137.

Millar, F. 1998b: 'Dura-Europos under Parthian Rule', *Das Partherreich und Seine Zeugnisse. The Arsacid Empire: Sources and Documentation. Beiträge Des Internationalen Colloquims, Eutin (27.-30. Juni 1996)*, Stuttgart, 473–492.

Moralee, J. 2004: *For Salvation's Sake: Provincial Loyalty, Personal Religion, and Epigraphic Production in the Roman and Late Antique Near East*, New York and London.

Mouton, B. 1992: 'La réhabilitation du site de Doura-Europos. Premier bilan. L'exemple du palais du stratège', *Dura-Europos Études 1990/Syria* 69, 29–48.

Newell, 1941: *The Coinage of the Western Seleucid Mints : From Seleucus I to Antiochus III*, New York.

Nock, A. D. 1952: 'The Roman Army and the Roman Religious Year', *Harvard Theological Review* 45, 187–252.

Noy, D. 2007: 'The Jews of Roman Syria: The Synagogues of Dura-Europos and Apamea', in S. N. C. Lieu and R. Alston (eds), *Aspects of the Roman East. Papers in Honour of Professor Fergus Millar*, Turnhout, 62–80.

Noy, D., and Bloedhorn, H. (eds) 2004: *Inscriptiones Judaicae Orientis*, Vol. 3, Syria and Cyprus, Tübingen.

Olin, M. 2000: '"Early Christian Synagogues" and "Jewish Art Historians". The Discovery of the Synagogue of Dura-Europos', *Marburger Jahrbuch Für Kunstwissenschaft 27*, 7–28.

Olin, M. 2002: 'The Road to Dura-Europos', *Books-Budapest Review of Books-English Edition 12*.

Olin, M. 2011: 'The Émigré Scholars of Dura-Europos', in G. Hoffman and L. Brody (eds), *Dura-Europos: Crossroads of Antiquity*, Chesnut Hill, 71–93.

Olin, M. R. 2001: *The Nation without Art: Examining Modern Discourses on Jewish Art*, Lincoln.

Ousterhout, R. G. 2011: *John Henry Haynes. A Photographer and Archaeologist in the Ottoman Empire 1881–1900*, London.

Pearson, H. F. 1939: *A Guide to the Synagogue of Doura-Europos*, Beirut.

Pedersen, S. 2015: *The Guardians: The League of Nations and the Crisis of Empire*, Oxford.

Peppard, M. 2016: *The World's Oldest Church: Bible, Art, and Ritual at Dura-Europos, Syria*, New Haven.

Perkins, A. 1973: *The Art of Dura-Europos*, Oxford.

Phang, S. E. 2007: 'Military Documents, Languages, and Literacy', in P. Erdkamp (ed.), *A Companion to the Roman Army*, Oxford, 286–305.

Pierce Kelley, C. 1994: 'Who Did the Iconoclasm in the Dura Synagogue?', *Bulletin of the American Schools of Oriental Research 295*, 57–72.

Pietrzykowski, M. 1985: 'The Origins of the Frontal Convention in the Arts of the Near East', *Berytus*, 55–59.

Pijoan, J. 1937: 'Review of the Parable of the Virgins from Dura-Europos', *The Art Bulletin 19*, 592–595.

Ploug, G. 1985: *Hama. Fouilles et Recherches de la Fondation Carlsberg 1931–1938. The Graeco-Roman Town*, Copenhagen.

Poidebard, A. 1934. *La trace de Rome dans le désert de Syrie. Le limes de Trajan a la conquête arabe. Recherches aériennes (1925–1932)*, Paris.

Pollard, N. 2004: 'Roman Material Culture across Imperial Frontiers? Three Case Studies from Parthian Dura-Europos', in *The Greco-Roman East: Politics, Culture, Society*. Yale Classical Studies 31, Cambridge, 119–144.

Pollard, N. 2007: 'Colonial and Cultural Identities in Parthian and Roman Dura-Europos', in R. Alston and S. N. C. Lieu (eds), *Aspects of the Roman East I*, Turnhout, 81–102.

De Pontbriand, S. 2012a: 'La cartographie d'Europos-Doura', P. Leriche, S. De Pontbriand, and G. Coqueugniot (eds), *Europos-Doura Varia* 1, 241–253.

De Pontbriand, S. 2012b: 'La résidence de Lysias à Europos-Doura. Un première approche', P. Leriche, S. De Pontbriand, and G. Coqueugniot (eds), *Europos-Doura Varia* 1, 77–92.

Punnett Peters, J. 1897: *Nippur or Explorations and Adventures on the Euphrates. The Narrative of the University of Pennsylvania Expedition to Babylonia in the Years 1888–1890*, Vol. I. First Campaign, London.

Queyrel, F. 2012: 'Le moule à statuette du secteur des maisons romaines à Europos-Doura', P. Leriche, G. Coqueugniot, and S. Du Pontbriand (eds), *Europos-Doura Varia* 1, 117–121.

Rajak, T. 2011: 'The Dura-Europos Synagogue: Images of a Competitive Community', in *Dura-Europos: Crossroads of Antiquity*, Chesnut Hill, 141–154.

Rajak, T. 2013: 'The Synagogue Paintings of Dura-Europos: Triumphalism and
    Competition', in S. Pearce (ed.), *The Image and Its Prohibition in Jewish Antiquity*,
    Oxford, 89–109.

Reeves, M. B. 2005: *The Feriale Duranum, Roman Military Religion, and Dura-Europos: A
    Reassessment*, Buffalo.

Remijsen, S., and Clarysse, W. 2008: 'Incest or Adoption? Brother-Sister Marriage in
    Roman Egypt Revisited', *The Journal of Roman Studies* 98, 53–61.

Rives, J. B. 1999: 'The Decree of Decius and the Religion of Empire', *The Journal of Roman
    Studies* 89, 135–154.

Rostovtzeff, M. I. 1919: 'Ancient Decorative Wall Painting', *Journal of Hellenic Studies* 39,
    144–163.

Rostovtzeff, M. I. 1926: *The Social and Economic History of the Roman Empire*, Oxford.

Rostovtzeff, M. I. 1927: 'Fouilles de Dour a-Eur op os, 1922–1923. Par Franz Cumont.
    [Haut-Commissariat de la République Française en Syrie et au Liban: Service des
    Antiquités et des Beaux Arts, Bibliothèque Archéologique et Historique, tome IX]
    (Paris: P. Geuthner. 1926. Pp. lxviii, 533, plates 124)', *American Historical Review* 32,
    836–841.

Rostovtzeff, M. I. 1932: *Caravan Cities*, New York.

Rostovtzeff, M. I. (ed.) 1934: *The Excavations at Dura-Europos Conducted by Yale
    University and the French Academy of Inscriptions and Letters. Preliminary Report of
    Fifth Season of Work, October 1931-March 1932*, New Haven.

Rostovtzeff, M. I. 1935a: 'ΠΡΟΓΟΝΟΙ', *Journal of Hellenic Studies* 55, 56–66.

Rostovtzeff, M. I. 1935b: 'Dura and the Problem of Parthian Art', *Yale Classical Studies* 5,
    155–304.

Rostovtzeff, M. I. 1935c: 'Deux notes sur des trouvailles de la dernière campagne de
    fouilles a Doura-Europos', *Comptes Rendus. Académie Des Inscriptions et Belles Lettres*,
    285–304.

Rostovtzeff, M. I. 1937: 'Rapport sur les Fouilles de Doura-Europos, Campagne de
    1936–1937', *Comptes Rendus. Académie Des Inscriptions et Belles Lettres*, 195–205.

Rostovtzeff, M. I. 1938: *Dura-Europos and Its Art*, Oxford.

Rostovtzeff, M. I. 1941: *Social and Economic History of the Hellenistic World*, Vol. 1,
    Oxford.

Rostovtzeff, M. I., Bellinger, A. R., Brown, F. E., and Welles, C. B. (eds) 1944: *The
    Excavations at Dura-Europos Conducted by Yale University and the French Academy of
    Inscriptions and Letters. Preliminary Report on the Ninth Season of Work, 1935–1936.
    Part 1, The Agora and Bazaar*, New Haven.

Rostovtzeff, M. I., Bellinger, A. R., Hopkins, C., and Welles, C. B. (eds) 1936: *The
    Excavations at Dura-Europos Conducted by Yale University and the French Academy
    of Inscriptions and Letters. Preliminary Report of Sixth Season of Work, October
    1932-March 1933*, New Haven.

Rostovtzeff, M. I., Brown, F. E., and Welles, C. B. (eds) 1936: *The Excavations at Dura-
    Europos Conducted by Yale University and the French Academy of Inscriptions and
    Letters. Preliminary Report of the Seventh and Eighth Seasons of Work, 1933–1934 and
    1934–1935*, New Haven.

Rostovtzeff, M. I., and Little, A. 1933: 'La maison des fresques de Doura-Europos',
    Mémoires de l'Institut National de France Académie des Inscriptions et Belles-Lettres 33,
    167–190.

Rothe, U. 2012: 'The "Third Way": Treveran Women's Dress and the "Gallic Ensemble"',
    American Journal of Archaeology 116, 235–252.

Rotroff, S. I., and Lamberton, R. 2006: *Women in the Athenian Agora*, Athens.

Rouselle, A. 2005: 'Le relief du fils de Shalman a Doura-Europos', P. Leriche, M. Gelin, and A. Dandrau (eds), *Doura Europos-Études V, 1993–1997*, 131–151.

Rousselle, A. 2005: 'Le relief du fils de Shalman à Doura-Europos', *Doura Europos Études 5*, 131–151.

Rowlandson, J., and Takahashi, R. 2009: 'Brother-Sister Marriage and Inheritance Strategies in Greco-Roman Egypt', *The Journal of Roman Studies* 99, 104–139.

Ruffing, K. 2000: 'Die Geschäfte des Aurelios Nebuchelos', *Laverna* 11, 71–105.

Ruffing, K. 2007: 'Dura Europos: A City on the Euphrates and her Economic Importance in the Roman Era', in M. Sartre (ed.), *Productions et échanges dans la Syrie grecque et romaine: actes du colloque de Tours, juin 2003*. Topoi Supple. 8, 399–411.

Russell, P. J. 1976: 'The Carved Bone Objects from Dura-Europos at the Yale University Art Gallery', New Haven.

Saliou, C. 1992: 'Les quatre fils de Polémocratès (P. Dura 19)', *Doura-Europos Études 1990, Syria, Tome LXIX*, 65–100.

Saliou, C. 2004: 'La form d'un îlot de Doura-Europos … l'îlot C7 revisité', in P. Leriche, M. Gelin, and A. Dandrau (eds), *Doura-Europos Etudes V, 1994–1997*, Paris, 65–78.

Saliou, C., and Dandrau, A. 1997: 'Données nouvelles sur les quartiers sud-est de Doura-Europos', in P. Leriche and M. Gelin (eds), *Doura-Europos Études IV*, Beirut, 95–106.

Salway, B. 1994: 'What's in a Name? A Survey of Roman Onomastic Practice from c. 700 B.C. to A.D. 700', *Journal of Roman Studies* 84, 124–145.

Sarre, F., and Herzfeld, E. 1911: *Archäologische Reise Im Euphrat- Und Tigris-Gebiet*, Berlin.

Scheffler, T. 2003: '"Fertile Crescent", "Orient", "Middle East": The Changing Mental Maps of Southwest Asia', *European Review of History: Revue Européenne d'histoire* 10, 253–272.

Schlumberger, D. 1960: 'Descendants non-méditerranéens de l'art grec', *Syria* 37, 253–319.

Scott, R. T. 1988: 'Frank Edward Brown, 1908–1988', *American Journal of Archaeology* 92, 577–579.

Seim, D. L. 2013: *Rockefeller Philanthropy and Modern Social Science*, London.

Seyrig, H. 1944: 'Antiquités Syriennes', *Syria* 24, 62–80.

Shaw, B. 1992: 'Under Russian Eyes', *Journal of Roman Studies* 82, 216–228.

Shapin, S. 1989: 'The Invisible Technician', *American Scientist* 77, 554–563.

Sherwin-White, S., and Kuhrt, A. 1993: *From Samarkhand to Sardis. A New Approach to the Seleucid Empire*, London.

Shoe, L. T. 1943: 'Architectural Mouldings of Dura-Europos', *Berytus* 8, 1–40.

Snow, C. E. 2011: 'Preservation of Art and Artifacts from Dura-Europos: A Conservator's Perspective', in G. Hoffman and L. Brody (eds), *Dura-Europos: Crossroads of Antiquity*, Chesnut Hill, 33–44.

Sommer, M. 2004: 'A Map of Meaning. Approaching Cultural Identities at the Middle Euphrates (1st to 3rd Centuries AD)', *Egitto E Vicino Oriente* 27, 153–183.

Sommer, M. 2006: 'Difference, Diversity, Diaspora. Locating the Middle Euphrates on Imperial Maps', *Mediterraneo Antico* 9, 417–436.

Sommer, M. 2007: 'Dura-Europos in a De-globalising Roman Empire', *Mediterraneo Antico* 10, 85–94.

Sommer, M. 2016: 'Acculturation, Hybridity, Créolité: Mapping Cultural Diversity in Dura-Europos', in T. Kaizer (ed.), *Religion, Society and Culture at Dura-Europos*, Cambridge, 57–67.

Spawforth, A. 2006: '"Macedonian Times": Hellenistic Memories in the Provinces of the Roman Near East', in D. Konstan and S. Saïd (eds), *Greeks on Greekness*, Cambridge, 1–26.

Stephens, F. J. 1937: 'A Cuneiform Tablet from Dura-Europos', *Revue d'Assyriolgie et d'archéologie Orientale* 34, 183–189.

Stern, K. B. 2010: 'Mapping Devotion in Roman Dura Europos: A Reconsideration of the Synagogue Ceiling', *American Journal of Archaeology* 114, 473–504.

Stern, K. 2012: 'Tagging Sacred Space in the Dura-Europos Synagogue', *Journal of Roman Archaeology* 25, 171–194.

Trigger, B. 2006: *A History of Archaeological Thought*, Cambridge.

'Two Forthcoming Yale Expeditions in the Orient', *Bulletin of the American Schools of Oriental Research* 1928: 17–17.

Valtz, E. 1984: 'Pottery from Seleucia on the Tigris', in *Arabie Orientale, Mésopotamie et Iran Méridonal: De l'age du fer au début de la période Islamique*, Paris, 41–48.

Valtz, E. 1991: 'New Observations on the Hellenistic Pottery from Seleucia-on-the-Tigris', in *Golf-Archäologie. Mesopotamien, Iran, Kuwait, Bahrain, Vereinigte Arabische Emirate und Oman*, International Archäologie 6, Göttingen, 45–56.

Valtz, E. 2002: 'Ceramica invetriata : caratteristiche ed evoluzione della produzione di *Seleucia ad Tigrim*', *Travaux de La Maison de l'Orient Méditerranéen* 35, 331–337.

Velud, C. 1988: 'Histoire des recherches à Doura-Europos. Contecte historique régional des fouilles de Doura entre les deux guerres mondials', *Doura-Europos Études 1988, Syria, Tome LXV*, 363–382.

Vokaer, A. 2009: 'Brittle Ware Trade in Syria between the 5th and 8th Centuries', in M. M. Mango (ed.), *Byzantine Trade, 4th–12th Centuries: The Archaeology of Local, Regional and International Exchange: Papers of the Thirty-Eighth Spring Symposium of Byzantine Studies, St John's College, University of Oxford, March 2004*, 121–136.

Vokaer, A. 2010: 'Cooking in a Perfect Pot. Shapes, Fabric and Function of Cooking Ware in Late Antique Syria', in S. Menchelli, S. Santoro, M. Pasquinucci, and G. Guiducci (eds), *Late Roman Coarse Wares, Cooking Wares and Amphorae in the Mediterranean: Archaeology and Archaeometry. Comparison between Western and Eastern Mediterranean. Volume I*. BAR S2185(I), Oxford, 115–129.

Webster, J. 2001: 'Creolizing the Roman Provinces', *American Journal of Archaeology* 105, 209–225.

Weitzmann, K. 1971: *Studies in Classical and Byzantine Manuscript Illumination*, H. L. Kessler (ed.), Chicago.

Weitzmann, K., and Kessler, H. L. 1990: *The Frescoes of the Dura Synagogue and Christian Art*, Washington.

Welles, C. B. 1941: 'The Epitaph of Julius Terentius', *Harvard Theological Review* 34, 79–109.

Welles, C. B. 1951: 'The Population of Roman Dura', in P. R. Coleman-Norton (ed.), *Studies in Roman Economic and Social History in Honor of Allan Chester Johnson*, Freeport, 251–273.

Welles, C. B. 1959: 'The Hellenism of Dura-Europos', *Aegyptus* 39, 23–28.

Wes, M. 1990: *Michael Rostovtzeff, Historian in Exile: Russian Roots in an American Context. Historia* 65, Stuttgart.

Wharton, A. J. 1994: 'Good and Bad Images from the Synagogue of Dura Europos: Contexts, Subtexts, Intertexts', *Art History* 17, 1–25.

Wharton, A. J. 1995: *Refiguring the Post Classical City. Dura Europos, Jerash, Jerusalem and Ravenna*, Cambridge.

Will, E. 1955: *Le relief cultuel gréco-romain: contribution à l'histoire de l'art de l'Empire romain*, Paris.

Will, E. 1959: 'Art parthe et art grec', *Etudes d'archéologie Classique II, Annales de l'Est.* Univ. de Nancy. Memoire 22, Paris, 783–795.

Will, E. 1988: 'La population de Doura-Europos: une évaluation', *Doura-Europos études 1988, Syria, Tome LXV*, 315–321.

Winks, R. W. 1996: *Cloak & Gown: Scholars in the Secret War, 1939–1961*, 2nd ed., New Haven.

Yarshater, E. 1983: *The Cambridge History of Iran*, Vol. 3 The Seleucid, Parthian and Sasanian Periods, Cambridge.

Yon, J. B. 2016: 'Women and the Religious Life of Dura-Europos', in T. Kaizer (ed.), *Religion, Society and Culture at Dura-Europos*, Cambridge, 99–113.

INDEX